THE CATHOLIC BIBLICAL QUARTERLY

MONOGRAPH SERIES

14

THE CREATION OF MAN: PHILO AND THE HISTORY OF INTERPRETATION

by

Thomas H. Tobin, S.J.

D1520745

EDITORIAL BOARD

Bruce Vawter, C.M., Chairman

THE CREATION OF MAN:
PHILO AND THE HISTORY
OF INTERPRETATION

by

Thomas H. Tobin, S.J.

The Catholic Biblical Association of America
Washington, DC 20064
1983

THE CREATION OF MAN:
PHILO AND THE HISTORY OF INTERPRETATION
by Thomas H. Tobin, S.J.

©1983 The Catholic Biblical Association of America
Washington, DC 20064

PRODUCED IN THE UNITED STATES

Library of Congress Cataloging in Publication Data

Tobin, Thomas H. 1945-
  The Creation of Man.

  (Catholic Biblical quarterly. Monograph series; 14)
  Originally presented as the author's thesis (doctoral—Harvard University,
1980)
  Includes bibliographical references and indexes.
  1. Bible. O.T. Genesis I-III—Criticism, interpretation, etc.—History.
2. Creation—Biblical teaching.   3. Man (Jewish theology)—Biblical teaching.
4. Philo, of Alexandria. I. Title. II. Series.
BS651.T58 1983   222'.1106   82-19891
ISBN 0-915170-13-2

TO MY MOTHER
AND THE MEMORY OF MY FATHER AND BROTHER

TABLE OF CONTENTS

PREFACE

The purpose of this study is to understand Philo's interpretation of the story of the creation of man in Genesis 1–3 against the background of the exegetical traditions which were available to him. It is also an analysis of the way in which the philosophical developments of the period influenced those traditions and their use by Philo. This study began as a thesis submitted to Harvard University in July 1980 and appears here in a somewhat revised form.

I have profited from the great learning and generous advice of a number of people. Above all, I have gained from the assistance of Prof. John Strugnell. He read successive drafts of the work and offered me detailed criticism at each point. He saved me from a number of obvious and not-so-obvious mistakes; those that remain are the ones he was unable to talk me out of. Profs. Zeph Stewart, Dieter Georgi, and George MacRae, S.J., also read drafts of the work and offered me much help. I also want to thank the Jesuits of John LaFarge House in Cambridge and Ignatius House in Chicago for their support of my work over the years. In addition, I owe a debt of gratitude to Loyola University of Chicago for its generous assistance in the preparation of the manuscript.

Unless otherwise noted, translations of ancient writers are from the Loeb Classical Library.

T.H.T.

Loyola University
Chicago, Illinois
June 1982

CHAPTER I

PHILO THE INTERPRETER AND TRADITION

Whatever else might be said about Philo of Alexandria, he clearly influenced the interpretation of the Bible for centuries. His impact on patristic exegesis was immense. Jerome thought that he should be included among the "ecclesiastical writers," and Eusebius related the legend that Philo came to Rome at the time of the Emperor Claudius to speak with the apostle Peter. Eusebius thought that this legend was not at all improbable since, according to him, Philo's *De Vita Contemplativa* was written about early Christian ascetics.[1] Pious legend would not allow a writer so influential on early Christian exegesis of the Bible to remain unconverted.

Philo's reviews, however, have not always been so positive. Not many years ago E. R. Dodds wrote of Philo as a philosopher that "any attempt to extract a coherent system from Philo seems to me foredoomed to failure; his eclecticism is that of a jackdaw rather than the philosopher."[2] A. J. Festugière's judgment, while less acerbic, was no less severe. After describing Philo's thought, he concluded:

> One can unfortunately read all of Philo without encountering a single original reflection that indicates some personal experience, anything that resembles the dialogue of the soul with itself about the spectacle of destiny or of men. There is nothing but the conventional, the banalities of the manual.[3]

On the other hand one has the judgment of H. A. Wolfson who thought that out of the innuendoes found in Philo's interpretations one could discover the systematic structure of his thought, a structure that was to become "the dominant force in the history of philosophy down to the seventeenth century."[4] One could go on almost indefinitely citing critics for and against

---

[1] Jerome, *De Vir. Ill.* 11; Eusebius, *Hist. Eccl.* 2.16.1–17.3. For a fuller account of these legends see J. E. Bruns, "Philo Christianus: The Debris of a Legend," *HTR* 66 (1973) 141–45.

[2] E. R. Dodds, "The *Parmenides* of Plato and the Origin of the Neoplatonic 'One,'" *Classical Quarterly* 22 (1928) 132.

[3] A. J. Festugière, *La révélation d'Hermès Trismégiste* (Paris: Gabalda, 1949), 2.534. The translation is my own.

[4] H. A. Wolfson, *Philo* (Cambridge: Harvard University Press, 1948), 1. vi–vii.

Philo, but the authors just cited suffice to give a sense of the variety of reactions that Philo has evoked.

Much of the variety in these reactions is due to the fact that Philo is being applauded or condemned for expressing or failing to express an original, consistent philosophical point of view. Unfortunately this has meant that Philo is being praised or condemned for something that he never set out to do in the first place. Almost none of Philo's works are philosophical treatises. Rather they are interpretations of the Bible, especially of the Pentateuch. Of the thirty-three works of Philo extant in Greek, all but seven are interpretations of biblical books. Philo was first of all an interpreter of the Bible. What he wrote was primarily about the meaning of the biblical text and was not an attempt to construct a philosophical system.

This is hardly a new insight. The Church Fathers, biblical exegetes themselves, recognized in Philo a fellow exegete and were deeply influenced by him. In more modern research on Philo, Carl Siegfried, in his still valuable study, *Philo von Alexandria als Ausleger des Alten Testaments*, written over one hundred years ago, saw Philo as an interpreter of the Bible and set out to study the methods that Philo used in those interpretations.[5] This same point has been made recently by Valentin Nikiprowetsky in *Le commentaire de l'écriture chez Philon d'Alexandrie*:

> Philo ought to be considered above all as an exegete who does not express his ideas except as a function of the scriptural text. He does not intend to develop a system but he wants to communicate the profound sense of the Mosaic Law which he follows verse by verse, above all keeping before his eyes the text on which he is working.[6]

The corollary of such an insight is that, to understand what Philo was about, one has to study the exegetical methods that he used in his interpretations. Only then can one evaluate fairly the success or failure of his efforts. Once again much of this work was begun by Carl Siegfried. Siegfried gave a thorough treatment of both the general hermeneutical principles and the specific rules that Philo used in his interpretations. Siegfried also showed how Philo's theological positions were consistent with his exegetical principles and rules.[7] While Siegfried's own methods have been criticized for being too wooden and inflexible, all subsequent commentators have been influenced by him.[8]

---

[5] C. Siegfried, *Philo von Alexandria als Ausleger des Alten Testaments* (Jena: Hermann Dufft, 1875).

[6] V. Nikiprowetzky, *Le commentaire de l'écriture chez Philon d'Alexandrie* (ALGHJ 11; Leiden: Brill, 1977) 181. The translation is my own.

[7] Siegfried, 160–272.

[8] Much of the work on Philo in the early part of this century centered on the matrices of

More recently scholars such as Christiansen, Pépin, Cazeaux, and Nikiprowetzky have dealt with the actual methods used by Philo and have tried to suggest ways in which those methods present consistent patterns of interpretation.[9] One might take the books of Irmgard Christiansen and Valentin Nikiprowetzky as indicative of the work that is being done. Christiansen maintains that Philo's interpretative methods are not arbitrary but that they rest on the consistent application of the Aristotelian *diairesis*. According to her, Philo applied to the interpretation of the biblical text the Aristotelian distinctions of genus versus species and subject versus various types of predication. Distinctions (διαιρέσεις) found at the literal, surface level of the text reflect analogous distinctions found at a deeper, more spiritual and allegorical level of the text. Through the use of the technique of *diairesis*, Philo can offer an allegorical interpretation of biblical texts that reveals their deeper, more universal meaning.[10]

While Christiansen's work concentrates on a specific technique of interpretation, Nikiprowetzky takes a much broader view and deals with Philo's overall methodology rather than with any specific technique. In Nikiprowetzky's opinion Philo uses the philosophical language of his own time, both in terms of vocabulary and in terms of concepts, in order to understand the higher wisdom found in the biblical text. The philosophical language is at the service of the exegesis of the Bible.[11] This accounts for Philo's "eclecticism." Like Hagar, the slave, symbol of the lower studies, who is at the service of Sarah, true wisdom, the philosophical language of the period should be at the service of the higher wisdom of Scripture. Because of this Philo feels that he can use philosophical concepts quite freely and turn them

---

Philo's thinking, that is, are his thought patterns basically Greek or are they Jewish? On the one hand, I. Heinemann, in his book *Philons griechische und jüdische Bildung* (Breslau: Marcus, 1932), denied that Philo depended on Palestinian *halakah* and claimed that his interpretations of legal texts were derived from Greek and Roman law. On the other hand, H. A. Wolfson, in his immensely learned book *Philo*, maintained that Philo not only knew of Palestinian Pharisaic Judaism but also that he was at home with it and followed it closely. Only in the past twenty years has the emphasis of research on Philo once again shifted to a study of Philo's exegetical methods.

[9] I. Christiansen, *Die Technik der allegorischen Auslegungswissenschaft bei Philon von Alexandrien* (Beiträge zur Geschichte der biblischen Hermeneutik 7; Tübingen: J. C. B. Mohr, 1969); J. Pépin, "Remarques sur la théorie de l'exégèse allégorique chez Philon," *Philon d'Alexandrie* (Colloques nationaux du Centre National de la Recherche Scientifique, Lyon, 11–15 Septembre, 1966; Lyon, 1967) 138–68; J. Cazeaux, "Aspects de l'exégèse philonienne," *RSR* 47 (1973) 262–69; V. Nikiprowetzky, *Le commentaire de l'écriture*.

[10] Christiansen's positions are neatly summarized in the theses placed at the beginning of each chapter of her book.

[11] Nikiprowetzky, *Le commentaire de l'écriture*, 191–92.

in different and apparently contradictory directions.[12] Philo's attention is focused on the exegesis of a scriptural text and not on a philosophical doctrine. Once this fact is recognized, Nikiprowetzky claims, one can then begin to study Philo profitably.

> Once this is admitted, a study of Philo has a chance of being more fruitfully directed when one chooses as a pivot an exegetical theme rather than a properly philosophical theme. As long as one makes a technical philosophical theme the center of one's research, one will above all come up against a disheartening eclecticism and insoluble contradictions. On the other hand, the doctrine of Philo appears much more clearly structured when one pursues the study of an exegetical motif through the various treatises of the commentary. The contradictions often fade away or are explained by exegetical necessity and, as (Philo) said, by the inexhaustible character of the biblical text.[13]

Philo's inconsistency and eclecticism disappear, according to Nikiprowetzky, once one realizes the primacy of the biblical text and the secondary, subordinate character of the philosophical concepts used to interpret the text.

Both the approach of Christiansen and that of Nikiprowetzky have been valuable because they emphasize the centrality of Philo's role as an interpreter of the biblical text. At the same time, however, there is an oddly ahistorical coloring to their work. The method that they use treats Philo's exegeses as if they were all of a piece, as if they were all from the pen of Philo himself. Put another way, they tend to treat Philo apart from the exegetical traditions on which he drew.[14] Yet from what Philo says about his own work and about the work of his predecessors, as well as from the fragments that we have of the second-century B.C. Jewish writer Aristobulus, we know that Philo's work forms part of a long and complex history. For instance, in dealing with laws that have to do with the punishments of assaults, Philo prefaces his interpretation with the following remark:

> This is the explanation commonly stated, but I have heard another from highly gifted men who think that most of the contents of the law-book are outward symbols of hidden truths, expressing in words what has been left unsaid. This explanation was as follows. . . .(*Spec.* 3.178.)

---

[12] Ibid., 183, 191.

[13] Ibid., 238. The translation is my own.

[14] This is especially true of Nikiprowetzky's work. It is especially pronounced in his article "Problèmes du 'Récit de la Création' chez Philon d'Alexandrie" (*REJ* 124 [1965] 271–306). In this article Nikiprowetzky tries to "harmonize" all of the various interpretations of the creation of the world and the creation of man. One can explain the *philosophical* inconsistencies found in Philo by appealing to the fact that Philo saw himself as an exegete and not a philosopher, but one cannot explain *exegetical* inconsistencies in that way. Philo's exegetical inconsistencies must be related to the traditions that he drew on and felt a responsibility toward.

Philo indicates in this way that both the interpretation that immediately precedes this section and the interpretation that immediately follows it are the work of other interpreters. References of this sort are not unusual in Philo.[15] Another type of example is provided by Philo's *Questions and Answers on Genesis and Exodus*. Each section of these works contains a question about a problem found in a biblical verse followed by a series of interpretations that solve that problem. In these interpretations Philo is clearly most interested in those solutions which are of an allegorical or symbolic nature. Often he simply indicates that the literal meaning of a verse is clear or gives a one sentence summary of that literal meaning. In both cases he then goes on to give much fuller allegorical interpretations.[16] One suspects that many, if not most, of the literal interpretations in the *Questions and Answers on Genesis* are not the work of Philo himself. A number of times Philo himself explicitly indicates that the literal interpretation is the work of others.[17] Given Philo's own interests, it is likely that the number of literal interpretations in the *Questions and Answers on Genesis* which are the work of previous interpreters is even larger than of those which Philo explicitly indicates are the work of others. These examples strongly suggest that Philo drew extensively on exegetical traditions in composing his own interpretations.

Philo, then, was not only an exegete but also an exegete within a tradition. He did not stand alone but was the representative of a tradition of interpretation. This means that when one talks about Philo's exegesis or Philo's exegetical methods without first trying to sort out what is Philo and what is traditional material, one risks throwing together under the name of Philo the work of several generations of interpreters. What one says about Philo may or may not be true of the traditions on which he drew. Any living, active tradition of interpretation is bound to develop or at least change in the course of several generations.

This insight is not new. The point was made at the beginning of the century by Wilhelm Bousset in his *Jüdisch-christlicher Schulbetrieb in Alexandria und Rom*.[18] In that book Bousset offered a number of examples in which Philo made use of and, in some cases, transformed traditional

---

[15] E.g., *Op.* 26, 67, 77, 131; *L. A.* 1.59; *L. A.* 3.78; *Sac.* 131; *Post.* 58; *Deus* 21–22, 133; *Agr.* 128–29; *Plant.* 36, 52–53, 69–72; *Sob.* 33; *Conf.* 2–24, 190–91.

[16] *Q. G.* 1.6, 11, 25, 37, 49; *Q. G.* 2.23, 24, 25, 34, 43, 46, 63, 72; *Q. G.* 3.1, 15, 24, 28, 29, 30, 32, 33, 45, 50; *Q. G.* 4.1, 11, 13, 15, 26, 37, 46, 54, 77, 80, 85, 89, 94, 111, 126, 134, 142, 149, 152, 159, 176, 182, 188, 190, 197, 203, 213, 225, 239, 240, 241, 243.

[17] *Q. G.* 1.8, 10, 32, 57, 93; *Q. G.* 2.28, 58, 64, 79; *Q. G.* 3.8, 11, 13, 52; *Q. G.* 4.2, 64, 145.

[18] W. Bousset, *Jüdisch-christlicher Schulbetrieb in Alexandria und Rom* (Göttingen: Vandenhoeck & Ruprecht, 1915) 8–154.

material. Nor is the insight surprising, since no one would really quarrel with
the fact that at some points Philo drew on previous exegetical traditions.
What is surprising, however, is how little work has been done to examine
thoroughly the traditional exegetical material and methods used by Philo.[19]
Only within the past ten years, thanks to the work of such scholars as
Robert G. Hamerton-Kelly and Burton L. Mack, has there been an interest
in systematically analyzing the various strands of traditional material found
in Philo.[20]

The attempt to understand the exegetical history of Alexandrian Judaism is not only important in order to understand Philo correctly, it is also
important if we are to understand early Christianity and Gnosticism, since as
Mack has pointed out:

> Studies in the origins of early Christianity and Gnosticism have indicated with
> increasing clarity the significance of Hellenistic Judaism as that religious milieu
> in which many of the theological concerns and language forms common to these
> three religious expressions were first molded and against which as a background
> the further developments in Gnosticism and Christianity are to be interpreted.[21]

In addition, such a study is valuable because it helps us to understand better
the way in which a tradition of interpretation develops and changes, how it
interacts with the thought patterns and concerns of the milieu in which it
exists, and how it transforms those patterns and concerns for its own purposes. It gives us a much more three dimensional view not only of Philo but
also of Alexandrian Judaism and its history. The present study is meant to
be an effort in that direction.

Obviously there are several ways to go about such a study. Given the
size of the Philonic *corpus*, inevitably one must set reasonable limits and
choose representative samples. One option is to choose a particular treatise
of Philo and to analyze the exegetical traditions found in that treatise.
Burton L. Mack profitably used this approach in his analysis of *De Congressu Eruditionis Gratia*.[22] Another approach is to analyze all of the various
interpretations of a given biblical text in an attempt to establish patterns and

---

[19] There were several scholars who did take note of Philo's use of tradition. I. Heinemann
(*Philons griechische und jüdische Bildung*, 137–54) and H. A. Wolfson (*Philo*, 1.57–73) are the
two most notable. Yet these exceptions highlight how little work has been done in this area.

[20] R. G. Hamerton-Kelly, "Sources and Traditions in Philo Judaeus: Prolegomena to an
Analysis of His Writings," *SP* 1 (1972) 3–26; B. L. Mack, "Exegetical Traditions in Alexandrian
Judaism: A Program for the Analysis of the Philonic Corpus," *SP* 3 (1974–75) 71–115; "Wei-
sheit und Allegorie bei Philo von Alexandrien," *SP* 5 (1978) 57–105.

[21] Mack, "Exegetical Traditions in Alexandrian Judaism," 71.

[22] Mack, "Weisheit und Allegorie," 57–105.

levels of interpretations. In this second approach one would have to choose a text for which there were multiple interpretations. Given such a text, one would have a good chance of reconstructing the history of the interpretation of that text. In turn such a reconstruction could be helpful in understanding the history of the interpretation of other texts whose interpretations were more fragmentary.

Of these two approaches I have chosen the second and will concentrate on the various interpretations of the creation of man found in Philo. Both approaches, it seems to me, are sound, but the variety of interpretations concerning the creation of man may offer us an opportunity to reconstruct in some detail the history of the interpretation of one of the most important biblical texts. In addition, the multiple interpretations of the creation of man contain enough conceptual and formal detail that one may be able to point to the intellectual milieux in which they developed. Finally, given the importance of the interpretation of the creation of man in early Christianity and in Gnosticism, insights into the history of the interpretation of the creation of man in Alexandrian Judaism may well deepen our understanding of the development of this doctrine in both early Christianity and Gnosticism.[23]

The principal interpretations of the creation of man are found in *Op.* 69–88, 134–150 and in *L. A.* 1.31–47, 53–55, 88–96. The former of these works, *De Opificio Mundi*, is an interpretation of the first three chapters of Genesis and so includes interpretations of the creation of the world and the creation and fall of man. *Legum Allegoriae 1*, an interpretation of Gen 2:1–17, is part of a larger work, *Legum Allegoriae*, in which both the creation and the fall of man are interpreted but which contains no interpretation of the creation of the world. Several interpretations of the creation of man are also found in sections of Philo's *Questions and Answers on Genesis* (1.4–22), a collection of interpretations grouped around a question involving a particular biblical verse. Finally, interpretations of the creation of man are found scattered throughout Philo's other treatises.

For the most part the interpretations can easily be distinguished formally one from the other. In *De Opificio Mundi* and *Legum Allegoriae* each interpretation involves an explanation of a particular verse or part of a verse and so, as Philo moves on to the interpretation of the next verse or the next part of a verse, one can easily see where one interpretation ends and the next

---

[23] E. Brandenburger, *Adam und Christus* (Neukirchen: Neukirchener Verlag, 1962); J. Jervell, *Imago Dei* (Göttingen: Vandenhoeck & Ruprecht, 1960); H.-M. Schenke, *Der Gott "Mensch" in der Gnosis* (Göttingen:Vandenhoeck & Ruprecht, 1962); R. Scroggs, *The Last Adam* (Philadelphia: Fortress, 1966); R. McL. Wilson, "The Early History of the Exegesis of Gen. 1.26," *Studia Patristica* I (ed. K. Aland and F. L. Cross; Berlin: Akademie Verlag, 1957) 420–437.

begins. When several interpretations of the same part of a verse are given
(e.g., *Op.* 136–139), Philo lists them serially and so one is easily distinguished from the other. This same procedure of listing interpretations
serially is also followed in the *Questions and Answers on Genesis*, and here
too one interpretation can be easily distinguished from another. When one
turns to the references to the creation of man scattered through the other
treatises of Philo, the situation becomes a bit more difficult. These scattered
references are usually part of a larger interpretation of some other biblical
verse and so must be disengaged from their contexts. But here too, by using
the interpretation as it is found in *De Opificio Mundi*, *Legum Allegoriae 1*,
or the *Questions and Answers on Genesis 1*, one can isolate these scattered
interpretations from their contexts.

In analyzing these various interpretations of the creation of man, one
must begin by distinguishing the various conflicting interpretations of the
creation of man. Here we are not talking about different formulations of one
interpretation but basic conflicts of interpretation. For instance, do Gen 1:27
and Gen 2:7 refer to the creation of the same man or of two different men?
Did God create man directly or through an intermediate figure? The answers
to these questions point to significantly different interpretations of the creation of man. At this point one must be careful to draw on only those
interpretations that appear several times in Philo. The multiple attestation
insures that one is dealing with real interpretations rather than with the
peculiarity of any one given text in Philo. Secondly, one must look for
patterns of dependence and development among these conflicting interpretations. At this point one is trying to see if these various interpretations are
more than simply unconnected, disparate interpretations. This involves trying to establish whether any given interpretation draws on the conceptual
structure and vocabulary of another interpretation and so is both dependent
on and a development of that other interpretation. Once the various patterns
of dependence and development have been established, the third step is to
determine which interpretations are Philo's own and which are the interpretations of his predecessors. This can be done in two complementary ways.
The first is simply to note which interpretations Philo tells us are not his own.
Those interpretations, and every interpretation shown to be prior to those
interpretations, by the analysis of the patterns of dependence and development are then pre-Philonic. The second way to distinguish the Philonic from
the pre-Philonic is to note which interpretations clash with a position that
spans the Philonic *corpus* and is therefore Philo's own position. By the use
of these two criteria one can distinguish with a fair amount of certainty those
interpretations which are Philo's own from those which are not.

While these three steps taken together can help us to establish the
patterns of development in the interpretation of the creation of man up to

Philo, they tell us practically nothing about the process of development or the reason for the development. For this we must go back and study each level of interpretation with much more care. The greater part of this study will be taken up with this sort of analysis. This involves the analysis of precisely what each level of interpretation is saying and how and why it says what it says. It also involves the analysis of the thought patterns used in the interpretations, and the relationship of those thought patterns to the biblical text and to the philosophical milieu of Alexandria during that period. This analysis will prove to be important, because these interpretations were attempts to be true both to the biblical text and to the best in the philosophical learning of the period. Finally, one must analyze why a development in interpretation took place. Any interpretation involves the solution of a problem presented by the text, and any development of interpretation involves not only the solution of a problem presented by the text but also the solution to a problem presented by the previous level of interpretation. An analysis of this alternation of problem and solution is crucial if one is to understand the process that created the development of the interpretations of the creation of man.

Finally, we must return to Philo and to the tradition of interpretation as a whole. At this point we must analyze how Philo worked with and made use of the exegetical traditions that were available to him. This will give a more accurate sense of how Philo functioned both as a representative of a tradition of interpretation and as an interpreter in his own right. It will also give us a chance to look at the development of the tradition as a whole from a somewhat different angle. From an analysis of how Philo edited and integrated these various interpretations into his own exegetical outlook, we may get a more nuanced conception of how these traditions were transmitted and what their function was. In this way we may be able to broaden our understanding of both Philo and the development of the Hellenistic Judaism of which he is the foremost representative.

Yet before we begin an analysis of the various interpretations of the creation of man found in Philo, something must be said about the philosophical milieu of Alexandria during this period. This is only an apparent detour. The Jewish quarter of Alexandria was not a ghetto, and Jews played an important part in the life of the most important city in the eastern Mediterranean.[24] This included the intellectual life of the city. The Jews of Alexandria developed their own learned tradition which lasted over a period of

[24] For a detailed treatment of the Jews of Alexandria, see V. A. Tcherikover and A. Fuks, *Corpus Papyrorum Judaicarum*, 3 vols. (Cambridge: Harvard University Press, 1957–64); P. M. Fraser, *Ptolemaic Alexandria* (Oxford: Clarendon, 1972), 1.54–58, 281–286, 687–716.

several centuries.[25] As early as the end of the third century B.C., Demetrius, an Alexandrian Jew, was writing a chronological history of the Jews.[26] The second century B.C. saw Artapanus, who wrote about figures such as Joseph and Moses in the form of an historical romance; Ezekiel the Poet, who wrote a drama about Moses and the exodus from Egypt in faultless Greek meter; and Aristobulus who sought to interpret the biblical text through Stoic concepts in a way that ridded it of anthropomorphisms.[27] For our purposes the most important of these figures is Aristobulus, because he points to the involvement of Jewish writers in the *philosophical* life of Alexandria. It is especially this aspect of Jewish involvement in the life of Alexandria that will be of help in understanding how Jewish interpreters developed their explanations of the scriptural text.

Even a very superficial reading of short passages from Philo reveals a great interest in philosophy. One can find in the writings of Philo Stoic, Peripatetic, Pythagorean, Platonic, and even Sceptical philosophical positions.[28] In fact, Philo, along with Cicero, serves as one of our most important witnesses to the philosophical trends of the late Hellenistic period as well as of the period of the early Empire. Furthermore, the philosophical milieu of the first century B.C. in Alexandria is one of the most important influences on the development of the interpretative tradition to which Philo fell heir.

Serious philosophical discussion seems to have come into its own in Alexandria only in the first century B.C. There was probably no lack of philosophers in the third and second centuries in Alexandria, yet, apart from the polymath Eratosthenes (ca. 274–194 B.C.), no prominent philosophical figure was associated with Alexandria during these two centuries.[29] Eratosthenes studied in Athens with both the Stoic Ariston of Chios (fl. 250 B.C.) and the sceptically inclined head of the Platonic Academy, Arcesilaus (ca. 316–242 B.C.). There seems to have been no "Platonist" (apart from Eratosthenes) or Peripatetic of note in Alexandria during these two centuries.[30] The fragments of the Alexandrian Jewish writer Aristobulus point to the presence of Stoicism in Alexandria in the middle of the second century

[25] M. Hengel, *Judaism and Hellenism* (Philadelphia: Fortress, 1974), 1.69.

[26] N. Walter, "Fragmente jüdisch-hellenistischer Exegeten: Aristobulos, Demetrios, Aristeas," (JSHRZ 3/2; Gütersloh: Gerd Mohn, 1975) 280–292.

[27] For Artapanus and Ezekiel, see J. H. Charlesworth, *The Pseudepigrapha and Modern Research* (Missoula: Scholars, 1976) 82–83, 110–11. For Aristobulus, see N. Walter, *Der Thoraausleger Aristobulos* (Berlin: Akademie Verlag, 1964).

[28] H. Chadwick, "Philo," *The Cambridge History of Later Greek and Early Medieval Philosophy* (ed. A. H. Armstrong; Cambridge: University Press, 1967) 137–57.

[29] Fraser, *Ptolemaic Alexandria*, 1.480–82.

[30] Ibid., 1.482–85.

B.C., and during the previous century the minor Stoic figure Sphaerus of Borysthenes (ca. 285–221 B.C.) spent some time in Alexandria and may even have died there.[31] In general, however, philosophy does not seem to have played a prominent role in the intellectual life of Alexandria during these two centuries.

The situation, however, in the first century B.C. is quite different. Here we find figures such as Antiochus of Ascalon (ca. 130–68 B.C.), Eudorus of Alexandria (fl. 30 B.C.) Arius Didymus (fl. 10 B.C.), Potamon of Alexandria (fl. 10 B.C.), and Aenesidemus of Cnossos (fl. 40 B.C.). Because the texts of all of these philosophers are fragmentary, it is impossible to sketch their positions in much detail, and it is difficult to describe with much precision the philosophical milieu of Alexandria during that period. Scepticism was represented by Aenesidemus of Cnossos who established a school in Alexandria about 45 B.C.[32] Aenesidemus made use of ten modes or tropes (τρόποι), ways of arguing that emphasized the variability and confusing character of phenomena.[33] These ten modes were used by Philo in *Ebr.* 171–205. Stoicism and the Peripatetic school also had advocates of their positions in Alexandria in the first century. These advocates served as the mediators of the Stoic and Peripatetic opinions summarized in Arius Didymus' *Epitome of Philosophical Doctrines.*[34] Peripatetic and especially Stoic doctrines are also found in Philo.

Obviously these various schools were never completely separate from one another; they influenced one another. This was also true of first-century B.C. Alexandria.[35] This blending, however, was of different sorts. The blend that interests anyone studying Philo is one in which the central position is given to Plato's physics or, more precisely, to certain interpretations of Plato's physics. This outlook goes under the name of Middle Platonism. The origins of this philosophical outlook are obscure and various figures (e.g.,

---

[31] Ibid., 1.481–82; N. Walter, *Der Thoraausleger Aristobulos*, 124–41.

[32] Fraser, *Ptolemaic Alexandria*, 1.491.

[33] D. L. 9.77–88; Sextus Empiricus, *Pyr.* 1.36–163. A sceptical attitude, if not Scepticism itself, seems to have had an important influence on the philosophy of the late Hellenistic period and the Imperial period. The sense that man was unable to come to firm conclusions about the structure of the world may have pushed philosophical reflection in the direction of the mystical. Knowledge of reality came to depend more on what was revealed and less on what could be reasoned to. See A. Wlosok, *Laktanz und die philosophische Gnosis* (Heidelberg: Carl Winter, 1960) 25–47.

[34] The most thorough treatment of Arius Didymus is still that of H. Diels, *Doxographi Graeci* (1879; rpt. Berlin: de Gruyter, 1929) 69–88.

[35] Fraser, *Ptolemaic Alexandria*, 1.486.

Posidonius, Antiochus, Eudorus) have been suggested as its founder(s). While scholars now tend to exclude Posidonius from the list, the origins of Middle Platonism still remain somewhat of a mystery.[36]

Yet evidence does suggest that Alexandria of the first century B.C. played an important role in that development. Philo himself is a witness to the strength of Middle Platonism in Alexandria in the first half of the first century A.D., and, since Philo was hardly the first one to hold such positions, one must look to earlier writers for clues to the background of his philosophical outlook. Such clues are to be found in Alexandria in the first century B.C. The most important figures are Antiochus of Ascalon, Eudorus of Alexandria, and Arius Didymus.

The first of these figures, Antiochus of Ascalon (ca. 130–68 B.C.), was in Alexandria for only a short period of time. He is less important for his specific philosophical opinions than he is for the basic change of orientation that he signals for Platonism. Antiochus studied with Philo of Larissa in Athens at the end of the second century. Philo of Larissa was a member of the sceptical New Academy, and Antiochus was for about twenty years a fairly orthodox follower of Arcesilaus and Carneades as interpreted by Philo of Larissa.[37] However, in 87–86 B.C., on a trip with the Quaestor L. Lucullus to Alexandria, Antiochus broke with the sceptical New Academy and sought to return to the doctrine of the "ancients," by which term he meant Plato, Speusippus, Xenocrates, Polemon, Aristotle, and Theophrastus.[38] Antiochus maintained the substantial unity of the positions taken by all of these philosophers.[39] Nevertheless his positions on physics and theology reflect a

[36] The influence of Posidonius (c. 135–50 B.C.) on Middle Platonism had been emphasized by W. Jaeger (*Nemesios von Emesa* [Berlin: Weidmann, 1914]) and K. Reinhardt (*Poseidonios* [Munich: C. H. Beck, 1921], *Kosmos und Sympathie* [Munich: C. H. Beck, 1926], "Poseidonios," PW 22, 558–926). However both L. Edelstein ("The philosophical System of Posidonius," *AJP* 57 [1936] 286–325) and A. D. Nock ("Posidonius," *Essays on Religion and the Ancient World* [Cambridge: Harvard University Press, 1972] 853–876) have shown that Posidonius still remained a Stoic and was not of fundamental importance for the development of Middle Platonism. G. Luck (*Der Akademiker Antiochos* [Bern: Paul Haupt, 1953]) emphasized the importance of Antiochus for the development of Middle Platonism, but J. Dillon (*The Middle Platonists* [Ithaca: Cornell University Press, 1977] 52–106) thinks that Antiochus, like Posidonius, remained essentially a Stoic. Both Dillon (115–135) and H. Dörrie, ("Der Platoniker Eudorus von Alexandreia," *Platonica Minora* [Munich: Wilhelm Fink, 1976] 297–309) emphasize the importance of Eudorus of Alexandria (fl. 30 B.C.) in the development of Middle Platonism.
[37] J. Dillon, *The Middle Platonists*, 53.
[38] Cicero, *Acad. Pr.* 11–15; *Acad. Post.* 13–43.
[39] Cicero, *Acad. Pr.* 14; *Acad. Post.* 15–18.

Stoic monism.[40] In that sense he cannot be seen as a founder of Middle Platonism. Yet his importance for the development of Middle Platonism should not be underestimated. He and his disciples turned away from the scepticism of the New Academy to a more dogmatic position. In addition he claimed that the position that he held was based on his reading and interpretation of the "ancients." Both this turn from scepticism and the turn to the authority of the "ancients" were important in establishing the groundwork for Middle Platonism.

The second figure is Eudorus of Alexandria (fl. 30 B.C.). Practically nothing is known of his life. He may have had contact with Antiochus himself, or the contact may have been through Antiochus' pupil Dion.[41] We know little more about his philosophical outlook, but what we know points to several developments that were crucial for the development of Middle Platonism.[42] In the first place Eudorus seems to have written a commentary on Plato's *Timaeus*.[43] Eudorus was not alone in being interested in the *Timaeus*. Several years earlier Cicero had translated the *Timaeus* into Latin.[44] This indicates a fairly wide philosophical interest in reading and interpreting Plato's *Timaeus*, an interest that began, perhaps, as early as the latter part of the second century B.C.[45] This is an important development,

---

[40] It appears from Cicero (*Acad. Pr.* 13–63 and *Acad. Post.* 13–43) that Antiochus thought that Stoicism was a correction of the Old Academy and not a new system (especially *Acad. Post.* 43). In this way, Antiochus could maintain an essentially Stoic outlook and yet claim to be in agreement with the "ancients." See A. A. Long, *Hellenistic Philosophy* (London: Duckworth, 1974) 226.

[41] Cf. P. M. Fraser, *Ptolemaic Alexandria*, 1.489 (Antiochus); J. Dillon, *The Middle Platonists*, 115 (Dion).

[42] The two most detailed treatments of Eudorus are H. Dörrie, "Der Platoniker Eudorus von Alexandreia," in *Platonica Minora*, 297–309 and J. Dillon, *The Middle Platonists*, 115–135.

[43] Plutarch, *De An. Pro. in Tim.* 1019e and 1020c.

[44] J. Dillon, *The Middle Platonists*, 108, 117–8. Cicero probably translated Plato's *Timaeus* into Latin in 45 B.C. Cicero (106–43 B.C.) seems to have been unaware of the kinds of philosophical developments that one finds in either Eudorus or in the *Timaeus Locrus* (a document to be discussed later in this chapter). While Cicero may not have kept abreast of every philosophical development, he certainly was aware of the revival of Pythagoreanism under Publius Nigidius Figulus (98–45 B.C.) in whose mouth he placed his Latin version of Plato's *Timaeus*. Cicero was in a position to have known of the kinds of philosophical developments that one finds in Eudorus or in the *Timaeus Locrus*.

[45] H. Dörrie ("Der Platonismus in der Kultur- und Geistesgeschichte der frühen Kaiserzeit" [*Platonica Minora*, 174–5]) places this renewed interest between 70 and 60 B.C. However, given the fact that both Panaetius and Posidonius show interest in Plato's *Timaeus*, this date is too late. The renewed interest in the *Timaeus* must have begun earlier, perhaps in the latter part of the second century B.C.

because much of the physics and theology of Middle Platonism is rooted in the interpretation of the *Timaeus.*

The second development to which Eudorus points is the return of the notion of transcendence. Neither the monism of the Stoics nor the agnosticism of the Sceptics (whether inside or outside of the New Academy) had room for a transcendent deity. A fragment from Eudorus suggests just such a restoration of transcendence.

> "It must be said that the Pythagoreans postulated on the highest level the One as a First Principle, and then on a secondary level two principles of existent things, the One and the nature opposed to this. And there are ranked below these all those things that are thought of as opposites, the good under the One, the bad under the nature opposed to it. For this reason these two are not regarded as absolute first principles by this School: for if the one is the first principle of one set of opposites and the other of the other, then they cannot be common principles of both, as is the (supreme) One." And again he says: "So in another way they said that the (supreme) One was the principle of everything, even of matter and of all existent things born of it (the One). This is the Supreme God (ὁ ὑπεράνω θεός)." Elsewhere, by way of clarification, Eudorus says that the (supreme) One established them (that is, the second One and its opposite) but adds that elements (στοιχεῖα) are derived from that One, elements that they call by many names. "I maintain then that the Pythagoreans allow that the (supreme) One is the principle of everything, but in another way they introduce in addition to it two highest elements. They call these two elements by many names. One of them is called by them ordered, limited, knowable, male, odd, right, and light; the one opposed to this is called disordered, unlimited, unknowable, female, left, even, and darkness. In this way the (supreme) One is a principle, but the One and the Unlimited Dyad are also elements, both 'Ones' being then principles. It is clear then that the One which is the principle of everything is other than the One which is opposed to the Dyad. The second One they also call the Monad." (Simplicius, *In Phys.*, I.5; Diels, 181. 7–30.)[46]

In this structure which Eudorus describes as Pythagorean, there is a One which utterly transcends the principles of existent things. This supreme One is called the Supreme God. While Eudorus describes the position as "Pythagorean," the reality might not have been so simple. Neither the old Pythagoreans nor the revived Pythagoreanism of the first century B.C. seems to have held that there was a supreme One above the second One and its opposite.[47] Eudorus may well have been more original than he lets on. In any

---

[46] The translation of the first half of the passage is from J. Dillon, *The Middle Platonists,* 126–7.
[47] Alexander Polyhistor *apud* D. L. 8.24–25; J. Dillon, *The Middle Platonists,* 127.

case, the notion of a supreme, transcendent God beyond the basic principles of existing things became a characteristic doctrine of Middle Platonism.

Yet the transcendence is of a peculiar sort. The emphasis on the transcendence of the supreme One creates the need for an intermediate realm in which one finds the proximate principles or causes for existing things. In the quotation from Eudorus this is the realm of the Monad and the Infinite Dyad. These two principles and the opposition between them are the proximate causes of the terribly precarious stability of the world of becoming and so are intermediate figures below the supreme One. The structure of this intermediate realm will be different for each Middle Platonist, but the existence of such a realm is characteristic of Middle Platonism.[48]

Whether or not Eudorus himself is the originator of this characteristically Middle Platonic scheme, at least he is a representative in late first-century B.C. Alexandria of an important philosophical option available to Jewish interpreters of the Bible.

Finally, Eudorus is a witness to the interweaving of the Platonic and the Pythagorean. In a sense the close connection of Platonic and Pythagorean concepts goes back to Plato himself. After all, the Timaeus in Plato's dialogue was a Pythagorean. More specifically, in this passage Eudorus ascribes a doctrine to the Pythagoreans that is probably an interpretation of the first three hypotheses of Plato's *Parmenides*.[49] Whether the interpretation was Eudorus' own or whether it was that of some Pythagorean is less important than the fact that we have an interpretation of a Platonic dialogue ascribed to Pythagoreans. In Middle Platonism one is often hardpressed to distinguish between the two.

The third figure is that of another Alexandrian, Arius Didymus. Arius Didymus lived in the late first century B.C. and was somewhat younger than Eudorus, whose work he made use of.[50] Arius Didymus was connected with the court of Augustus and was probably more important in that role than he was ɾ s a philosopher. Among other things he wrote a work entitled *On the Doctrines of Plato*. Only one fragment of this summary of Plato has been

---

[48] Cf. Albinus, *Didaskalikos* X, p. 164, 16–27; Apuleius, *De Dog. Plat.* 193–4; Numenius, Fr. 21 (des Places).

[49] E. R. Dodds, "The *Parmenides* of Plato and the Origin of the Neoplatonic 'One,'" 129–142, especially 132–6. The relationship of Middle Platonism to Pythagoreanism is murky, to say the least. Positions characterized as Pythagorean were certainly a part of Middle Platonism, but how and when these positions entered the Platonic tradition is not clear. Cf. H. Thesleff, *An Introduction to the Pythagorean Writings of the Hellenistic Period* (Abo: Abo Akademi, 1961); W. Burkert, *Lore and Science in Ancient Pythagoreanism* (Cambridge: Harvard University Press, 1972); H. J. Krämer, *Der Ursprung der Geistmetaphysik* (Amsterdam: Schippers, 1964); and *Platonismus und hellenistische Philosophie* (Berlin: de Gruyter, 1971).

[50] P. M. Fraser, *Ptolemaic Alexandria*, 1.489–90.

preserved, but it will be helpful in locating several of the interpretations found in Philo's comments on the creation of man.[51] Since it is unlikely that Arius Didymus was an original philosopher, his description of Plato's doctrines probably represents a fairly common interpretation of such doctrines in late first-century B.C. Alexandria.

A document that illustrates many of these developments is "Timaeus Locrus'" *On the Nature of the World and of the Soul.*[52] This document purports to be the original words of the Pythagorean Timaeus who is the main character in Plato's dialogue. In reality the situation is quite different. The *Timaeus Locrus* is dependent on Plato's *Timaeus* and is an interpretation of Plato's dialogue. In his recent commentary on this work, Matthias Baltes has argued by means of a number of parallels with the extant fragments of Eudorus that the *Timaeus Locrus* may have originated in the circle of Eudorus.[53] The work was probably written then in the late first century B.C. in Alexandria. The opening sections illustrate both the revival of belief in a transcendent deity and the development of an intermediate figure between that transcendent deity and the world.

> Timaeus the Locrian said the following: There are two causes of all things, Mind (νόος) for everything that happens according to reason (κατὰ λόγον) and Necessity (ἀνάγκα) for that which happens by force (βίᾳ) according to the powers of bodies. Of these the one has the nature of the good and is called God and the principle (ἀρχά) of the best things, while the others, being secondary and contributory causes, are to be subsumed under Necessity. The totality of things is threefold: Idea, Matter, and the Sense Perceptible which is the offspring of the other two. The Idea is eternal, unchanging and immovable, indivisible and of the nature of the Same, intelligible and a paradigm of things which

---

[51] Arius Didymus *apud* Eusebius, *Praep. Evang.* 11.23.3–6.

[52] Timaeus Locrus, *De Natura Mundi et Animae* (ed. W. Marg; Leiden: Brill, 1972). For the sake of convenience this document will be referred to as the *Timaeus Locrus*. It was written in Doric.

[53] M. Baltes, *Timaios Lokros, Über die Natur des Kosmos und der Seele* (Leiden: Brill, 1972) 23. Baltes draws this conclusion from a series of parallels between the *Timaeus Locrus* and the fragments of Eudorus. The first of these parallels (the number 384 as the basic number for the division of the soul) goes back to Crantor (ca. 335–275 B.C.). A second parallel (the description of the Idea as male and matter as female) goes back to Xenocrates (ca. 396–314 B.C.) A third (a Stoic definition of passion as πλεονάζουσα ὁρμή) is common to both Eudorus and the *Timaeus Locrus*. Finally both Eudorus and the *Timaeus Locrus* show a great deal of interest in mathematical questions, especially those concerned with the division of the soul. The first two parallels, both of which go back to the period of the Old Academy, are peculiar enough to make it improbable that both Eudorus and the *Timaeus Locrus* are drawing separately on Crantor and Xenocrates. It seems to me that Dillon (*The Middle Platonists*, 131) is being too sceptical when he thinks that Eudorus and the *Timaeus Locrus* are drawing separately on the Old Academy.

are made and which are in flux. Thus must one speak of and contemplate the Idea. Matter is that which receives impressions (ἐκμαγεῖον), the mother and nurse, and the one who brings forth the third kind of being. When Matter has taken to itself the likenesses (ὁμοιώματα), and, as it were, has been stamped by them, it produced those things which have been made. He (Timaeus) said that Matter was eternal but not immovable, of itself formless and patternless but receiving every form. Because of its relationship to bodies, it is divisible and of the nature of the Different. Matter is called place and space. These two then are principles, of which the Form (τὸ εἶδος) has the character of the male and father while Matter has that of the female and mother. The third (the Sense Perceptible) is the offspring of these two. Because they are three, they are apprehended in three different ways: the Idea by mind (νόος) through scientific knowledge, Matter by a kind of spurious reasoning since it cannot be known directly but only by analogy, and what is begotten from these by sense perception and opinion.

Before the heaven, according to this account, came into being, the Idea and Matter already existed, as well as God, the maker of the better. Because the elder is better than the younger and the ordered than the disordered, when God who is good saw that Matter received the Idea and was changed in all kinds of ways but not in an orderly fashion, he wanted to order it and to bring it from an indefinite to a defined pattern of change, so that the differentiations of bodies might be proportional and Matter would no longer be changed arbitrarily. (*Timaeus Locrus* 93a–94c.)

One finds in this opening section both a transcendent deity, Mind (νόος), and between this transcendent Mind and the world comes the Idea (ἰδέα). The Platonic ideas have coalesced into a single figure, the Idea, which serves as the model, the archetype for the visible world. The intermediate figure is different from that found in the fragment from Eudorus. In Eudorus the intermediate figure was the Monad rather than the Idea. This is not at all unusual. The structure and function of the intermediate realm varies from Middle Platonist to Middle Platonist. What is constant is the existence of that realm and its mediating role between the highest deity and the visible world.[54]

What evidence there is, then, points to the Alexandria of the first century B.C. as the place of origin for some of those philosophical positions which are characteristic of Middle Platonism. Eudorus himself may or may not have been the originator of some of these positions, but the least we can say is that such speculation was part of the philosophical milieu of the city, especially in the latter half of the first century B.C.

[54] See footnote 48.

Jewish interpreters must have found such speculation very attractive. The fact that such speculation once again emphasized the transcendence of the supreme deity must have come as a welcome alternative to the prevailing Stoic monism. The way in which this movement from a Stoic to a Middle Platonic point of view took place will become clearer when we analyze the levels of interpretation of the story of the creation of man as those levels are found in Philo. In addition, much of this speculation seems to have taken place in connection with the interpretation of Platonic texts, especially of the *Timaeus*. In that sense, not only the speculation itself but also the form that the speculation took offered a helpful model for Jewish interpreters. Just as Middle Platonic thought took the form of an interpretation of Platonic texts, and again especially of the *Timaeus*, so too Jewish explanations of the origin of the world took the form of interpretations of the early chapters of Genesis. Middle Platonism then offered helpful models, both in terms of content and in terms of form, to Jewish interpreters of the creation story in Genesis.[55]

Middle Platonic thought always had a strong religious coloring to it, and Jewish interpreters must also have found that religious coloring attractive. The standard Middle Platonic formulation of the purpose of life, the goal of ethics, was "likeness or assimilation to God" (ὁμοίωσις θεῷ). The formula was derived from Plato's *Theaetetus* (176b) and is found in a fragment from Eudorus.

> Socrates and Plato agree with Pythagoras that the goal is assimilation to God (ὁμοίωσις θεῷ). Plato defined this more clearly by adding "in so far as possible" (κατὰ τὸ δύνατον); and it is only possible by wisdom (φρόνησις), that is to say, as a result of virtue. (Stobaeus, *Ecl. Eth.* II.49, 8–12.)

The same formulation is found in Philo and, like Eudorus, Philo refers to Plato's *Theaetetus*.

> This truth found noble utterance in the *Theaetetus*, where a man highly esteemed, one of those admired for their wisdom, says: "Evils can never pass away; for there must always remain something which is antagonistic to good. Having no place among the gods in heaven, of necessity they hover around the mortal nature and this earthly sphere. Wherefore we ought to fly away from earth to heaven as quickly as we can; and to fly away is to become like God (ὁμοίωσις θεῷ), as far as this is possible; and to become like him is to become holy, just and wise." (*Fug.* 63.)

---

[55] The term "form" is used here very broadly since we do not know precisely what the interpretations of Plato looked like in the late first century B.C. (e.g., whether or not they were line by line interpretations). What is important, however, is that the way in which philosophical reflection was carried on in Middle Platonism was through the interpretation of Platonic texts.

While such a formulation of the purpose of life is not restricted to Middle Platonism, it is the characteristic formula for Middle Platonists.[56] It is a formula that places the philosophical thought of Middle Platonists in a highly religious context. Philosophical reflection is part of a process by which one is assimilated to the divine or becomes like the divine. In general, as Antonie Wlosok has shown, the Middle Platonic thought of the latter part of the first century B.C., especially in Alexandria, is deeply affected by a Platonism (influenced by Neopythagoreanism) in which cult myths and mystery rites are reinterpreted and allegorized. This interest in the reinterpretation of cult myths and mystery rites also reflects the intensely religious character of much Middle Platonic thought.[57] The attraction, then, of Middle Platonism for Jewish interpreters was not simply its conceptual structure but also the religious sensibility that was a crucial part of that framework. The specific ways in which successive generations of Jewish interpreters made use of these concepts will become clearer as we analyze more closely the various levels of interpretation of the accounts of the creation of man.

---

[56] J. Dillon, *The Middle Platonists*, 43–4. For the use of this formula by later Stoics, see H. Merki, ΟΜΟΙΩΣΙΣ ΘΕΩ (Fribourg: Paulusverlag, 1952) 8–17.

[57] Wlosok, *Laktanz und die philosophische Gnosis*, 50–60.

CHAPTER II

STAGES OF INTERPRETATION

As one begins to read Philo's interpretation of man's creation in *De Opificio Mundi*, the text seems quite straightforward. In *Op.* 69-71 Philo interprets Gen 1:26-27 which tells of man's creation as the image of God. According to him the "image" of God includes only man's mind and not his body, since God is not anthropomorphic and so has no body. Philo then goes on to deal with the problem of the "us" in "Let *us* make man . . ." (Gen 1:26). According to him the "us" refers to helpers whom God used to create the lower parts of man, the parts from which evil could originate. In this way God is not responsible for any evil actions that man might commit (*Op.* 72-75). Man is then completely formed. God has created the human mind as his own image, and his helpers have created the rest of man.

All of that seems quite clear until one comes to the interpretation of the second description of man's creation in Gen 2:7 (*Op.* 134-135). One then discovers that one has been thinking of the wrong "man." What appeared to be the creation of man, mind and body, in Gen 1:26-27 now turns out to be quite different. The "man" made in Gen 1:26-27 is still made in the image of God but is now an idea, a seal, incorporeal, neither male nor female, and by nature incorruptible (*Op.* 134). He is an intelligible, heavenly man. One also discovers that only in Gen 2:7 is the earthly, corruptible, sense perceptible, mortal man created. He is formed from earth into which is breathed a divine spirit (πνεῦμα θεῖον); and, because of this, the earthly man is on the borderline between the mortal and the immortal (*Op.* 135). One can look back to *Op.* 69-75 in the hope of finding some clue which would indicate that Philo's interpretation of Gen 1:26-27 really was about the creation of an intelligible, heavenly man, but no clues are to be found. Taken by itself, *Op.* 69-75 assumes that there is but a single creation of man and that man is made up of soul and body. The interpretation of Gen 2:7 in *Op.* 134-135, however, claims that there are not one but two creations of "man." The first, described in Gen 1:26-27, is the creation of an intelligible, heavenly man; the second, described in Gen 2:7, is the creation of an earthly, sense perceptible man. We have, then, two very different interpretations of the creation of man. The fact that the interpretation of Gen 2:7 in *Op.* 134-135 tries to turn the creation of

20

man in Gen 1:26–27 into the creation of a heavenly man cannot disguise the reality that the interpretation of Gen 1:26–27 in *Op.* 69–75 knows of only one creation of man.

When one turns to other passages in Philo, especially those in the *Legum Allegoriae*, in the hope of clarifying this problem, the situation becomes more rather than less confusing. One finds that even within these two different interpretations of the creation of man (that is, the double creation of man and the single creation of man), the interpretations are not unified. In addition to an interpretation of Gen 2:7 which distinguishes between a heavenly man and an earthly man, there is also an interpretation of Gen 2:7 in which there is only a single creation of man. Such an interpretation is found in *L. A.* 1.36–40. In this interpretation God breathes a divine spirit into the dominant part of man's soul, his mind. In *L. A.* 1.36–40 there is no indication that the creation of man in Gen 2:7 is the creation of an *earthly* man distinct from the prior creation of a *heavenly* man in Gen 1:26–27. Within a structure of interpretation, then, that recognizes only a single creation of man, two interpretations exist: One, rooted in Gen 1:26–27, emphasizes man as an image (εἰκών); the other, rooted in Gen 2:7, emphasizes the divine spirit (πνεῦμα θεῖον) as the central element in man's creation. The philosophical affinities of each of these two interpretations are quite different. The interpretation of the term "image" (εἰκών) in Gen 1:26–-27 is Platonic while the term "spirit" (πνεῦμα) in Gen 2:7 receives a Stoic interpretation. Yet the fact that they often appear together with their concepts and vocabulary combined (*Det.* 80–90; *Plant.* 14–27; *Mut.* 223; *Op.* 139, 145–146; *Spec.* 1.171) indicates that they are referring to the same single creation of man.[1]

Even within these two interpretations of the single creation of man, differences can be discerned. In most of the interpretation of Gen 1:26–27 as a single creation (*Op.* 24–25; *L. A.* 3.95–96; *Her.* 230–231; *Spec.* 1.80–81; *Spec.* 3.83, 208; *Q. G.* 2.62), man is not created directly as an image of God but rather as the image of an image. That "image" of God which serves as a paradigm for the creation of man is called the *Logos*. In this interpretation man is an image of the *Logos* who is in turn an image of God. However, in *Op.* 69–71 and *Op.* 72–75 *et par.* there is no intermediate *Logos* figure. In *Op.* 69–71 man is created as an image of God himself. In *Op.* 72–75 *et par.*, man is created by God and his powers but there is no *Logos* figure, and man is not created as an image of God's powers.

---

[1] The importance of these quite different philosophical affinities will become clearer in Chapters III and IV. For the moment it is enough to note that the philosophical interpretations given to these two terms point to distinct interpretations of the one creation of man.

In addition, the interpretations that lack the intermediate *Logos* figure are all anti-anthropomorphic. They are interpretations meant to refute an objection which claims that the text is predicating something human and so something unworthy of God. For instance, *Op.* 69–71 sets out to answer the objection that if man is created in the image of God, then God must have a body, since man, his image, has a body. The objection is overcome by claiming that only man's mind and not his body is an image of God.[2] However, none of the interpretations in which the *Logos* serves as an intermediate figure between God and man is anti-anthropomorphic. There are, then, two distinct interpretations or at least stages of interpretation within the interpretative history of Gen 1:26–27, one with and one without the intermediate *Logos* figure.

A similar phenomenon is present, although less clearly so, in the interpretation of Gen 2:7. The structure of *L. A.* 1.36–38, like that of *Op.* 69–71, *Op.* 72–75 *et par.*, is anti-anthropomorphic. The interpretation denies the "monstrous folly" that God's breathing of the spirit (πνεῦμα) into man at his creation involved the use of inbreathing organs such as mouth or nostrils. The other interpretations of Gen 2:7 which still maintain a single creation of man are not anti-anthropomorphic in structure.[3] These other interpretations are also far more developed in that they go well beyond the interpretation of man's creation as an inbreathing of spirit to discuss the "divine spirit" (πνεῦμα θεῖον) as a "fragment" (ἀπόσπασμα) of the divinity. *L. A.* 1.36–38, then, stands apart from the other interpretations of Gen 2:7 as a single creation.

Finally, these interpretations are not isolated oddities. With the exception of *L. A.* 1.36–38, each interpretation is attested in several different passages in Philo. Even *L. A.* 1.36–38, since it is an anti-anthropomorphic interpretation, is at least structurally similar to *Op.* 69–71 and to *Op.* 72–75. This multiple attestation indicates that they are distinct interpretations or at least distinct stages of interpretation; they are not the result of a fit of forgetfulness on the part of Philo. The following table lists the passages in Philo which represent the various interpretations:

---

[2] The same is true of *Op.* 72–75 *et par.* God made use of helpers in the creation of the lower parts of man not because God had any need of helpers but because he was to have no part in the evil deeds of man which originated in man's lower parts.

[3] *L. A.* 1.39–40; *L. A.* 1.161; *Her.* 281–83; *Som.* 1.33–34; *Spec.* 4.123.

A. Gen 1:26–27
  1. Anti-anthropomorphic and no *logos* figure
  Op. 69–71
  Op. 72–75
  Conf. 168–82
  Mut. 27–32
  Fug. 68–72
  2. *Logos* figure present and not anti-anthropomorphic
  Op. 24–25
  L. A. 3.95–96
  Her. 230–31
  Spec. 1.80–81
  Spec. 3.83
  Spec. 3.207
  Q. G. 2.62
B. Gen 2:7
  1. Anti-anthropomorphic and use of "spirit"
  L. A. 1.36–38
  2. Spirit as a "fragment"
  L. A. 1.39–40
  L. A. 3.161
  Her. 281–83
  Som. 1.33–34
  Spec. 4.123
  Q. G. 2.59
C. Gen 1:26–27 and Gen 2:7 combined
  Det. 80–90
  Plant. 14–27
  Mut. 223
  Op. 139
  Op. 145–146
  Spec. 1.171
  Virt. 203–05

A variety also exists within those interpretations of the creation of man which distinguish between the creation of an intelligible, heavenly man in Gen 1:26–27 and the creation of a sensible, earthly man in Gen 2:7. The double creation of man first occurs in *Op.* 134–135 and in the parallel passages in *L. A.* 1.31–32 and *Q. G.* 1.4. In all of these passages, the man created in Gen 1:26–27 is the man created after the Image of God, that is, the *Logos*. This man is immortal, an object of thought only, neither male nor female, and incorruptible (Op. 134; *L. A.* 1.31; *Q. G.* 1.4). However, the man created in Gen 2:7 is an earthly man into whom God breathed a divine spirit. That man consists of body and soul, is either male or female, and is by nature mortal (*Op.* 134–135; *L. A.* 1.31–32; *Q. G.* 1.4). The distinction in these passages is between a heavenly *man* and an earthly *man*.

However, as one reads other passages in which Gen 1:26–27 and Gen 2:7 are interpreted as a double creation, one notices the presence of a rather different interpretation. This other interpretation emerges in the distinction between the man whom God made and placed in the garden to guard it and till it (Gen 2:15) and the man whom God molded and simply placed in the garden (Gen 2:8).[4] The man mentioned in Gen 2:15 is taken to be the man created in Gen 1:26–27 while the man mentioned in Gen 2:8 is taken to be the man created in Gen 2:7. The distinction, however, is interpreted not as a distinction between two *men* but between two *minds*. The man of Gen 2:7–8 is the "molded mind" (ὁ πλαστὸς νοῦς) (*L. A.* 1.55) or the "earthly and perishable mind" (ὁ γήινος καὶ φθαρτὸς νοῦς) (*L. A.* 1.90). On the other hand, the man of Gen 1:26–27/2:15 is the "pure mind" (ὁ καθαρὸς νοῦς) that God takes to himself and does not allow to go outside of himself (*L. A.* 1.89). Such a mind has no part in perishable matter but is of a purer and clearer kind (*L. A.* 1.88). This purer mind is then associated with virtue (ἀρετή) (*L. A.* 1.53, 89; *Plant.* 44–46) and finally is even assimilated to the figure of the *Logos* (*Conf.* 40–41, 62–63, 146–47).

Within those interpretations of the creation of man as a double creation, we have two quite distinct interpretations, one that maintains a double creation of *man* and the other that maintains a double creation of *mind*. As with the single creation of man, these interpretations of the creation of "man" as a double creation are not isolated, odd interpretations but are conscious, intentional efforts to interpret the text of Genesis. The following table lists these interpretations.

A. Double Creation of *man*:
　　Op. 134–35
　　L. A. 1.31–32
　　Q. G. 1.4; 2.56
　　Q. G. 1.8a
B. Double Creation of *mind*:
　　L. A. 1.42
　　L. A. 1.53–55
　　L. A. 1.88–89
　　L. A. 1.90–96
　　L. A. 2.4
　　Plant. 44–46
　　Conf. 41
　　Conf. 62–63
　　Conf. 146

[4] *L. A.* 1.53–55, 88–89, 90–96.

At first one wonders what sense can be made out of all of these various, conflicting interpretations of the creation of man. Yet, as one reads them over carefully, patterns begin to appear by means of which one can see how one interpretation depends on another interpretation and yet goes beyond it. As this pattern of dependence and development repeats itself, an outline of the history of the interpretation of the creation of man emerges. Once this interpretative history has been clarified, one can then begin to see what belongs to the various levels of tradition which Philo drew on for his own interpretations.

The first pattern that emerges is the dependence of interpretations of the creation of man as a double creation on those that reflect only a single creation of man. The passages in which one finds Gen 1:27 and Gen 2:7 interpreted as a description of a double creation try only to explain why Gen 1:27 refers to the creation of a heavenly man and why Gen 2:7 refers to the creation of an earthly man. The fact that the man in Gen 1:27 was made as an image of the *Logos* and the fact that the man created in Gen 2:7 was made through the inbreathing of a divine spirit is not argued but assumed. Put another way, what requires proof is that these two descriptions of the creation of man (Gen 1:27 and Gen 2:7) refer to the creation of *two different* men, one heavenly and the other earthly; what are assumed to be correct are the interpretations of Gen 1:27 as the creation of man as the image of *Logos* and of Gen 2:7 as the creation of man through the inbreathing of a divine spirit. The interpretation of Gen 1:27 and Gen 2:7 as a double creation of man takes for granted the basic thought patterns and vocabulary of those interpretations which take Gen 1:27 and Gen 2:7 to refer to a single creation of man.

The heavenly man created in Gen 1:27 is the man created according to the Image of God, that is, according to the *Logos* (*Op.* 134–35; *L. A.* 1.31–32; *Q. G.* 1.4). This is most clearly expressed in *Q. G.* 1.4.

> But the man made in accordance with (God's) form is intelligible and incorporeal and a likeness of the archetype, so far as this is visible. And he is a copy of the original seal. And this is the *Logos* of God, the first principle, the archetypal idea, the pre-measurer of all things. (*Q. G.* 1.4.)

In this interpretation the *Logos* is the archetype, the seal, the pattern according to which man is made. The thought patterns and the vocabulary used to describe the *Logos* are the same as those used in *L. A.* 3.95–96, *Her.* 230–31, etc. In those latter passages we find, however, only a single creation of man. The passages that explain Gen 1:27 as the creation of a heavenly man take for granted the existence of an interpretation of Gen 1:27 in which man is created in the image of the *Logos*. Likewise the heavenly man is described as a copy or likeness of the *Logos*. This description, *except* for the heavenly character of the man, reflects the description in *L. A.* 1.95–96, *Her.* 230–31, etc. These latter passages, however, take the man mentioned in Gen 1:27 to refer to the creation of a single man. Once again the pattern of interpretation exemplified by *Q. G.* 1.4 takes for granted the interpretation found in *L. A.* 1.95–96, *Her.* 230–31, etc. Passages that explain the creation of the heavenly man take up the structure of the interpretation of Gen 1:27 as a single creation but push it in a different direction. That different direction is justified by an interpretation of the phrase "male *and* female" (ἄρσεν καὶ θῆλυ) in Gen 1:27 (*Op.* 134). This is taken to mean that not only is the man mentioned in Gen 1:27 created after the image of God, but he is also prior to any sexual differentiation and so not part of the sensible world. This distinguishes the man created in Gen 1:27 from the one formed in Gen 2:7, who is sexually differentiated, since, after the creation of the man in Gen 2:7, woman is created in Gen 2:21–22. Passages such as *Op.* 134–35 and *L. A.* 1.31–32, in which Gen 1:27 is interpreted as a description of the creation of a heavenly man, assume the existence of an interpretation of Gen 1:27 in such passages as *L. A.* 3.95–96, *Spec.* 1.80–81, *Q. G.* 2.62, etc., in which the explanation refers to the creation of a single man who is identical with the man created in Gen 2:7.

A similar phenomenon takes place with the creation of the *earthly* man in Gen 2:7. Passages such as *Op.* 134–135 and *L. A.* 1.31–32 take for granted an interpretation of Gen 2:7 in which man is created through the inbreathing of a divine spirit. *Op.* 134–135 and *L. A.* 1.31–32 argue only that the man created in Gen 2:7 is an *earthly* man distinct from the *heavenly* man created in Gen 1:27. This interpretation assumes the existence of the kind of interpretation found in *L. A.* 1.36–40 where only a single creation of man is mentioned. This new interpretation, however, moves in a different direction. That new direction is justified by an interpretation of Gen 2:7 which says that man is compounded of *earth* and divine spirit. This is taken to mean that he is composed of *body* and soul (*Op.* 134–135). No mention of body, however, is made in the text of Gen 1:27 and so the man created in Gen 1:27 must not be corporeal or sense perceptible. If that is the case, then the man created in Gen 2:7 must be distinct from the man created in Gen 1:27. The former is sensible while the latter is intelligible. Once again, passages such as *Op.* 134–135 and *L. A.* 1.31–32, in which Gen 2:7 is interpreted as the creation of a earthly, sensible man distinct from the creation of an intelligible, heavenly man, assume the existence of passages such as *L. A.* 1.36–40, *Spec.* 4.123, etc., in which Gen 2:7 is taken to refer to the creation of a single man identical with the man created in Gen 1:27.

Interpretations, then, of the creation of man as a double creation take over prior interpretations of Gen 1:27 and Gen 2:7 as complementary accounts of the creation of a single man and re-interpret them to refer to the creation of two different men, one heavenly and the other earthly. Accounts of the double creation of man depend, then, on prior accounts of the single creation of man.[5]

Within the interpretation of a double creation, some are accounts of a double creation of *man* (e.g., *Op.* 134–135; *L. A.* 1.31-32; *Q. G.* 1.4); others are of a double creation of *mind* (e.g., *L. A.* 1.53–55; *L. A.* 1.88–89). The latter depend on the former. In the first place, since Gen 1:26–27 and Gen 2:7 are accounts of the creation of man (or in this case, men), interpretations of those creations as creations of minds are developments of accounts that interpret them as the creation of men. Secondly, all of the other interpretations of Gen 1:26–27 and Gen 2:7 take both passages to refer to the creation of man and not of mind. Here are included all of the interpretations of Gen 1:26–27 and Gen 2:7 as a single creation. The tradition of interpretation is a tradition about the creation of man and not of mind. Thirdly, and most significantly, one can watch in a passage such as *L. A.* 1.88–89 the shift from "man" to "mind" take place.

> "And the Lord God took the *man* whom he had made, and placed him in the garden to till and guard it" (Gen 2:15). "The *man* whom God made (ὅν ἐποίησεν)" differs, as I have said before, from the one that "was molded (τοῦ πλασθέντος)": for the one that was "molded" is the more earthly *mind*, the one that was "made" the less material, having no part in perishable matter, endowed with a constitution of a purer and clearer kind.
>
> This pure *mind*, then, God takes, not suffering it to go outside of himself, and, having taken it, sets it among the virtues that have roots and put forth shoots, that he may till them and guard them. For many, after beginning to practise virtue, have changed at the last; but on the man to whom God affords secure knowledge, he bestows both advantages, both that of tilling the virtues, and also that of never desisting from them, but of evermore husbanding and guarding each one of them. So "tilling" represents practising, while "guarding" represents remembering. (*L. A.* 1.88–89.)

While the text of Gen 2:8,15 says "man," the interpretation shifts the meaning to that of "mind." A similar shift can be observed in *L. A.* 1.53–55. This shift indicates that, within interpretations of the double creation, interpretations of a double creation of "mind" are developments of interpretations of a double creation of "man."

When one turns to the interpretations of the creation of man as a single

---

[5] There are several passages that help us to understand the transition from the single to the double creation of man (*Op.* 76, 129–30; *Her.* 163–64; *L. A.* 2.11–13). However they do not directly affect the basic reconstruction of the history of the interpretation of the creation of man as it is found in Philo. These passages will be examined in Chapter V.

creation, two major interpretations emerge.[6] The first of these is an interpretation of Gen 1:26–27 in which man is created in the Image of God, and that
Image is God's *Logos*.[7] The second is an interpretation of Gen 2:7 in which
God breathes into man a divine spirit which is a "fragment" (ἀπόσπασμα) of
the divinity.[8] One suspects that originally these two interpretations were
quite separate. The interpretations of Gen 1:26–27 are Platonic in their
thought structure. Man is an image in the sensible world of a paradigm in the
intelligible world. The relationship of the intelligible world to the sensible
world is conceived of in thoroughly Platonic terms.[9] On the other hand, the
interpretation of Gen 2:7 in which man has a divine spirit, a fragment of the
divinity, is Stoic in outlook.[10] Granted that these are different interpretations
of the same text, the quite different philosophical outlooks of the two interpretations still speak against their coming from the same hand. In addition,
as often as not they appear separately in the text of Philo. In a number of
passages one finds only the interpretation of Gen 1:26–27 (*Op.* 24–25; *L. A.*
3.95–96; *Her.* 230–231; *Spec.* 1.80–81; *Spec.* 3.83, 207; *Q. G.* 2.62), while in
others one finds only the interpretation of Gen 2:7 (*L. A.* 1.36–40;
L. A. 3.161; *Her.* 281–283; *Som.* 1.33–34; *Spec.* 4.123). Originally, then, the
two interpretations were probably separate.

Yet the two interpretations are combined and are seen as two complementary interpretations of a single creation of man in a number of passages.[11] The question is whether this combination was made by Philo himself
or whether it occurred prior to Philo and became part of the tradition of
interpretation on which Philo drew. The latter is the more likely alternative
for two reasons. First of all, the interpretations which maintain a double
creation of man draw on *both* the interpretation of Gen 1:26–27 and the
interpretation of Gen 2:7. This suggests that the combination of the two
interpretations had already become traditional and that it was that traditional combination which was turned in a different direction by the interpretations of the creation of man as a double creation. Secondly, in some of the
passages in which the two interpretations are combined, there is an attempt
to interpret Gen 2:7 in the light of the interpretation of Gen 1:26–27.[12] In

---

[6] For the moment I am leaving out of consideration the anti-anthropomorphic interpretations listed in footnote 2.

[7] *Op.* 24–25; *L. A.* 3.95–96; *Her.* 230–31; *Spec.* 1.81; *Spec.* 3.83, 207; *Q. G.* 2.62.

[8] *L. A.* 1.39–40; *L. A.* 3.161; *Spec.* 4.123; *Som.* 1.33–34.

[9] See Plato's *Timaeus* 30a–d.

[10] See A. A. Long, *Hellenistic Philosophy*, 155–158 for the Stoic concept of
"spirit" (πνεῦμα).

[11] *Det.* 80–90; *Plant.* 14–27; *Mut.* 223; *Op.* 139, 145–46; *Spec.* 1.171.

[12] E.g., *Mut.* 223; *Op.* 146; *Det.* 83.

other passages, the two interpretations are simply combined, without giving precedence to either of them.[13] For instance, in *Her.* 56 the two interpretations are set side by side, and there is no attempt to interpret one in the light of the other:

> Thus he says plainly "the soul of every flesh is the blood" (Lev 17:11). He does well in assigning the blood with its flowing stream to the riot of the manifold flesh, for each is akin to the other. On the other hand, he did not make the substance of the mind depend on anything created, but represented it as breathed upon by God. For the Maker of all, he says, "blew into his face the breath of life, and man became a living soul" (Gen 2:7); just as we are also told that he was fashioned after the image of his Maker (Gen 1:27).

In *Mut.* 223, however, the interpretation of Gen 2:7 is seen in the light of Gen 1:26–27.

> Now "reasoning" as a name is but a little word, but as a fact it is something most perfect and most divine, a fragment of the soul of the universe, or, as it might be put more reverently following the philosophy of Moses, a faithful impress of the divine Image.

Again, this suggests that the simple combination of the two interpretations was traditional. That traditional balance was then altered to give primacy to the interpretation of Gen 1:26–27. As we shall see later, that alteration was probably made by Philo himself.[14]

The remaining interpretations are structurally very similar; they are all anti-anthropomorphic interpretations.[15] Each is an attempt to answer an objection that the biblical text of either Gen 1:26–27 or Gen 2:7 attributes something improper to God, something that reduces God to the level of a human being. A solution is then proposed that interprets the text in such a way that the uniqueness, the otherness of God, is preserved. In each case the solution involves the use of an appropriate concept derived from either Platonic or Stoic philosophy.[16] In two of the three cases (*Op.* 69–71 and

---

[13] E.g., *Op.* 139; *Her.* 55–56; *Spec.* 1.171.

[14] *Her.* 281–83 is a clear example of the way in which Philo himself is uncomfortable with the Stoic interpretation of "spirit" in Gen 2:7. The reasons for this discomfort and the various ways in which Philo reinterpreted Gen 2:7 will be discussed in Chapter IV.

[15] *Op.* 69–71, 72–75; *Conf.* 168–182; *Mut.* 27–32; *Fug.* 68–72; *L. A.* 1.36–38. A passing anti-anthropomorphic reference is also made to Gen 1:26–27 in *Som.* 1.73–74. It is dependent, however, on the interpretation found in *Op.* 69–71.

[16] Platonic: *Op.* 69–71, image (εἰκών), *Tim.* 30a–d; *Op.* 72–75 *et par.*, helpers in the creation of the lower parts of man, *Tim.* 41a–44d. Stoic: *L. A.* 1.36–38, spirit (πνεῦμα), A. A. Long, *Hellenistic Philosophy*, 155–158.

L. A. 1.36–38), the interpretations form the basis from which all of the other interpretations mentioned developed. *Op.* 69–71 takes Gen 1:26–27 to mean that the mind of man (not his body) is an image of God. There is no *Logos* figure intermediate between the two. Later interpretations develop this basic interpretation by means of the insertion of the *Logos* figure. *Op.* 69–71 represents a more primitive formulation. In much the same way, *L. A.* 1.36–38, which interprets the breath (πνοή) that God breathed into man in Gen 2:7 as a divine spirit, serves as the basis from which later interpreters developed the notion that this spirit was a divine fragment (e.g., *L. A.* 3.161 and *Som.* 1.34). This indicates that, since none of the other levels of interpretation are anti-anthropomorphic, the anti-anthropomorphic interpretations represent one of the earliest levels of interpretation available to us in Philo. The third anti-anthropomorphic interpretation (*Op.* 72–75; *Conf.* 168–182; *Mut.* 27–32; *Fug.* 68–72), despite its multiple attestation, is a rather isolated interpretation. As an interpretation of the phrase "Let *us* make man . . ." in Gen 1:26, it attempts to show that the "us" refers to God's helpers or powers (δυνάμεις) who created the lower parts of man in order that God himself might not be held responsible for man's evil deeds since those deeds originate in the desires of those lower parts. In all of the other interpretations, however, these helpers go unmentioned; the only intermediate figures between God and man at man's creation are the *Logos* and then later the heavenly man. *Op.* 72–75 *et par.*, however, know nothing of these other figures (i.e., the *Logos* and the heavenly man). In other words, the interpretation of Gen 1:26 found in *Op.* 72–75 *et par.* stands apart from all of the developments of interpretation of Gen 1:26–27 which have been mentioned in this chapter. The anti-anthropomorphic interpretation of the phrase "let *us* make man . . .," like the other two anti-anthropomorphic interpretations of the creation of man (*Op.* 69–71 and *L. A.* 1.36–38), probably represents the earliest level of tradition available to us in Philo of the creation of man.[17]

The following table gives a schematic outline of the development of the interpretations of the creation of man and their interrelationship.

[17] There are two other anti-anthropomorphic passages which will be dealt with in the next chapter: *Op.* 148–50; *Q. G.* 1.21. Both are interpretations of the first man's giving of names to the animals (Gen 2:19). They are not significant, however, for the reconstruction of the interpretative history of the creation of man.

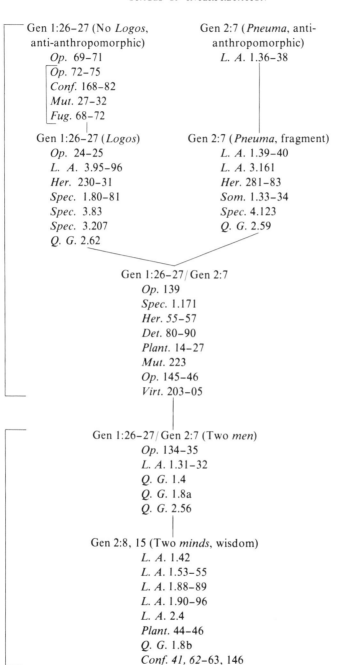

SINGLE CREATION

Gen 1:26–27 (No *Logos*,
    anti-anthropomorphic)
      Op. 69–71
      Op. 72–75
      Conf. 168–82
      Mut. 27–32
      Fug. 68–72

Gen 2:7 (*Pneuma*, anti-
    anthropomorphic)
      L. A. 1.36–38

Gen 1:26–27 (*Logos*)
    Op. 24–25
    L. A. 3.95–96
    Her. 230–31
    Spec. 1.80–81
    Spec. 3.83
    Spec. 3.207
    Q. G. 2.62

Gen 2:7 (*Pneuma*, fragment)
    L. A. 1.39–40
    L. A. 3.161
    Her. 281–83
    Som. 1.33–34
    Spec. 4.123
    Q. G. 2.59

Gen 1:26–27/Gen 2:7
    Op. 139
    Spec. 1.171
    Her. 55–57
    Det. 80–90
    Plant. 14–27
    Mut. 223
    Op. 145–46
    Virt. 203–05

DOUBLE CREATION

Gen 1:26–27/Gen 2:7 (Two *men*)
    Op. 134–35
    L. A. 1.31–32
    Q. G. 1.4
    Q. G. 1.8a
    Q. G. 2.56

Gen 2:8, 15 (Two *minds*, wisdom)
    L. A. 1.42
    L. A. 1.53–55
    L. A. 1.88–89
    L. A. 1.90–96
    L. A. 2.4
    Plant. 44–46
    Q. G. 1.8b
    Conf. 41, 62–63, 146

Finally, one must ask at what point in this history of interpretation Philo appears. It is important to keep in mind what is not involved in this question. The question is not about which interpretations Philo accepts and which he rejects. All of the interpretations that have been mentioned appear in Philo, and none of them are openly rejected by him. Philo is a traditional interpreter. He feels a responsibility not only to the biblical text but also to the interpretations of that text by his predecessors. He seldom openly rejects their interpretations, although he may reinterpret them in such a way that they more closely resemble his own viewpoint. Philo feels bound by their work. That work has a certain "canonical" value for him. The question, then, about which interpretations are the work of Philo is about which interpretations or which kinds of interpretation Philo himself initiated or wrote and not which interpretations he accepted or rejected. This is important to keep in mind lest we think that the only interpretations that were important to Philo were his own interpretations. On the contrary, as a traditional interpreter, the interpretations of his predecessors were as important to him as his own.

There are two ways of trying to answer the question. The first is to ask whether Philo explicitly tells us which interpretations are the work of previous interpreters. If our reconstruction of the development of the interpretation of man's creation is roughly correct, then any interpretation of man's creation that Philo attributes to a predecessor and every interpretation prior to that interpretation must be pre-Philonic.

Philo mentions a number of times that a given interpretation is that of "some others" (τινές), but he never mentions them by name.[18] An example of such a reference is quite helpful to us in sorting out Philo from his predecessors. The example is found in *Q. G.* 1.8, an interpretation of Gen 2:8: "And the Lord God planted a garden in Eden, in the east; and there he put the man whom he had molded."

> (Gen 2:8) Why does he place the molded man in Paradise, but not the man who was made in his image?
> *Some*, believing Paradise to be a garden, have said that since the molded man is sense-perceptible, he therefore rightly goes to a sense-perceptible place. But the man made in his image is intelligible and invisible, and is in the class of incorporeal species.

---

[18] The mention of these other interpreters is not just a rhetorical device. They refer to real interpretations and are not simply foils for Philo's own interpretation. This is clear from *Q. G.* 1.8 given in the text. The first interpretation fits in well with the kind of explanation found in *Op.* 134–35 and *L. A.* 1.31–32.

But I would say that Paradise should be thought a symbol of wisdom. For the earth-formed man is a mixture, and consists of soul and body, and is in need of teaching and instruction, desiring, in accordance with the laws of philosophy, that he may be happy. But he who was made in his image is in need of nothing, but is self-hearing and self-taught and self-instructed by nature. (*Q. G.* 1.8).

At the moment, what is important is that Philo gives an interpretation of Gen 2:8 which he explicitly describes as someone else's interpretation. Present in that interpretation is the distinction between the intelligible man of Gen 1:26 and the sense perceptible man of Gen 2:7. Thus, the distinction between the intelligible, heavenly man, and the earthly, sense perceptible man found in passages such as *Op.* 134–135, *L. A.* 1.31–32, and *Q. G.* 1.4 are the work of previous interpreters; they are pre-Philonic. Similarly, all of the interpretations that lead up to and serve as a basis for that interpretation are pre-Philonic.

Because of its compressed character, the meaning of the second part of *Q. G.* 1.8 is not altogether clear. The two major elements in the interpretation are the notion of Paradise as a symbol of wisdom and the earthly man's need of teaching and instruction. The earthly man is in Paradise because he needs to be taught and instructed in wisdom. Both of these elements also appear in *Plant.* 44–46, where Paradise is a figure of the virtues and the sensible man of Gen 2:7 is the middle *mind* (μέσος νοῦς) that must choose between good and evil. The same identification of the man of Gen 2:7 with the *mind* that is in need of acquiring virtue is developed in *L. A.* 1.88–89, 90–96. The second half of *Q. G.* 1.8 represents (although less clearly) the same kind of shift from the notion of the earthly *man* to the notion of an earthly *mind* in need of instruction that takes place in *Plant.* 44–46 and *L. A.* 1.53–55, 88–89, 90–96. These passages will be analyzed more closely later.[19] But for the moment, what is important is that the interpretation found in *Q. G.* 1.8b and which Philo claims as his own is closely related to those interpretations which transform the two *men* of Gen 1:26–27 and Gen 2:7 into symbols of *mind* and *virtue.* It is in this area of interpretation, an area represented by the last set of passages on the chart on p. 31 that one comes upon Philo's own contribution to the interpretation of the creation of man.[20]

One comes to much the same conclusion when one asks the question about the overall interpretation found in *De Opificio Mundi* and *Legum Allegoriae.* This is the second way one can use to sort out the pre-Philonic

---

[19] See Chapter VI, section A.

[20] Another example in which Philo distinguishes himself from his predecessors is found in *Her.* 281–83. This passage will be analyzed in detail in Chapter IV.

from Philo's own contribution to the interpretation of the creation of man.
The basic structure of interpretation in *De Opificio Mundi* and *Legum
Allegoriae* is likely to reveal Philo's own viewpoint. That basic structural
viewpoint is that of the "allegory of the soul." This type of interpretation is
quite different from the interpretation that we have mentioned up until
now. Up until now the interpretations have taken the text of Genesis to refer
to events in the external world, i.e., the creation of the world and the creation of man. While the figures involved in the interpretations may have been
either heavenly figures such as the *Logos* or earthly figures such as the man
created in Gen 2:7, all of them belonged to the external world. Without
rejecting this kind of interpretation, the allegory of the soul emphasizes that
the figures described in the text of Genesis are also symbols of faculties and
processes that are within each individual. The allegory of the soul is essentially a method of interpretation in which the figures described in the text of
Genesis as figures in the external world are internalized and taken to refer to
internal, spiritual realities.[21] In this allegory, the man created in Gen 2:7
becomes a symbol of "mind" (νοῦς), the woman of "sense perception"
(αἴσθησις), and the serpent of "pleasure" (ἡδονή). Figures of the external
world, Adam, Eve, and the serpent, are now taken to refer to the interior life
of the individual human being. This viewpoint dominates all three books of
the *Legum Allegoriae* and *Op.* 151–170 which is a summary of what is found
in the *Legum Allegoriae*.[22] This viewpoint, then, represents Philo's own
interpretation of the creation and fall of man. It is also the viewpoint of
L. A. 1.53–55, 88–89, and 90–96 in which the earthly *man* of Gen 2:7
becomes the earthly *mind* and in this way can be integrated into the allegory
of the soul, the over-arching Philonic interpretation of the creation and fall
of man. Philo's own viewpoint, then, emerges in these interpretations of
Gen 2:8, 15. At the same time, the contrast highlights the pre-Philonic character of the other interpretations of the creation of man. However, the
allegory of the soul does not involve the rejection of these other interpretations of the text of Genesis, interpretations that refer to the external world.
Rather, there are two levels of interpretation, one "literal" (which refers to
events in the external world) and the other "allegorical" or "symbolic"
(which refers primarily to interior processes and events). Philo considers

---

[21] The nature and function of the allegory of the soul will be dealt with in more detail in
the last chapter of this study. For the moment it is enough to have a general notion of its
meaning and to know that it represents Philo's own viewpoint.

[22] The same conclusion, that is, that the Philonic stratum of interpretation is at the level
of the allegory of the soul, was arrived at by B. L. Mack ("Weisheit und Allegorie," 80–82).
Mack drew this conclusion from an analysis of *De Congressu Eruditionis Gratia*.

both of these levels of interpretation legitimate. But he is more interested in the allegorical level of interpretation, and it is that level which dominates *Legum Allegoriae* and the latter part of *De Opificio Mundi*.[23] This second approach, then, leads us to the same conclusion as did the first: The passages in which the two *men* become two *minds* are Philonic, and the other interpretations are not; they are the work of Philo's predecessors.

By a careful reading of the interpretations of the creation of man that occur in Philo, one can sort out the various levels in the history of the interpretation of the creation of man and one can point out at which level Philo's own interpretation enters in. Although this is helpful, one is still close to the level of brute facts. One still needs to understand how and why the interpretations of the creation of man developed in the way that they did. One needs also to understand the relationship of this development to the religious and cultural milieu in which these interpretations were developed, that is, to the milieu of Alexandria of the first century B.C. and the early first century A.D. Finally, one needs a clearer sense of how traditional interpreters like Philo and his predecessors went about their work, how they maintained the delicate balance between continuity and change that is the task of any interpreter who feels responsible to a tradition.

---

[23] This is not clearly visible in the *Questions and Answers on Genesis and Exodus*. Both literal and allegorical interpretations are given for each verse and both types of interpretation are considered valid. However, Philo devotes much more space to the allegorical interpretation.

Philo's notion of an "allegorical" interpretation involves 1) the internalization of the interpretation and 2) the recognition of multiple levels of interpretation. This was by no means the only conception of allegory in the ancient world. Most allegorists rejected the validity of the literal level of interpretation. Many did not interpret texts "allegorically" by internalizing the meaning of the text. Rather they took the text to refer to physical processes in nature. See J. Pépin, *Mythe et allégorie* (Paris: Aubier, 1958) 125–31, 146–67.

In this study I shall use the term "allegory" to refer only to those interpretations which characterize themselves as "allegorical." An interpretative technique may seem to be allegorical; but if it is never referred to as such, the interpreter does not take it to be an allegorical interpretation. In the interpretations of the creation of man in Philo, only at the level of Philo himself, that is, only at the level of the allegory of the soul, does the term appear.

CHAPTER III

ANTI-ANTHROPOMORPHIC INTERPRETATIONS

People of one cultural and religious heritage have always found it diffi-cult to live among a people who do not share that heritage. They often need to defend that heritage in terms that the people among whom they live would find acceptable. That process, however, is by no means simply a matter of external pressure. The cultural minority itself often makes its own the out-looks and the criteria of acceptability of the majority culture.[1] It is not surprising then that some of the earliest biblical interpretations that we possess which were written by Jews of the Hellenistic world attempt to answer objections raised by that world. For the educated class of the Hellen-istic world a God who appeared to be anthropomorphic in character was objectionable. For several centuries Homer had been attacked because he represented the gods as human in form and in faults and had been defended because his stories about the gods contained deeper, non-anthropomorphic truths.[2] In a sense the problem of anthropomorphisms was not a new one for Jewish writers. After all, the author of Second Isaiah had already been concerned to show that nothing was comparable to the reality of God.[3] Yet what was new for the Jewish interpreter living in the Hellenistic world was the way in which the problem was to be solved. The concepts used in solving the problem were drawn from the philosophical thought patterns of the Hellenistic world.

A. *The Pattern of the Anti-Anthropomorphic Interpretation*

Some of the earliest Jewish interpretations of the story of the creation of man found in Philo were just such attempts to answer accusations that God

---

[1] See V. Tcherikover, "Jewish Apologetic Literature Reconsidered," *Eos* 48 (1956) 169–93. Tcherikover emphasizes that Jewish apologetic literature was for internal rather than external consumption. The intended audience was the Jewish community and not the Gentile world. While this is much less true by the time we get to Philo, it is certainly true for the anti-anthropomorphic interpretations found in Philo and Aristobulus.

[2] F. Buffière, *Les mythes d'Homère et la pensée grecque* (Paris: Société d'édition "Les Belles Lettres," 1956); Pépin, *Mythe et allégorie.*

was human in form. One of the clearest examples of this anti-anthropo-morphic type of interpretation is found in *Op*. 69–71. These sections inter-pret Gen 1:26–27: "Let us make man after our image and likeness." The objection, of course, was that if man was like God then God must be like man (ἀνθρωπόμορφος). The response was that this image (εἰκών) referred not to the human body but only to the human mind (νοῦς).

> No, it is in respect of the mind, the sovereign element of the soul, that the "image" is used; for after the pattern of a single Mind, even the Mind of the Universe as an archetype, the mind in each of those who successively came into being was molded. It is in a fashion a god to him who carries and enshrines it as an object of reverence; for the human mind evidently occupies a position in men precisely answering to that which the great Ruler occupies in all the world. (*Op*. 69.)

Only the human mind is an "image" of God and not the human body. God is the archetype and the human mind is the image of that archetype.[4] In this way the interpreter thought that he had overcome the apparent anthropomorphism.[5]

The pattern of interpretation in this passage is quite simple and repre-sents the pattern found generally in this kind of exegesis:

1) Reference (either by quotation or by paraphrase) to the scriptural text.
2) Rejection of what appears to be an anthropomorphism.
3) Suggestion of an acceptable, non-anthropomorphic interpretation, the con-ceptions for which are drawn from the philosophical viewpoints of the period.[6]

A second and equally clear example of this pattern occurs in *Op*. 149–150, an interpretation of Gen 2:19: "(God) led them (the animals) to the man to see what he would call them; and whatever the man called every living creature, that was its name." After referring to this text, the objection is raised: How could God, who knows everything, be in doubt about what something should be called? A solution is then suggested:

> Not that he was in any doubt—for to God nothing is unknown—but because he knew that he had formed in mortal man the natural ability to reason of his own

---

[3] Isa 40:12–31.

[4] It is clear from the phrase "it is in respect of the mind that the 'image' is used" that εἰκών in this passage means "copy" (*Abbild*) and not "model" (*Vorbild*).

[5] The interpreter does not seem to have been aware that even the fact that man's mind is an image of God could be considered as an anthropomorphism.

[6] Mack, "Exegetical Traditions in Alexandrian Judaism," 81. This is essentially the struc-ture suggested by Mack.

motion, so that he himself might have no share in faulty action. No, he was putting man to the test, as a teacher does a pupil, kindling his innate capacity, and calling on him to put forth some faculty of his own, that by his own ability man might confer titles in no wise incongruous or unsuitable but bringing out clearly the traits of the creature who bore them. (*Op.* 149.)

After a rejection of the unacceptable interpretation that God was ignorant of something, the suggestion is made that, because God had given man the natural ability to reason (ἡ λογικὴ φύσις), he now puts that faculty to the test by having man assign appropriate names to the various animals. This verse is interpreted in the same way in *Q. G.* 1.21.[7]

The same anti-anthropomorphic pattern is found in *L. A.* 1.36–38, an interpretation of Gen 2:7: "(God) breathed into his (man's) face a breath of life. . . ." After rejecting as a monstrous folly the anthropomorphic notion that God had a mouth or nostrils, an alternate interpretation is given:

Yet the expression clearly brings out something that is in accord with reality (φυσικώτερον). For it implies of necessity three things, that which inbreathes, that which receives, that which is inbreathed; that which inbreathes is God, that which receives is the mind, that which is inbreathed is the spirit (πνεῦμα). What, then, do we infer from these premises? A union of the three comes about as God projects the power that proceeds from himself through the mediant spirit till it reaches the subject. (*L. A.* 1.36–37.)[8]

Once again we have the rejection of an anthropomorphism followed by the suggestion of a suitably non-anthropomorphic interpretation.

The final and by far the most complex example of this pattern takes us back to the interpretation of Gen 1:26, but this time of the phrase "Let *us* make man. . . ." Two questions would have arisen naturally for the Hellenistic Jew of that period, the identity of "us" and why God needed helpers to create man. An interpretation of the "us" appears in four places in Philo: *Op.* 72–75; *Conf.* 168–182; *Mut.* 27–32; *Fug.* 68–72. In all four places the interpretation is basically the same. God did not need helpers in order to create man but it was fitting that he should make use of such helpers because of the peculiar character of man (*Op.* 72; *Conf.* 175; *Fug.* 70). Of all of the creatures made by God, only man was capable of turning from virtue to vice (*Op.* 72–73; *Conf.* 178; *Fug.* 70). Creatures above man, such as unembodied souls or the spirits who inhabited the heavenly bodies partook only of virtues (*Op.* 73; *Conf.* 176–177). Creatures below man, such as animals and plants,

---

[7] The giving of names described in Gen 2:19–20 is not strictly part of the creation of man. Yet it remains outside of the allegory of the soul and is much more in keeping with the interpretations of the creation of man than with the allegorical interpretations of the fall.

[8] For the meaning of the term φυσικώτερον, see Hengel, *Judaism and Hellenism*, 1.164.

partook neither of virtue nor of vice, because they lacked the prerequisite of mind that would have enabled them to be either virtuous or its opposite (*Op.* 73; *Conf.* 177). Man however was capable of both virtue and vice. Because of this peculiarity of man, it was fitting for God to make only that part of man which was the highest and to leave to helpers (that is, to his Powers, δυνάμεις) the creation of the lower parts of man, the parts from which vice could originate (*Op.* 74; *Conf.* 179; *Mut.* 30–31; *Fug.* 69). In this way whatever was good in man could be assigned to God, while whatever was evil could be attributed to someone else, that is, to these helpers (*Op.* 75; *Conf.* 179–180; *Mut.* 30–31; *Fug.* 70).

These four passages are also similar from a structural point of view. In all four passages the problem of the meaning of the phrase "Let *us* make man" is solved by a distinction. In two of the cases (*Op.* 73; *Conf.* 176–178) the distinction is based on the different types of creatures made by God.

Op. 73	*Conf.* 176–178
Plants and animals devoid of reason (ζῷα ἄλογα)	The unreasoning part of creation (ἄλογον)
Living beings who partake only of virtue (ζῷα νοερά)	Reasoning part of creation which is immortal (λογική, ἀθάνατον εἶδος)
Those of a mixed nature (μικτῆ φύσις)	Reasoning part of creation which is mortal (λογική, φθάρτον εἶδος)

The solutions based on this distinction are also similar. In the case of the first two types it is fitting for God to be the sole creator; but, because man is capable of both wisdom and folly, of both good and evil (*Op.* 74; *Conf.* 178), it is proper for God to create only the better principle (*Op.* 74) or the principle that leads to right actions (*Conf.* 179), while the creation of the rest should be given to fellow-workers (συνεργοί) or subordinates (ὑπηρέται, ὕπαρχοι) (*Op.* 75; *Conf.* 179). In the other two passages (*Mut.* 27–32 and *Fug.* 68–72), the distinction and its consequences are of a similar nature but restricted to a consideration of man's capacity for both good and evil (*Mut.* 30; *Fug.* 70). In three of the four passages (*Conf.* 171–75; *Mut.* 28–29; *Fug.* 69), these helpers are identified with God's powers (δυνάμεις) at work in the created world. This identification of the helpers immediately precedes, in all three cases, the distinction mentioned above. Finally two of the four passages (*Op.* 72 and *Conf.* 168) begin by indicating that without caution one may end up attributing something scandalous to God, that is, that he was in need of helpers in creating man. This problem is more fully developed in the passage from the *De Opificio Mundi*. The point of the question concerns the reason why God used helpers in the creation of man when he had no need of such helpers for the rest of creation. The other two passages

(*Mut.* 27–32 and *Fug.* 68–72) do not begin by specifically stating that problem. Yet both of these passages are short summaries and are treated as secondary confirmations for the interpretations of other passages, *Mut.* 27–32 for Gen 17:1 and *Fug.* 68–72 for Gen 48:15–16.[9] They are interpretations whose validity is taken for granted and so now can be used to explain other biblical verses. Their present form then is secondary. Because the interpretation of Gen 1:26 found in these two passages is taken for granted, the statement of the problem that originally gave rise to the interpretation has been omitted.

These four passages, then, from the viewpoint of both content and structure, have a good deal of stability. Each makes the same points and does so with the same argument constructed in basically the same order. We have in these four passages an exegesis of Gen 1:26 that had become traditional and that Philo used and altered only to a limited extent. The structure of that traditional interpretation was the following:

A. Reference to Gen 1:26 (*Op.* 72).
B. Rejection of the notion that God needed helpers (*Op.* 72; *Conf.* 168).
C. Alternate interpretation:
   1. Identification of God's Powers (δυνάμεις) as the ones to whom he is speaking (*Conf.* 171–175; *Mut.* 28–29; *Fug.* 69).
   2. Distinction which serves as the basis of the solution (*Op.* 73; *Conf.* 176–178; *Mut.* 30; *Fug.* 70).
   3. Application of the distinction to the creation of man (*Op.* 74; *Conf.* 179; *Mut.* 31; *Fug.* 69–71).
   4. Purpose: to show that God has no part in evil (*Op.* 75; *Conf.* 179–180; *Mut.* 31–32; *Fug.* 70).

The pattern of these passages and their outlook clearly reflect the pattern and the outlook found in the other anti-anthropomorphic passages discussed above (i.e., *Op.* 69–71, 149–150; *L. A.* 1.36–38). Section A is a reference to the biblical text; Section B involves the rejection of an anthropomorphism; and Section C represents a suitable non-anthropomorphic interpretation of Gen 1:26, one which uses categories taken from the philosophy of the period and so would be acceptable to the educated class of the Hellenistic world. This same pattern is present in all of the anti-anthropomorphic interpretations of verses from the first three chapters of Genesis.[10]

---

[9] *Mut.* 27–32 is part of a larger interpretation of the different relationships that God has to good men and evil men. *Fug.* 68–72 is part of a discussion of how God leaves the execution of punishments to subordinate ministers.

[10] The other anti-anthropomorphic interpretations of verses from Genesis 1–3 are the following: *Op.* 13–14; *L. A.* 1.2–7, 43–44; *L. A.* 3.4–10, 51–55, 203–208; *Q. G.* 1.42, 53, 54, 55. *L. A.* 2.19–25 and *L. A.* 3.65–68 are not really anti-anthropomorphic interpretations. This

The similarity, however, among the anti-anthropomorphic interpretations of the creation of man goes beyond that of pattern. They also share several other characteristics. In the first place, they are isolated interpretations in the sense that they cannot be completely integrated into a larger context of interpretation. For instance, in *Op.* 69–71 the human mind is created as the image of God; man's mind is an image of God, the Mind of the universe. In all of the other interpretations of this verse that occur in Philo, man's mind is created according to the image of God and that image is God's *Logos* (e.g., *Op.* 24–25; *L. A.* 3.95–96; *Her.* 230–231; *Spec.* 1.80–81; *Spec.* 3.83). In these interpretations man's mind is not an image of God but the "image of an image." Similarily, the interpretation of the "us" in Gen 1:26 plays no role at all in the interpretation of the biblical verses that have to do with the actual creation of man. On the contrary, the creation of the sensible part of man's soul and of his body are all created either by God himself or by his *Logos* (e.g., *L. A.* 3.95–96; *L. A.* 2.19–25; *Q. G.* 1.53). The same can be said for two other anti-anthropomorphic interpretations (*Op.* 149–150 and *Q. G.* 1.21). Both of these passages are interpretations of man's giving of names to the animals (Gen 2:18–20). Adam, the man, gives the animals their names not because God is in any doubt about what the animals should be called but because God is testing man's ability to reason. This specifically anti-anthropomorphic interpretation cannot be integrated into Philo's allegory of the soul in which Adam, now as a symbol of mind, gives names to various objects (*L. A.* 1.91–92; *Mut.* 63–64; *Q. G.* 1.22).[11] The anti-anthropomorphic interpretation of the giving of names is not part of a larger context of interpretation. Finally, *L. A.* 1.36–38 (on the meaning of "breathed into") is one of a series of isolated interpretations of Gen 2:7. Although *L. A.* 1.39–40 is in continuity with *L. A.* 1.36–38 in that both are Stoic interpretations, *L. A.* 1.36–38 is a much simpler interpretation of the Stoic notion of spirit, while *L. A.* 1.39–40 points to a much more developed notion of spirit as a "divine fragment."[12] The isolated character of these

---

becomes clear when one compares these two passages with their parallels in the *Questions and Answers on Genesis* (*L. A.* 2.19–25 // *Q. G.* 1.24, 25, 27; *L. A.* 3.65–68 // *Q. G.* 1.47–48). None of the passages in *Q. G.* 1 suggests an anti-anthropomorphic interpretation; rather Philo has cast his allegorical interpretations of these passages in the pattern of an anti-anthropomorphic exegesis in L. A. 2.19–25 and L. A. 3.65–68. The anti-anthropomorphic structure of the interpretations is secondary. This procedure is enlightening because it points to the fact that such a pattern did exist and so could be imitated.

[11] *Op.* 149–50 must also be distinguished from *Op.* 148, an interpretation in which the problem of anthropomorphisms is completely forgotten. In *Op.* 148 the interpreter speaks quite unselfconsciously about man being made by "divine hands." *Op.* 149–50 then is a separate interpretation.

[12] See Chapter IV, section B.

anti-anthropomorphic interpretations suggests that this type of interpretation is *ad hoc*. They are isolated interpretations and not part of a consistent attempt to explain longer texts.[13] Other interpretations may be developed from them (e.g., from *Op.* 69–71 and *L. A.* 1.36–38), but they themselves are fairly basic attempts to solve particular exegetical problems and are not part of a larger context of interpretation.

A second characteristic of these anti-anthropomorphic passages is that they do not appeal to a two-level type of interpretation. Rather the interpretation is given as the one meaning of the text. There is no consciousness of the presence of levels of meaning (i.e., literal and allegorical). For instance, when Gen 1:26 is interpreted in *Op.* 69–71, the claim that the human mind and not the human body is a likeness of the Mind of the universe is a claim about the one meaning of the verse, and there is no indication that the author is aware of other levels of interpretation. This is true for all of the anti-anthropomorphic interpretations of the creation of man.[14] One finds in the anti-anthropomorphic interpretations of the creation of man neither the sense that the text is open to multiple levels of interpretation nor the technical terminology associated with the allegorical interpretations of Homer. Terms such as ὑπόνοια or ἀλληγορία simply to not occur in these interpretations.[15]

A third characteristic is that there is a commonality in the terminology used in these anti-anthropomorphic passages. This does not mean that exactly the same expressions are used in all of the passages to indicate the type of interpretation nor does it mean that the expressions used are found only in this kind of interpretation. Yet a series of expressions are used in these anti-anthropomorphic interpretations that cluster around the notions of what is "proper" or "fitting." Such terminology includes the following:

οἰκεῖος: *Op.* 13, 74 (3), 149; *L. A.* 1.4; *Conf.* 180
ἀνοικεῖος: *Op.* 74 (2), 149; *L. A.* 3.204
ἐμπρεπές, τὸ πρέπον: *Conf.* 175, 176, 179, 180
προσηκόντως, προσήκειν: *Conf.* 179, 180[16]

[13] Mack, "Exegetical Traditions in Alexandrian Judaism," 81.
[14] See footnote 10. The same is true for all of the anti-anthropomorphic interpretations of Genesis 1–3. In *De Opificio Mundi* and the *Legum Allegoriae* where an awareness of multiple levels in the text seems to exist, these elements have been added to an earlier anti-anthropomorphic interpretation that did not have that awareness. This is true of *L. A.* 3.4–10 where *L. A.* 3.6b is the original anti-anthropomorphic interpretation (cf. *L. A.* 3.51) and of *L. A.* 1.43–44 where *L. A.* 1.43b–44 is the original anti-anthropomorphic interpretation.
[15] These and other terms such as σύμβολον and συμβολικῶς will appear in the interpretation of Genesis 1–3 only at the level of the allegory of the soul.
[16] Examples of this terminology are drawn not only from interpretations of the creation

The use of such expressions in this type of interpretation is quite under-standable since the problem being dealt with is the attribution of something improper or unsuitable to God and the solution is to interpret the passage in such a way that only what is proper or fitting is attributed to God. For example, in the interpretation of Gen 1:26, an explanation of the verse must be given which shows that God is not in need of helpers in creating man but that the use of such helpers is fitting and proper in order to prevent an improper attribution to God of responsibility for the creation of evil.

Finally, these anti-anthropomorphic interpretations do not involve, for the most part, a detailed, word-by-word exegesis of the text. Rather the interpretation represents a probable suggestion that the passage can be properly understood when juxtaposed to concepts taken from the Hellenistic philosophy of the period. A clear example of this is found again in L. A. 1.36–37, an interpretation of Gen 2:7:

> "Breathed into," we note, is equivalent to "inspired" or "besouled" the soulless; for God forbid that we should be infected with such monstrous folly as to think that God employs for inbreathing organs such as mouth or nostrils; for God is not only not in the form of man, but belongs to no class or kind. Yet the expression clearly brings out something that accords with reality (φυσι-κώτερον). For it implies of necessity three things, that which inbreathes, that which receives, that which is inbreathed; that which inbreathes is God, that which receives is the mind, that which is inbreathed is the spirit (πνεῦμα).

There is no attempt at justification in terms of a specific explanation derived from the text about why "breathed into" means "inspired" or "besouled." It is simply stated that such an explanation is in accord with reality (φυσι-κώτερον). When something occurs in the text that is perceived as anthropo-morphic, the solution to the problem is an interpretation whose concepts are derived from the philosophy of the period. The justification for the use of any given philosophical concept is its appropriateness in interpreting the verse in Genesis. In this case, we have the appropriateness of the notions of active cause, passive recipient, and medium of causality as applied to the triad of God, man, and "inbreathing." The same is true of the passages that interpret the "us" of Gen 1:26. There is no textual justification given to show why the "us" of Gen 1:26 must represent God's Powers or why their partici-pation in the creation of man should absolve God of any responsibility for evil. Rather the interpreter simply claims that the explanation is a "plausible and reasonable" one (πιθανὴν καὶ εὔλογον) (Op. 72), or that it is fitting (ἐμπρεπές) that God should converse with his Powers (Conf. 175). The same

of man but from all of the anti-anthropomorphic interpretations of Genesis 1–3. This is to give a clearer picture of the widespread use of such terminology.

use of the notion of probability is characteristic of the other anti-anthropomorphic passages concerned with the creation of man.[17]

In general, then, the anti-anthropomorphic interpretations of God's creation of man follow a simple pattern in which the alleged anthropomorphism is rejected and then a solution is suggested. These interpreters are dealing with a real problem, that is, the problem of anthropomorphisms; and they try to solve that problem by using the conceptual tools available to them. The conceptual framework for the solution is drawn from the philosophy of the period and is chosen for its appropriateness in solving the problem at hand. At this fairly early stage, the use of philosophical concepts is still somewhat clumsy. The solutions offered are very much *ad hoc*, and there is little or no textual justification for the interpretation. Rather the text from Genesis is juxtaposed to a philosophical concept that is deemed suitable in a given context. The result of such a juxtaposition is seen as the only real explanation of the meaning of the text; it is never just one legitimate explanation among others.

B. *The Milieu of the Anti-Anthropomorphic Interpretations*

There is no direct evidence that would allow us to limit these interpretations with much precision to a particular time or place or to know precisely the purpose for which they were written. However, a comparison of this type of interpretation, both in terms of pattern and in terms of content, with other literature, both Jewish and non-Jewish, yields at least a few plausible suggestions.

In terms of content two of the four groups of passages are influenced predominantly by Platonic concepts. These two sets of passages are: *Op.* 69–71 on Gen 1:26–27; and *Op.* 72–75, *Conf.* 168–182, *Mut.* 29–32; *Fug.* 68–72 on Gen 1:26. As we saw earlier, *Op.* 69–71 is an interpretation of the phrase κατ' εἰκόνα of Gen 1:26–27, an interpretation which claims that the likeness of man to God is not in terms of body but in terms of mind, the sovereign element of the soul (ὁ τῆς ψυχῆς ἡγεμὼν νοῦς). This sovereign mind holds the same relationship to the rest of man as does the Mind of the whole, God, toward the whole universe. In fact, the divine mind is the archetype of the human mind. The interpreter then goes on to describe the mind's ascent through the heavens to the intelligible sphere, to the place of the patterns and the originals of the world of sense (τὰ παραδείγματα καὶ αἱ ἰδέαι τῶν αἰσθητῶν), and finally, in a Corybantic frenzy, beyond even this

---

[17] *Op.* 77–78, 82 seem to be expansions of the outlook and vocabulary of *Op.* 69–71. They are part of a series of four explanations as to why man was created last. However they do not provide much help in understanding the development of this exegetical tradition.

realm toward God, the great king himself. This final stage, however, remains incomplete, for the dazzling rays of God are too much for the eye of the human mind. While the description of νοῦς as ἡγεμών is found in Plato (*Leg.* XII. 963a), the use of the concept ἡγεμών for the highest part of the soul is also Stoic.[18] The real Platonic character of the passage is reflected in the description of the relationship of the human mind to the divine Mind. The relationship is one of macrocosm to microcosm in which the divine Mind is the archetype of the human mind.[19] In *Tim.* 30a-c Plato describes the purpose of the ordering of the world in the following way:

> Now it was not, nor can it ever be, permitted that the work of the supremely good should be anything but that which is best. Taking thought, therefore, he (the Demiurge) found that, among things that are by nature visible, no work that is without mind (ἀνόητον) will ever be better than one that has mind, when taken as a whole, and moreover that mind cannot be present in anything apart from soul. In virtue of this reasoning, when he framed the universe, he fashioned mind within soul (νοῦς ἐν ψυχῇ) and soul within body, to the end that the work he accomplished might be by nature as excellent and perfect as possible. This, then, is how we must say, according to the likely account (λόγον τὸν εἰκότα), that this world came to be, by the providence of God, in very truth, a living creature with soul and reason (ἔμψυχον ἔννουν).[20]

Later in the *Timaeus* (46d), the individual human mind is described in much the same way:

> For we must declare that the only existing thing which properly possesses mind (νοῦς) is soul, and this is an invisible thing, whereas fire, water, earth and air are all visible bodies.

We have in both passages the contrast both in the cosmos and in the individual human being of visible versus invisible, with mind and soul set over against the sensible element of the cosmos and the human body. This is the same contrast that appears in *Op.* 69:

> For after the pattern of a single Mind, even the Mind of the universe as an archetype, the mind in each of those who successively came into being was

---

[18] See R. Arnaldez, *Les oeuvres de Philon d'Alexandrie* (Paris: Editions du Cerf, 1961), 1.186.

[19] Plato does not use the terms "macrocosm" and "microcosm." The term μικρὸς κόσμος is first used by Aristotle (*Ph.* 8.2, 252b). But the parallelism between man and the cosmos is an important element in the *Timaeus*. See A. Olerud, *L'idée de macrocosmos et de microcosmos dans le Timée de Platon* (Uppsala: Almqvist, 1951) 13–42. Olerud's discussion of the *Timaeus* is far more adequate than is his attempt to trace these concepts to Iranian patterns of thought.

[20] Translations of the *Timaeus* are from F. M. Cornford, *Plato's Cosmology* (New York: Humanities Press, 1937).

molded. It is in a fashion a god to him who carries and enshrines it as an object of reverence; for the human mind evidently occupies a position in men precisely answering to that which the great Ruler occupies in all the world. It is invisible while itself seeing all things.

The use of the term "mind" (νοῦς) to describe God is also consistent with the outlook of the *Timaeus*. The Demiurge is identified with "mind" in *Tim.* 47e–48a. This identification is also found in the *Timaeus Locrus* (93a), a late first-century B.C. Middle Platonic summary of Plato's *Timaeus*.

Op. 69–71 however lacks the concept of some sort of intermediate figure between the supreme God and the world. Such a concept was characteristic of Middle Platonism.[21] The Demiurge of the *Timaeus* was often identified with the intermediate figure, and the supremely transcendent God was identified with the Good of the *Republic* and the One of the first hypothesis of the *Parmenides*.[22] At a later stage in the development of the exegetical traditions connected with Gen 1:26–27, man's creation according to the image of God will be interpreted to mean that the "image" (εἰκών) is the *Logos* of God and so man is created in the likeness of the *Logos*, an intermediate figure, rather than in the likeness of the supreme God himself (e.g., *L. A.* 3.95–96). But in the case of *Op.* 69–71, this development has not yet taken place. The mind of man is created in the likeness of the Mind of the universe, a Mind identical with the Demiurge, the supreme God of the *Timaeus*. There is no intermediate figure. *Op.* 69–71 then reflects the renewed interest in Plato, especially in the *Timaeus*, that began perhaps as early as the end of the second century B.C. But it reflects that interest prior to the development of the intermediate figure that became so characteristic of Middle Platonism.[23]

A second, clearly Platonic concept present in this section of the *De Opificio Mundi* is the ascent of the soul through the heavenly realms to the intelligible world. This image is drawn from the *Phaedrus* (246a–249d) where Plato describes the ascent of the soul by means of the image of the winged charioteer and his two winged horses. In *Op.* 69–71 the mind ascends on "soaring wing" (πτηνὸς ἀρθείς), an image central to Plato's description (*Phaedrus* 249c). In addition, the description of the ascent both in Plato's

---

[21] Cf. *Timaeus Locrus* 93a–95a; Albinus, *Didaskalikos* X, p. 164, 16–27; Apuleius, *De Dog. Plat.* 193–94; Numenius, Fr. 11 (des Places).

[22] Cf. Albinus, *Didaskalikos* X, p. 165, 27ff.; Numenius, Frs. 16, 20 (des Places). For suggestions in this area, see Dillon, *The Middle Platonists*, 46; Baltes, *Timaeus Lokros* 32; Dodds, "The *Parmenides* of Plato and the Origin of the Neoplatonic 'One,'" 129–42.

[23] That intermediate figure first appears in writers of the late first century B.C. (e.g., Eudorus of Alexandria, *Timaeus Locrus*).

Phaedrus (249c, 253a) and in this section of the *De Opificio Mundi* (71) is put in the language of religious enthusiasm (κορυβαντιῶντες, *Op.* 71; τελεταί, *Phdr.* 249c; Βάκχαι, *Phdr.* 253a). The image of the ascent of the soul as such is by no means restricted to Platonism. In fact it is a commonplace. Yet the use of the image of the "soaring wing" and the ascent of the soul beyond the sensible world to the intelligible world clearly indicate strong Platonic influence in this particular case.[24]

The second group of passages (*Op.* 72–75; *Conf.* 168–182; *Mut.* 29–32; *Fug.* 68–72) also draws heavily on Plato's *Timaeus* (41a–44d). After telling how the Demiurge made the world-soul, the heavenly bodies that serve as the "body" for the world-soul, and finally the traditional gods (*Tim.* 34a–40d), Plato goes on to describe the creation of the human body and soul. The Demiurge addresses the gods and tells them that in order to complete his creation he must now make mortal creatures, among whom he includes man (*Tim.* 41c–d). That part of man which is immortal will be made by the Demiurge himself while the rest, the mortal part, will be fashioned by the newly-made gods (*Tim.* 41c–d; 42d–e). In this way these newly-made gods will imitate the power (δύναμις) that the Demiurge used when he made them (*Tim.* 41c). All of this happens in order that the Demiurge might be guiltless of any future wickedness that man might do (*Tim.* 42d), for man is the only creature capable of living justly or unjustly (*Tim.* 42d). The parallels between this passage from the *Timaeus* and the passages from Philo are obvious. The phrase from Gen 1:26, "Let *us* make man . . .", offers an obvious point of contact with this section of the *Timaeus* and so the use of the *Timaeus* to provide the conceptual framework for interpreting Gen 1:26 seems quite natural. The identification of the figures to whom God speaks as God's Powers (δυνάμεις) is not found in the *Timaeus,*, but again it was a natural enough identification for a Jewish writer since the Septuagint often renders the Hebrew יהוה צבאות as κύριος τῶν δυνάμεων. It is to these heavenly powers then that God speaks (*Conf.* 171–173; *Mut.* 28–29; *Fug.* 69). It was also made easier by an identification, common during that period, of the traditional Greek gods with the various powers that either controlled the universe or served as the means by which the supreme God exercised control. Such an identification is found in such diverse sources as Diogenes Laertius' description of Stoicism and the pseudo-Aristotelian treatise *De Mundo.*[25]

---

[24] The metaphor of the ascent of the mind is by no means restricted to Plato or Platonism. In fact it is a literary commonplace (e.g., Xenophon, *Mem.* 1.4.17; Horace, *Carm.* 1.28,4ff). For a discussion of these passages, see R. M. Jones, "Posidonius and the Flight of the Mind through the Universe," *CP* 21 (1926) 98–101.

[25] D. L. 7.147; *De Mundo* 397b–398a.

The interpretation of the phrase "Let *us* make man" of Gen 1:26 then clearly draws on the *Timaeus* and reflects a renewed interest in the interpretation of Plato.

The two other anti-anthropomorphic texts (*L. A.* 1.36–38; *Op.* 149–150/*Q. G.* 1.21) that are concerned with the creation of man are Stoic rather than Platonic. *L. A.* 1.36–38 is an interpretation of the phrase "breathed into" of Gen 2:7:

> "Breathed into," we note, is equivalent to "inspired" or "be-souled" the soulless; for God forbid that we should be infected with such monstrous folly as to think that God employs for inbreathing organs such as mouth or nostrils; for God is not only not in the form of man, but belongs to no class or kind. Yet the expression clearly brings out something that is in accord with nature.

> For it implies of necessity three things, that which inbreathes, that which receives, and that which is inbreathed; that which inbreathes is God, that which receives is the mind (νοῦς), that which is inbreathed is spirit (πνεῦμα). What then do we infer from these premises? A union of the three comes about, as God projects the power (δύναμις) that proceeds from Himself through the mediant spirit till it reaches the subject.

> And for what purpose save that we may obtain a conception of him? For how could the soul have conceived of God, had he not breathed into it and mightily laid hold of it? For the mind of man would never have ventured to soar so high as to grasp the nature of God, had not God himself drawn it up to himself, so far as it was possible that the mind of man should be drawn up, and stamped it with the impress of the powers that are within the scope of its understanding.

The most clearly Stoic element is the notion of the "spirit" (πνεῦμα) by which God's power is communicated to man. The notion of πνεῦμα as a vehicle for the *Logos* of the universe was a common Stoic notion that probably originated with Chrysippus and was widely used thereafter in Stoic circles.[26] The image of the ascent of the mind is also present. At first glance this might point once again to Platonic influence. Yet on closer examination the ascent of the mind in this passage lacks that peculiar element that would indicate Platonic influence, the ascent beyond the *sensible* to the *intelligible* world.[27] The use of the metaphor in this passage, in fact, maintains a quite un-

---

[26] Long, *Hellenistic Philosophy*, 155–58.

[27] Jones, "Posidonius and the Flight of the Mind," 100, 105. Jones quite rightly emphasizes the Platonic influence on most of the uses of the image of the ascent of the mind in Philo. However, *L. A.* 1.36–38 fails to meet the criterion used by Jones himself to establish Platonic influence on the commonplace metaphor of the ascent of the mind. The criterion is whether or not there is a movement beyond the sensible realm to the intelligible world. In *L. A.* 1.36–38 there is no such movement to the intelligible world.

Platonic continuity between God, his power, and the human mind.[28] Since the metaphor continues the Stoic notion of the πνεῦμα as God's power extending out to draw up man's mind, there is no need to go beyond the bounds of popular Stoic influence to explain the use of the metaphor in *L. A.* 1.36–38.

The final anti-anthropomorphic passage is an interpretation of Gen 2:19, the giving of names (*Op.* 149–150; *Q. G.* 1.21). In this interpretation God tests man by having him give names to the various sorts of creatures. God does this because he knows that he has planted in man the natural ability to reason (ἡ λογικὴ φύσις) (*Op.* 149), an ability that he also describes as an "innate capacity" (ἐνδιάθετος ἕξις). Man is able to complete the task successfully because this natural ability to reason can "receive the impressions made by bodies and objects" (τὰς φαντασίας τῶν σωμάτων καὶ πραγμάτων) in their sheer reality (*Op.* 150).[29] The conceptual framework of this passage is also Stoic and there is no indication of the presence of Platonic material. Both the terms used and the close connection of the reasoning power with the impressions made by objects are typically Stoic conceptions.[30]

In reviewing the philosophical concepts and vocabulary of these passages, the predominant influences are obviously Stoic and Platonic. The passages influenced by Platonism use material drawn from the *Timaeus* and the *Phaedrus*, dialogues central to the development of Middle Platonism in the first century B.C. Yet they draw on fairly basic elements in Plato (e.g., the parallelism of cosmos and man and the creation of the lower part of man through the use of helpers) and do not contain the intermediate figure so characteristic of most Middle Platonic theories. This suggests that these passages come fairly early in the revival of Platonism. Since the intermediate figure appears late in the first century B.C., these passages are prior to that date, although it is impossible to say by how much. They represent the first Jewish attempt to use the concepts and vocabulary of the revival of Plato to overcome the apparent anthropomorphisms of the biblical text. The Stoi-

---

[28] The monism of Stoicism will continue to be a problem for Hellenistic Jewish interpreters. The problem becomes more and more acute as the interpreter appropriates more and more the conceptual patterns and vocabulary of Stoicism (see Chapter IV). In *L. A.* 1.36–38 the use of Stoic categories is not yet so thorough as to exclude a sense of divine transcendence.

[29] The same basic viewpoint is found in *Q. G.* 1.21: "For God was not in doubt; but, since he gave mind to the first-born noble man in accordance with which, becoming knowledgeable, he could reason naturally, like a teacher he guides his pupil to a suitable display of learning and he sees the excellent offspring of his soul." See J. R. Harris, *Fragments of Philo Judaeus* (Cambridge: Cambridge University Press, 1886) 13.

[30] For a description of Stoic epistemology, see Long, *Hellenistic Philosophy*, 123–31, 172–73.

cally oriented passages are much harder to date. Since the trend of the interpretations becomes, as we shall see, progressively more Platonic, these Stoically influenced interpretations may be somewhat earlier.[31] Just how much earlier becomes a bit clearer when one turns from content to a more formal analysis of these passages.

When one turns from a comparison of the content of these passages with Greek philosophical texts to a comparison at a more formal or structural level, one is drawn first toward Aristobulus. The fragments of this Jewish writer are preserved in Eusebius' *Praeparatio Evangelica* and in his *Historia Ecclesiastica*. As with most fragmentary material, dating is quite difficult. At the end of the nineteenth century Paul Wendland maintained that the fragments of Aristobulus were forgeries that were dependent on Philo and so obviously later than Philo.[32] In recent years, however, Nikolaus Walter has shown that the fragments of Aristobulus were genuine. They are not dependent on Philo but represent the work of Aristobulus, an Alexandrian Jew who lived in the middle of the second century B.C.[33]

The most helpful sections of Aristobulus for our purposes are the anti-anthropomorphic passages. These sections are part of a discourse supposedly addressed to Ptolemy VI Philometor (181–145 B.C.). In it Aristobulus asks the king to take the biblical accounts in a way that is in keeping with reality (φυσικῶς) and not to fall into mythical or merely human conceptions (*Praep. Evang.* 8.10.2). These mythical conceptions are the result of interpreting the text only in a very literal way (τῷ γραπτῷ) (*Praep. Evang.* 8.10.2). Aristobulus uses the terms φυσικῶς and τῷ γραπτῷ to distinguish a proper interpretation from an excessively literal, incorrect one. The two terms do not indicate levels of meaning in the text. For instance, in a passage such as Exod 13:9, "For with a strong hand God brought you out of Egypt," "hand" clearly refers to the power of God (δύναμις θεοῦ) and *not* to a "hand" in any literal sense (*Praep. Evang.* 8.18.8). For Aristobulus the exodus is a particular example of the fact that all things exist and are controlled by a divine power (θεῖα δύναμις) (*Praep. Evang.* 13.12.5,7).[34]

---

[31] The extent of the Platonizing trend will become clearer in Chapters IV and V.

[32] Paul Wendland, *De gnomologiorum graecorum historia atque origine commentatio*, Pt. IX (Bonn: 1895), cols. 229–234.

[33] Walter, *Der Thoraausleger Aristobulos*, 58–88; "Fragmente jüdisch-hellenistischer Exegeten," 259–62.

[34] In still another interpretation Aristobulus claims that one can speak of the constitution of the world as a "divine establishment" (θεῖα στάσις) only in the sense that God provided the world with its stability, its position and so all things are subject to him (Eusebius, *Praep. Evang.* 8.10.9–12). The thought of this section is not altogether clear. It makes most sense if one assumes that the supposed anthropomorphism is not that God "stands" but that the constitu-

The longest anti-anthropomorphic passage in Aristobulus is an interpretation of Exod 19:18–20, God's fiery descent upon Mount Sinai. He wants to clarify the real meaning of God's descent (κατάβασις) and so avoid attributing anything improper to God. In order to do this he emphasizes certain details in the text. For instance, the crowd that stood around the blazing mountain was so large that it would have taken five days' journey to pass through them, and yet all of them could see the blazing mountain. This shows that God's descent was not local (τοπική), for God is everywhere (*Praep. Evang.* 8.10.14–15). Likewise, while the mountain was on fire, nothing on it was consumed, a clear indication that this was no ordinary fire (*Praep. Evang.* 8.10.16). Nothing unsuitable is attributed to God, yet the validity of the text is maintained. This is the only one of the anti-anthropomorphic interpretations in Aristobulus that contains textual justifications for the interpretations that are given. Finally, there is no awareness in any of Aristobulus' interpretations that there might be multiple levels of meaning in the biblical text. He sees himself as giving the only real meaning of the text before him.[35]

These anti-anthropomorphic interpretations in Aristobulus are quite similar to the anti-anthropomorphic interpretations of the creation of man found in Philo. The basic pattern is the same in that both reject an improper anthropomorphic interpretation and then suggest an acceptable non-anthropomorphic interpretation. In both cases the conceptual framework is drawn from available philosophical notions. In the case of Aristobulus, the dominant concept is the Stoic notion of δύναμις which permeates all of reality, a notion close to that found in *L. A.* 1.36–37 (*Praep. Evang.* 8.10.2,8; 13.12.5,7).[36] The Stoic character also links him to *Op.* 149–150/*Q. G.* 1.21. The interpretations which Aristobulus offers, like those found in the passages from Philo, do not, with one exception, involve a textual justification of the interpretation; rather Aristobulus offers these interpretations as a suitable way to explain an otherwise objectionable passage. Aristobulus refers to his interpretation as a "fitting explanation" (λόγος καθήκων) (*Praep. Evang.* 8.10.1). In addition, both Aristobulus and the passages in Philo seem to represent a series of *ad hoc* solutions to particular problems. There is no indication that these interpretations are part of a larger attempt

---

tion of the world is somehow "divine" (θεῖα). In that case Aristobulus maintains that the world can be called a "*divine* establishment" only in the sense that *God* gave the world its "position" (στάσις) but not in the sense that the world is divine.

[35] See Hengel, *Judaism and Hellenism*, 1.164; 2.107.

[36] Although the dominant conception used by Aristobulus (δύναμις) as an interpretative tool is Stoic, his concept of God is not. For Aristobulus God transcends Nature, while, for the Stoic, God and Nature are two sides of the same coin.

to give an overall explanation of the biblical text. Finally, neither Aristobulus nor these anti-anthropomorphic passages from Philo are conscious of a biblical text with multiple levels of meaning. Both understand themselves as giving the only correct meaning (φυσικῶς, *Praep. Evang.* 8.10.1; 13.12.9 and φυσικώτερον, *L. A.* 1.36) of the text.

While there are a number of similarities between Aristobulus and these passages from Philo, the passages from Philo are somewhat more developed than are the anti-anthropomorphic passages in Aristobulus. In Aristobulus there is a simple equivalence between, for instance, God's "hand" and his "power." In the passages from Philo, however, the use of philosophical concepts is more fully exploited. For instance, in *L. A.* 1.36–38 one finds not only the use of the Stoic concept of πνεῦμα as the medium of communication of God's power to man but also the development of the image of the flight of man's mind to God based on the communication of that divine spirit. Again, the interpretation of the phrase "let *us* make man" from Gen 1:26 in *Op.* 72–75 *et par.* is a good deal more developed than anything found in Aristobulus. From the viewpoint of technique, Aristobulus is the *terminus post quem* for these anti-anthropomorphic passages in Philo .[37]

Both the anti-anthropomorphic passages from Aristobulus and those from Philo have a good deal in common with the allegorical interpretations of Homer such as one finds in Heraclitus, Pseudo-Plutarch, and Cornutus.[38] All three of these works have important features in common with the anti-anthropomorphic passages in Aristobulus and Philo, such as the *ad hoc* character of the interpretations, their consistently anti-anthropomorphic style, their use of common, especially Stoic, philosophical notions, and the characterization of an interpretation as "suitable" or "proper."[39]

On the other hand, these collections of Homeric allegories are considerably more developed than are the passages from either Aristobulus or Philo. There is also more textual justification in the Homeric allegories for the interpretations than one finds in the passages from Philo.[40] This should not

---

[37] I have avoided using the *Letter of Aristeas* to help understand these passages from Philo. The pertinent section would have been 148–71. These lines contain a defence and an ethical interpretation of certain dietary regulations in the Mosaic Law. The problem is that they are interpretations of legal texts and the development of the interpretation of such texts is different than that for non-legal texts such as the creation of man.

[38] Heraclitus, *Allégories d'Homère* (ed. F. Buffière; Paris: Société d'édition "Les Belles Lettres," 1962); Cornutus, *Theologiae Graecae Compendium* (ed. C. Lang; Leipzig: Teubner, 1881); Pseudo-Plutarch, *De vita et poesi Homeri*, in *Plutarchi Chaeronensis Moralia* (ed. G. N. Bernardakis; Leipzig: Teubner, 1894), 7.329–462.

[39] Heraclitus, *Quaes. Hom.* 7.12, 13; 9.2; 11.1; 13.5; 14.6; Cornutus, *Theol. Graec.* 26.16, 20; 27.7; Ps.-Plutarch, *Vit. Hom.* 93, 94, 101, 104.

[40] See Heraclitus, *Quaes. Hom.* 6–16; Ps.-Plutarch, *Vit. Hom.* 93–98.

be surprising since the three collections, all from the first century A.D., are part of a long and well-developed tradition of Stoic allegorization of Homer.[41] Yet because they are in continuity with that history and have important similarities with the anti-anthropomorphic interpretations in Aristobulus and Philo, they point to the kinds of models that Hellenistic Jews of the last centuries B.C. must have used as they began to interpret the apparently anthropomorphic passages in their own religious texts.

Two other significant differences between the Homeric allegories and the anti-anthropomorphic texts in Aristobulus and Philo also contribute to our understanding of the development of Hellenistic Jewish exegesis. The first of these differences concerns technical vocabulary. One finds in the Homeric allegories a developed use of a technical vocabulary, especially the use of the terms ἀλληγορία and ἀλληγορεῖν.[42] The use of these two terms became common in the course of the first half of the first century B.C. and subsequently maintained that position.[43] The first occurrence of the term is in Cicero's *Orator* (94):

> When there is a continuous stream of metaphors, a wholly different style of speech is produced (*alia fit plane oratio*): consequently the Greeks call it ἀλληγορία.[44]

It is clear from this passage that by the time Cicero wrote the *Orator* (ca. 46 B.C.), the term ἀλληγορία had already become fairly common. Prior to that time the term ὑπόνοια was used to describe such interpretations. In addition such terms as "symbol" (σύμβολον) and "symbolically" (συμβολικῶς) were often used. All of this vocabulary, however, is missing from Aristobulus, the anti-anthropomorphic passages in Philo, and, as we shall see in the next two chapters, from all of the interpretations of the creation of man prior to the allegory of the soul. The reason for this reticence on the part of Jewish interpreters is not clear. It is difficult to believe that, while they were aware of the techniques used in the allegorization of Homer, they were ignorant of the technical vocabulary used. Jewish interpreters may well have felt uncomfor-

---

[41] Cf. Pépin, *Mythe et allégorie*, 156–57; Buffière, *Les mythes d'Homère et la pensée grecque*, 67–77; Heraclitus, *Allégories d'Homère*, xxix–xxxii; C. Thompson, *Stoic Allegory of Homer: A Critical Analysis of Heraclitus' Homeric Allegories* (Yale Dissertation, 1973). Thompson, while concentrating on Heraclitus, also analyzes parallel sections in Pseudo-Plutarch and Cornutus and shows the ways in which each of the three authors appropriates the Stoic allegorical tradition in his own particular way.

[42] E.g., Heraclitus, *Quaes. Hom.* 5.1, 16; Ps.-Plutarch, *Vit. Hom.* 70; Plutarch, *De Is. et Os.* 32.

[43] Buffière, *Les mythes d'Homère et la pensée grecque*, 45ff.

[44] Translation by H. M. Hubbell, in Cicero, *Brutus and Orator* (LCL; Cambridge: Harvard University Press, 1962) 375.

table characterizing their interpretations of the biblical texts as anything
other than the "real" (φυσικῶς) interpretation.[45] This may especially have
been the case since Alexandria, which was the center for the development of
Hellenistic Jewish exegesis, was also the center of opposition to Stoic allegory.[46] In any case, the techniques of Stoic allegory were used but not the
technical vocabulary of allegory.

The anti-anthropomorphic interpretation in Philo also differs from
those essentially Stoic allegories in that a good number of them are heavily
influenced by Platonism. In addition, the interpretations become more and
more Platonic as time goes on, while the Stoic elements either drop out or
are revised.[47] This indicates that a significant shift has begun to take place
and that the shift was connected with the revival of interest in the interpretation of Plato. While still using the techniques of their predecessors (e.g.,
Aristobulus) which were derived from the Stoic interpretation of Homer,
Hellenistic Jewish exegetes began to draw the content of their interpretations
from Platonic rather than from Stoic sources. It is difficult to date such a
shift. However, because it took place after Aristobulus but before the latter
part of the first century B.C., one cannot be far wrong if one places this shift
in the first half of the first century B.C.

If the dating of these passages from Philo is not altogether clear, neither
is the purpose to which they were put. There are no obvious clues in the
passage themselves. But several characteristics suggest that they were written
for a Jewish audience sympathetic to the kind of interpretation found in
these passages. There is no indication that the anti-anthropomorphic interpretations are responses to the objections of any specific group. The objections raised are only rhetorical in nature (e.g., one might ask . . . , one might
wonder . . . , etc., *Op.* 69, 72; *Conf.* 168). They appear to be quite uncontro-
versial explanations of the biblical text in the categories of Hellenistic philosophy. The interpretations are stated; they are not argued. This means that
such interpretations were probably not intended for a non-Jewish audience
that most likely would have required some sort of justification, whether they
were sympathetic to Judaism or not.[48] In addition, the intended Jewish
audience seems to have been basically sympathetic to this kind of interpreta-

[45] This reticence in using the technical vocabulary of allegory continues until one reaches
the level of the allegory of the soul. The reason for this reticence as well as the reason for the
final introduction of allegorical technical terms will become a bit clearer in the last chapter of
this study.

[46] See Pépin, *Mythe et allégorie*, 168–72.

[47] See Chapter IV, sections B and C.

[48] This is also true of Aristobulus. Although addressed to Ptolemy VI Philometor, the
real audience was Jewish (Walter, *Der Thoraausleger Aristobulos*, 132–34).

tion. One finds in these passages none of the theoretical justification found in Aristobulus (*Praep. Evang.* 8.10.1–6). Evidently the kind of interpretation found in these passages from Philo had become a quite acceptable, non-controvesial form of interpretation. They served the purpose of developing an already existing sense among Hellenistically educated Jews in Alexandria that the biblical accounts could be understood in a way that was congruent with Greek philosophical notions.

The earliest level of interpretation of the creation of man available to us in Philo, is the anti-anthropomorphic interpretation. These interpretations have a similar pattern, one which rejects an unsuitable anthropomorphic interpretation and in its place suggest a fitting non-anthropomorphic interpretation whose conceptual framework is drawn from the philosophical concepts of the period. Some of the passages draw on Platonism while others draw on Stoic concepts. The similarity of pattern and the divergence in content indicate that in the first half of the first century B.C., a shift began to take place in Hellenistic Jewish exegesis. An exegesis based on a Stoic philosophical viewpoint began to give way to Platonic influences which reflect the revival of interest in the interpretation of Plato. This shift in Hellenistic Jewish exegesis reflects a corresponding shift that took place in the philosophical viewpoints of the Hellenistic world.

CHAPTER IV

THE SINGLE CREATION OF MAN

The anti-anthropomorphic interpretations of the last chapter were specific interpretations that answered specific objections. They were isolated interpretations that did not form part of an effort to interpret the whole of a given text; they interpreted only a single verse, often only a single word. These interpretations did not affect nor were they affected by the interpretation of other texts. In this chapter, however, we will look at interpretations of the creation of man in which broader, more coherent and integrated explanations of the text were developed. Once again these explanations drew on contemporary philosophical developments, especially those of Middle Platonism.[1] In the second half of the first century B.C., Middle Platonism developed significantly. Although Middle Platonism was not a unified movement all of whose philosophical positions can be clearly identified, structurally most Middle Platonists developed some sort of intermediate figure between God as the ultimate, intelligent source of order and the sensible world.[2] This intermediate figure was the proximate source of order in the sensible world. Such a figure was also to find a place in Jewish interpretations of the creation story. During this period the relationship of educated Alexandrian Jews to their Hellenistic environment grew and this growing relationship must have fostered an attempt to move beyond isolated, piecemeal interpretations to a more coherent framework of interpretation.[3] The

---

[1] Dillon (*The Middle Platonists*, 84–114) has shown that a number of the central characteristics of Middle Platonism emerged in the latter half of the first century B.C. They did not begin with either Posidonius or Antiochus of Ascalon.

[2] Ibid., 45–49. It is also true that Pythagoreanism played an important role in this development. Such a role and its mediation through a figure such as Xenocrates (c. 396–314 B.C.) has been emphasized by H. J. Krämer (*Der Ursprung der Geistmetaphysik*, 92–119).

[3] This relationship and the problems it created are well illustrated by Philo's family. Philo himself certainly received a Greek education and probably knew little or no Hebrew. Yet Philo was firmly committed to his own Jewish religious tradition. The same, however, cannot be said for his own nephew, Tiberius Julius Alexander, whose name indicated his outlook. He was completely Hellenized. He served as the Roman procurator of Judaea (46–48), as prefect of Egypt (66), and as chief of Titus' staff at the siege of Jerusalem in A.D. 70. Alexandrian Jews

interpretation of Gen 1:26-27 develops in such a way that it can be integrated into an overall interpretation of the creation of the world. The more Stoically influenced interpretation of Gen 2:7 found in Philo also develops beyond the anti-anthropomorphic but is then integrated into the Platonic interpretation of Gen 1:26-27 as a complementary formulation of the creation of man. The Platonizing tendency of this exegetical tradition becomes clear at this level of interpretation.[4] Both of these interpretations, however, still describe the creation of the same man, that is, they still describe the single creation of man.

A. *The Interpretation of Gen 1:27 and the* Logos *Figure*

In *Op.* 69-71 the mind of man was created as the image of God. The relationship of man's mind to the rest of his soul and to his body was analogous to the relationship of God to the universe. The pattern of man's mind was directly related to God Himself. In the next stage of development in the interpretation of Gen 1:27, man is no longer created directly as the image of God Himself but rather as the image of an image, that is, man is created according to the image of God's *Logos* (Reason). The *Logos* in its turn is an image of God.

> Having said what was fitting on these matters, Moses continues, "the birds he did not divide" (Gen 15:10). He gives the name of birds to the two reasons (λόγους), both of which are winged and of a soaring nature. One is the archetypal reason (ἀρχέτυπος) above us, the other the copy (μίμημα) of it.
>
> Moses calls the first the "image of God" (εἰκὼν θεοῦ), the second the cast (ἐκμαγεῖον) of that image. For God, he says, made man not the "image of God" but "*according to* the image" (κατ᾽ εἰκόνα) (Gen 1:27). And thus the mind in each of us, which in the true and full sense is the "man," is an expression at third hand (τρίτος τύπος) from the Maker, while between them is the *Logos* (Reason) which serves as paradigm (παράδειγμα) for our reason, but itself is the representation (ἀπεικόνισμα) of God. (*Her.* 230-231.)

throughout most of the Ptolemaic period and into the early Roman period were probably able to attend the Greek *gymnasia* for their education. This affected only a small minority of Jews in Alexandria, yet it was out of this group that the interpretations we are analyzing came. In addition one must remember the importance of the *gymnasia*: they provided one with an entrance into educated, Alexandrian society. See V. Tcherikover's introduction in *CPJ*, 1.27-39.

[4] The tendency of the Jewish interpretations came to be Middle Platonic rather than Stoic for obvious reasons. Stoic monism and materialism were next to impossible to reconcile with Judaism. The relationship of Jewish interpreters in Alexandria to Greek culture and thought was not uncritical. They thought that Judaism, properly understood, was far superior to anything Greek thought had to offer. Yet the relationship of Jewish interpreters to Middle Platonism was not an adversary relationship. The best of Greek thought was found in a more sublime form in the Jewish Scriptures. See Wolfson, *Philo*, 1.17-27.

Much of the language of *Op*. 69–71 is retained but is turned in a different direction. In *Op*. 69–71 the mind of man is made as an image of the Mind of the universe, a Mind which serves as the archetype in accord with which each human mind is formed (*Op*. 69). However in *Her*. 230–231, the archetype of the human mind is no longer God, the Mind of the Universe, but His *Logos*. The *Logos* stands between God and man and is the representation (ἀπεικό-νισμα) of God and the paradigm (παράδειγμα) of the human mind. Thus human reason is the copy (μίμημα) or the cast (ἐκμαγεῖον) not of God himself but of his *Logos*. The exegetical justification for this interpretation rests on the meaning of the phrase κατ᾿ εἰκόνα. In *Op*. 69–71, the phrase simply meant that man was created "*as* the image" of God. The image of God is man's mind. However in *Her*. 230–231, the κατά in the phrase κατ᾿ εἰκόνα is taken to mean not "*as* an image" but "*according to* or *after* an image." If that is the case, then the image according to which man is created must be something other than man himself. It must also be something other than God since the image is not God himself but his *image*. The image must be a *tertium quid* and that *tertium quid* is God's *Logos*.[5]

This same interpretation of Gen 1:27 is also found in *Op*. 24–25, *L. A*. 3.95–96, *Spec*. 1.80–81., *Spec*. 3.83, 207, and *Q. G*. 2.62. The concepts and the vocabulary of all seven passages are very similar. The *Logos* of God is the image of God (*Op*. 25; *Spec*. 1.81; *Spec*. 3.83) and the archetype of the human mind (*Op*. 25; *L. A*. 3.96; *Spec*. 3.83; *Q. G*. 2.62). In addition, the divine *Logos* is the paradigm of our minds as well as of other things (*L. A*. 3.96; *Spec*. 3.83) and the representation of God in the creation of the sensible world (*L. A*. 3.96). In turn, the human mind is the "image of an image" (εἰκὼν εἰκόνος) (*Op*. 25; *L. A*. 3.96) or the cast of that image (*Spec*. 3.83). In relation to God, the *Logos* is an image or representation and in relation to man a paradigm or archetype. This pattern is consistent throughout these passages and is distinguishable both from the creation of man directly as the image of God and also from the double creation of man. According to this interpretation, the man who is created in Gen 1:27 is the earthly man or more precisely the man prior to any distinction between a heavenly man and an earthly man. (See diagram on next page)

Let us first look at the overall conceptual framework of these passages. Within such a framework we can understand more clearly the role of the figure of the *Logos*.

The overall conceptual framework of these passages is clearly derived from Plato's *Timaeus*. What comes into being in the sensible world reflects a

---

[5] This use of a detail in the text as a pivot around which the interpretations of that and other texts revolve, becomes crucial at this level of interpretation.

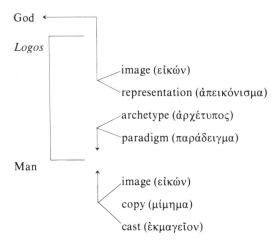

paradigm derived from the world of ideas. Terms such as paradigm, copy, and image are all used by Plato in the *Timaeus* to explain the relationship of the world of becoming to the intelligible world. The same is true of the contrasting pair of terms νοητός/αἰσθητός.[6] The realm of the intelligible is the pattern for the realm of sense perception.

More specifically, this framework is derived from those sections of the *Timaeus* that have to do with cosmology rather than with anthropology. The creation of man in the *Timaeus*, unlike the ordering of the world, is not described in terms of paradigms and copies. In the *Timaeus* the highest faculty of man is formed by the Demiurge himself while the forming of the rest of man is handed over to the the newer, subordinate gods (*Tim.* 41a-d). In the formation of man there is no mention of the paradigms used as models in the making of the world. Plato may well have thought that there was an intelligible paradigm of man, but that concept is not explicitly mentioned in his description of man's creation in the *Timaeus*.[7]

The Platonic framework of paradigm and copy for these passages in Philo is also cosmological rather than anthropological. This is also reflected in the passages themselves in Philo. The majority of the passages from Philo that have been mentioned in connection with this interpretation of the creation of man occur either as part of a discussion of the creation of the world

---

[6] παράδειγμα: *Tim.* 29b, 31a; μίμημα: *Tim.* 40d, 48e, 50c, 51b; εἰκών: *Tim.* 29b, 37d, 92c; νοητός: *Tim.* 48c, 51c, 92c; αἰσθητός: *Tim.* 28b, 37b, 52a, 92c.

[7] See Plato, *Rep.* 514a–532d, the passage about the cave which may include "man" among the ideas; cf. Aristotle, *Metaph.* 1.9.13, 991a.

(*Op.* 25; *L. A.* 3.96) or mention the creation of the world (*Her.* 235; *Spec.* 1.81). The framework for the interpretation of the creation of man in these passages is also derived from a cosmological framework. In this cosmological interpretation, the first day of creation is distinguished from the other days. On the first day of creation the intelligible world is created and on the rest of the days the sensible world is created. This distinction is based on what appeared to the interpreter as an anomaly in the text of Genesis. The first day of creation is called "day *one*" while the other days are called "second," "third," etc. The use of the cardinal rather than the ordinal number indicated that what took place on "day one" differed from what took place on the other days. What was different was that on "day one" the intelligible world was created and only on the second day did God begin to create the sensible world (*Op.* 15–36).[8] This creation took place through the medium of the *Logos.* This cosmological framework is in turn derived from the cosmology of Plato's *Timaeus.*

The interpretation of the creation of the world through the use of the Platonic distinction between paradigm and copy is not the only model of creation, not even the only Platonic model, found in Philo, and it is important to distinguish this model from others used in Philo. Ursula Früchtel has made a valuable contribution to the clarification of these models as they are found in Philo and of their relationship to Plato.[9] The first of these models is that of creation through division: This model appears most prominently in *Her.* 130–236. Drawing on the distinctions of Platonic logic found especially in the *Sophist* and the *Politicus,* she sees the ordering of the world as a process of division.[10] In this process the figure of the *Logos* is the one who does the dividing (ὁ τομεύς).[11] Another model is that of the world as God's temple (ἱερὸν θεοῦ). This model appears especially in *Spec.* 1.66ff. and

---

[8] It is important to keep this division in mind (i.e., "day one" versus the other days of creation) because at the next major stage of development (i.e., the double creation of man) the break between the creation of the intelligible world and the creation of the sensible world will be placed at Gen 2:5 (*Op.* 129–30). As will be seen in Chapter V, this change is necessitated by the double creation of man.

[9] U. Früchtel, *Die kosmologischen Vorstellungen bei Philo von Alexandrien* (ALGHJ 2; Leiden: Brill, 1948). I have described these models in a somewhat different order than they are given in Früchtel.

[10] Plato, *Plt.* 281c–282c; *Sph.* 253d–e.

[11] Früchtel, *Die kosmologischen Vorstellungen,* 51–52. This use of division is also found in Antiochus of Ascalon (Cicero, *Fin.* 5.16) and Seneca (*Ep.* 58.8–15). Christiansen (*Die Technik der allegorischen Auslegungswissenschaft,* 77–98) has emphasized that, in addition to Plato's dialectic, Aristotle's categories are also used as principles of division. The appearance of this technique in both Seneca and Antiochus of Ascalon indicates that this technique was a possession common to a number of authors.

Mos. 2.67ff. The tent in the wilderness and the temple are symbols of the structure of the world. While this model is not directly Platonic, it does draw on the Platonic distinction of intelligible world/sensible world. The inner part of the tent represents the intelligible world while the outer parts represent the sensible world. In this model the *Logos* serves as a mediator through which man can ascend from the sensible world to the intelligible world and finally to a vision of God.[12] A third model is that of the world as a plant created by God (φυτὸν θεοῦ). This model appears most prominently in *Plant.* 1–31. The world is a single organism, a cosmic plant in which the role of the *Logos* figure is to bind the whole plant into a single unified whole. This model draws on both Platonic and Stoic conceptions.[13]

The one remaining model found in Philo is what Früchtel refers to as the "city of God" (πόλις θεοῦ). In this model God is compared to an architect who builds a city based on a preconceived plan. In the same way, God created the sensible world based on an already existing paradigm, the intelligible world. When the world is looked on as the "city of God," the *Logos* is the fundamental idea that contains all of the other ideas or paradigms which serve as models for the world of sense perception and the instrument (ὄργανον) through which the sensible world is created.[14] This model is found most prominently in *De Opificio Mundi*.

Früchtel wants to derive this model from passages in Plato's *Republic* (500c ff.) in which the philosopher as artist forms a city based on a heavenly model (παράδειγμα).[15] The metaphor of the artist, however, was a common analogy used to explain the relationship of the Platonic ideas to the sensible world. The same analogy appears in both Cicero and Seneca.[16] This common metaphor about the creation of the world does not dominate the cosmological outlook of the *De Opificio Mundi*, and the use of this metaphor is restricted to only a few passages in the *De Opificio Mundi*.[17] The basic cosmological pattern of the *De Opificio Mundi* is that the sensible world is created as a copy of a paradigm found in the intelligible world, that is, the central cosmological pattern of the *Timaeus*. Früchtel is right in seeing the cosmological pattern in the *De Opificio Mundi* as distinct from the second model in which the world is seen as a temple, but she is wrong in claiming that the model is derived from the *Republic* rather than from the *Timaeus*.

---

[12] Früchtel, *Die kosmologischen Vorstellungen*, 69–115.
[13] Ibid., 53–61.
[14] Ibid., 7–40.
[15] Ibid., 10–14.
[16] Cicero, *Orat.* 8–10; Seneca, *Ep.* 65.3–10.
[17] *Op.* 17–22.

Once this is understood, the concepts and vocabulary of all of the passages about the creation of man in Philo clearly reflect this fourth cosmological model of paradigm and copy. The terms used to describe the relationship of the man created in Gen 1:27 to the *Logos* and the world of ideas all fit into the cosmological model derived from Plato's *Timaeus*. These include such terms as:

κόσμος νοητός	*Op.* 24
παράδειγμα	*L. A.* 3.96; *Her.* 231
σφραγίς	*Op.* 25	*Det.* 86
ἀρχέτυπος	*L. A.* 3.96; *Her.* 230; *Spec.* 3.83	*Det.* 86; *Spec.* 1.171; *Plant.* 20
ἀπεικόνισμα	*L. A.* 3.96; *Her.* 231	*Plant.* 20
εἰκών	*Op.* 25; *L. A.* 3.96; *Her.* 231; *Spec.* 3.83 *Spec.* 1.81	*Det.* 82, 86; *Mut.* 223
μίμημα	*Op.* 25; *Her.* 230	*Det.* 83; *Op.* 139
ἐκμαγεῖον	*Her.* 231; *Spec.* 3.83	*Mut.* 223; *Op.* 146[18]

Man is a copy, a cast, an image, and a representation of the intelligible realm; on the other hand this realm is the paradigm, the archetype, and the seal for the creation of man. These passages do not contain concepts or vocabulary taken from the other three cosmological models. This indicates that this interpretation of the creation of man is a distinct tradition rooted in an equally distinct interpretation of the creation of the world.[19] This distinctiveness is retained even when one of these passages is found in an interpretation based on another cosmological model. For example, the passage quoted above (*Her.* 230–231) occurs in a large, allegorical section devoted to the notion of creation by division (*Her.* 130–236). But that allegorical interpretation does not affect the outlook or the vocabulary of the interpretation of Gen 1:27 (*Her.* 230–231). The *Logos* as paradigm for the creation of man does not become the *Logos* who creates by division, which is his role in the overall framework of *Her.* 130–236.[20] The conceptual framework and much

---

[18] I have also included in this list the occurrences of these terms in those passages which combine the interpretation of Gen 1:27 with that of Gen 2:7. They are the passages that come after the slash mark.

[19] This also includes the passages which combine the interpretations of Gen 1:27 and Gen 2:7. This strengthens the notion that this interpretation of Gen 1:27 was originally quite distinct.

[20] The same is true of *Plant.* 18–22. This passage interprets Gen 1:27 and Gen 2:7, but the interpretation is not affected by the fact that it is placed in a larger section which interprets the creation of the world by means of the metaphor of the cosmic plant (*Plant.* 1–27). The *Logos* involved in the creation of man is the Archetype (*Plant.* 20) and not the Bond (ὁ δεσμός) that holds creation together, which is the role that it plays in the larger passage (e.g., *Plant.* 9).

of the crucial vocabulary of these interpretations of Gen 1:27, then, form a distinct tradition rooted in a cosmology derived from Plato's *Timaeus*.[21]

Although both the overall conceptual framework and much of the vocabulary are rooted in the *Timaeus*, the central figure of the *Logos* is not. We must now turn to that figure. The *Logos* is the one in whose image (εἰκών) man has been fashioned and through whom both man and the sensible world have been made by God (e.g., *L. A.* 3.96). As I indicated earlier, the role of the *Logos* in the creation of man must be seen within the context of its function in the creation of the world. The primary context for the *Logos* is cosmological; the figure is then secondarily used in the context of the creation of man.

The figure of the *Logos* as it is found in Philo is complex both in terms of its functions and in terms of its origins. Several of these functions have already been mentioned in connection with the work of Ursula Früchtel. Yet they do not exhaust the roles played by the *Logos* in Philo. For instance, the *Logos* is closely associated in a number of passages with the figure of Wisdom.[22] Both the *Logos* and Wisdom are given the same attributes, e.g., image, beginning, vision of God (*Conf.* 146; *L. A.* 1.43). Because of the number of times that this identification occurs, Jewish wisdom speculation clearly represents one of the roots of the concept of the *Logos* in Philo.[23] Similarly the *Logos* takes on many of the attributes of the *Logos* as it was understood in Stoicism. The *Logos* can be the one who fills up all things with its being (*Her.* 188). The *Logos* can also be described as putting on the world as a garment (*Fug.* 110). In these passages, as in Stoicism, the *Logos* is the principle of rationality that pervades the universe.[24] In many ways the functions given to the *Logos* in Stoicism are quite similar to those given to Wisdom in Jewish wisdom literature. That functional similarity between the two may well have been one of the primary reasons the *Logos* figure was introduced into Judaism. The *Logos* figure offered educated Jews a way of speaking of Wisdom that was comprehensible to educated non-Jews.[25]

The very complexity of the *Logos* figure in Judaism indicates that once the figure had been introduced into Judaism it became the carrier of a variety

---

[21] Within those interpretations which are highly allegorical (e.g., *Conf.* 146), these models of creation are joined together. But the fact that they remain unaltered in some highly allegorical interpretations points to the fact that they were originally quite distinct interpretations.

[22] *L. A.* 2.86; *L. A.* 1.65; *Som.* 1.65–66; *Som.* 2.242–45; *Fug.* 97, 109; *Post.* 122; *Deus* 134–35.

[23] The importance of this factor has been emphasized by Mack (*Logos und Sophia* [Göttingen: Vandenhoeck & Ruprecht, 1973]).

[24] D. L. 7.134; Cicero, *Nat. D.* 1.36.

[25] H. F. Weiss, *Untersuchungen zur Kosmologie des hellenistischen und palestinischen Judentums* (TU 97; Berlin: Akademie Verlag, 1966) 264–65.

of different functions. The figure could be interpreted within a Platonic framework or as a Stoic principle of rationality or as a further stage within Jewish Wisdom speculation. All of these functions appear in Philo's writings. In addition, any given function might be only vaguely related to the original reasons for its introduction into Jewish religious thought. While originally connected with Stoicism, the *Logos* may be interpreted in a basically Platonic framework which gives very little indication of its Stoic origins.[26] Because of this fact I cannot hope to solve the problems connected with the long and complex history of the *Logos*. What can be done is to provide a context within which its use in connection with the creation of man in Gen 1:27 becomes intelligible.

In the case of the texts connected with the creation of man in Gen 1:27, the *Logos* clearly functions within the Platonic cosmology of the *Timaeus* in which the sensible world is made after the patterns of the ideal world. Terms that Plato used to characterize the world of ideas are now used to characterize the *Logos*: archetype, paradigm, intelligible.[27] In fact the *Logos* becomes the archetypal idea in which all of the other ideas are contained. The *Logos* unifies the world of ideas under one rubric. What had been a realm, the world of ideas, now becomes a figure, the *Logos*.[28]

The term used most often to describe the figure of the *Logos* is that of "image" (εἰκών). The term is never used in Plato to refer to the ideal world but only to refer to the sensible world.[29] Yet in Plato there is no comparable intermediate *figure* between the demiurge and the sensible world, only the *ideas* which are paradigms for the objects in the sensible world. However, once one has introduced an intermediate figure, one is forced to characterize its relationship both to the primal deity and to the sensible world. Obviously the text of Gen 1:27 conditions the exegete to use the term "image" to describe the *Logos*. Yet the term, as it is interpreted in these passages from Philo, does no injury to the Platonic usage; it simply expands the use one step farther. If the man of Gen 1:27 is an image of the *Logos*, that is, of the realm above, then the *Logos* too is an image of the realm above it, that is of God himself. In these passages the term "image" is used consistently to point

---

[26] One must not prematurely group everything Philo says about the *Logos* together. One should first sort out the various interpretations given to the *Logos* and try to place them in their proper philosophical and religious milieu. In these particular passages from Philo on the *Logos*, the figure is rooted in Middle Platonism and not in Stoicism or in Wisdom speculation.

[27] ἀρχέτυπον: *L. A.* 3.96; *Op.* 25; *Spec.* 3.83; *Spec.* 1.171; παράδειγμα: *L. A.* 3.96; *Her.* 231; *Spec.* 3.83; *Det.* 87; *Op.* 139; νοητός: *Op.* 25.

[28] *Spec.* 3.83; *Op.* 145; *Spec.* 1.171; *Op.* 25.

[29] See H. Willms, ΕΙΚΩΝ (Münster: Aschendorff, 1935) 77; Wolfson, *Philo*, 1.238; F. W. Eltester, *Eikon im Neuen Testament* (Berlin: Töpelmann, 1958) 33.

to the relationship of the *Logos* to that higher realm, the realm of God himself.[30] In this way the Platonic use of the term is not altered structurally; it still refers to a reflection or copy (*Abbild* and never *Vorbild*) in a lower realm of something belonging to a higher realm. The use of the term "image," then, brings out the intermediate character of the *Logos* figure in a way that is consistent with the Platonic structure of paradigm and copy.

Finally, the *Logos* is that through which (δι' οὖ) the sensible world was made (*Spec.* 1.81). In another passage the *Logos* is referred to as the "instrument" (ὄργανον) by means of which God made the world and man (*L. A.* 3.96). God created the world by using the *Logos* as his instrument. The notion of the *Logos* as the instrument used in creation appears only in passing in passages describing the creation of man (*Spec.* 1.81; *L. A.* 3.96). But the notion of the *Logos* as the instrument through which creation takes place will help us to understand the milieu out of which the *Logos* figure emerged and so will help us to understand, albeit indirectly, the role of the *Logos* in the creation of man.

These three characteristics of the *Logos* (unifier of the world of ideas, instrument of creation, intermediate figure) all help us to locate the figure within the development of Middle Platonism in the second half of the first century B.C.

The first characteristic, that is, the *Logos* as unifier of the ideas, is illustrated by a fragment of Arius Didymus' *On the Doctrines of Plato* preserved by Eusebius, Stobaeus, and the second-century A.D. Middle Platonist Albinus.[31] Arius Didymus was connected with the court of Augustus and flourished in the late first century B.C. For our purposes, what is important is that he was an Alexandrian, that he studied philosophy there before coming to the court of Augustus, and that he wrote a book summarizing the doctrines of Plato.[32] Toward the end of the fragment preserved in Eusebius, Arius discusses the integration of the ideas.

---

[30] This analysis is confirmed by the interpretations of some of these passages by Willms (56–74). Εἰκών still has the meaning of "copy" (*Abbild*). This is not always the case in Philo. The term can also mean "model" (*Vorbild*) (*Som.* 1.79). This use of the term (i.e., as "model") is also found in *Timaeus Locrus* 99d and in Plutarch, *Quaest. Conv.* 8.2.1.

[31] Eusebius, *Praep. Evang.* 11.23; Stobaeus, *Dox. Graec.* 447; Albinus, *Didaskalikos* XII, pp. 166.35–167.12. This fragment of Arius Didymus is quoted *verbatim* in Eusebius and Stobaeus and in a close paraphrase in Albinus. Albinus, however, never mentions that he is using a source. This has led Dillon (*The Middle Platonists*, 269) to suggest that Albinus' *Didaskalikos* is essentially a "new edition" of Arius Didymus' *On the Doctrines of Plato*. R. E. Witt (*Albinus and the History of Middle Platonism* [Cambridge: University Press, 1937] 95–103) also thinks that Albinus is heavily dependent on Arius Didymus. While there is no way to be certain, Albinus' *Didaskalikos* may reflect fairly closely Arius Didymus' *On the Doctrines of Plato*.

[32] Plutarch, *Praec. ger. reipubl.* 18; *Ant.* 80; Cassius Dio, 51.16.3.

As therefore, the particular archetypes (τὰ κατὰ μέρος ἀρχέτυπα), so to say, precede the bodies which are perceived by sense (τῶν αἰσθητῶν σωμάτων), so the Idea which includes in itself all ideas (τὴν πάσας ἐν ἑαυτῇ περιέχουσαν) being most beautiful and most perfect, exists originally as the pattern (παρά-δειγμα) of this present world; for that (the present world) has been made by its creation like this Idea, and wrought according to the providence of God out of the universal essence (ἐκ τῆς πάσης οὐσίας). (Eusebius, *Praep. Evang.* 11.23.)[33]

Instead of a series of ideas serving as paradigms, all of the individual ideas are integrated into one Idea which serves as a paradigm for the formation of the sensible world as a whole. As in Philo, there is a certain ambiguity in the sense that the individual ideas still exist yet there is an attempt to integrate them under one rubric into a unified whole. In Arius Didymus' case that rubric is the Idea; in these passages from Philo it is the *Logos*. A bit earlier in the fragment, Arius Didymus also makes use of the metaphor of the Idea as a seal (σφραγίς) from which many copies and images (ἐκμαγεῖα καὶ εἰκόνες) are made. All three terms occur also in the passages from Philo and have the same meaning. Of particular significance is the use of the term "seal" as a metaphor to describe the relationship of the world of ideas to the sensible world. It is the earliest use of this metaphor to describe the relationship of the ideas to the sensible world.[34] Both in terms of outlook and vocabulary, then, this fragment from Arius Didymus has a good deal in common with these interpretations of Gen 1:27 found in Philo.

Secondly, the *Logos* is the instrument (ὄργανον) through which God made the sensible world (*L. A.* 3.96; *Mig.* 6). A similar formulation is found in *Sac.* 8. In this formulation, the phrase "through which" (δι' οὗ) serves to explain the relationship between God and his *Logos* in the formation of the sensible world. The *Logos* is that "through which" the world was formed. This formulation, however, is most fully developed in *Cher.* 125–127.

> God is the cause (αἴτιον) not the instrument (ὄργανον), and that which comes into being is brought into being through an instrument (δι' ὀργάνου), but by a cause (ὑπο δε αἰτίου). For to bring anything into being needs all these con-jointly, the "by which" (τὸ ὑφ' οὗ), the "from which" (τὸ ἐξ οὗ), the "through which" (τὸ δι' οὗ), the "for which" (τὸ δι' ὅ), and the first of these is the cause (τὸ αἴτιον), the second the material, the third the tool (τὸ ἐργαλεῖον), and the fourth the end or object.
>
> If we ask what combination is always needed that a house or city should be built, the answer is a builder, stones or timber, and instruments (ὄργανα). What

---

[33] Translation by E. H. Gifford, *Eusebii Pamphili Evangelicae Praeparationis Libri XV* (Oxford: University Press, 1903), 3/2, 589.

[34] F. J. Dölger, *Sphragis* (Studien zur Geschichte und Kultur des Altertums, V, 3/4; Paderborn: Schöningh, 1911) 56–58. The metaphor is also found in Plutarch, *De Is, et Os.* 54.

is the builder but the cause "by which"? What are the stones and timber but the material "from which"? What are the instruments but the means "through which"? And what is the end or object of the building but shelter and safety, and this constitutes the "for which."

Let us leave these merely particular buildings, and contemplate that greatest of houses or cities, this universe. We shall see that its cause is God, by whom it has come into being, its material the four elements, from which it was compounded, its instrument (ὄργανον) the Word of God (λόγος θεοῦ), through which (δι' οὖ) it was framed, and the final cause of the building is the goodness of the architect. It is thus that truth-lovers distinguish, who desire true and sound knowledge. But those who say that they possess something through God, suppose the Cause, that is the Maker, to be the instrument, and the instrument, that is the human mind, they suppose to be the cause. (*Cher.* 125–127.)

This elaborate discussion of the types of causality is meant to be a refutation of the human mind's claim (symbolized by Adam) that with sense perception (Eve) it has begotten something (Cain) through the agency of God (διὰ τοῦ θεοῦ) (Gen 4:1). But according to *Cher.* 125–127, God can never be an instrument, only a cause. This highly developed consideration of causality appears to be a pre-Philonic unit introduced at this point by Philo into his own allegorical interpretation of the birth of Cain. The reason for saying this is that the causality discussed in *Cher.* 125–127 is the causality involved in the making of the world as a whole and not the causality involved in any particular act such as the engendering of Cain or, allegorically, the working of the human mind with sense perception. In addition, if one were to assume that *Cher.* 125–127 was closely connected with the context in which it occurs, then the logic of the passage would lead one to say that the human mind would be correct to claim that, with sense perception, it has brought something forth through the agency of the *Logos*, since it is the *Logos* and not God who is properly the "through which." That is quite obviously not the case in this passage. Rather it is only very loosely connected with its present context and is pre-Philonic.[35] This schema on causality, however, and especially the role of the *Logos* as the instrument through which God framed the world, provides evidence helpful in locating this particular function of the *Logos*.

This passage in Philo is part of a philosophical *topos* that became quite common in the first century B.C., a *topos* that Willy Theiler refers to as a "metaphysics of prepositions."[36] Examples of such a schema are found in Seneca (*Ep.* 65.8–10), in Aetius (*apud* Stobaeus, Diels 287b–288b), and in

---

[35] W. Theiler, *Die Vorbereitung des Neuplatonismus* (Berlin: Weidmann, 1930) 29–31.
[36] Ibid., 31–37.

Varro (*apud* Augustine, *De Civ. D.* 7.28).[37] The appearance of such sche-
mata in these three authors and in Philo points to the first century B.C. as the
period of origin. Theiler suggests Antiochus of Ascalon (ca. 130–68 B.C.) as
the originator of the schema because it appears in Varro, a Roman disciple
of Antiochus.[38] Whoever the originator was, the scheme, with all of its
variations, is certainly colored by Platonism in the sense that in all three
authors (Varro, Aetius, and Seneca) one of the causes is always the
Platonic ideas.[39] The scheme became a common-place scholastic formulation in Middle Platonism. It is in this kind of formulation that appears
in *Cher.* 125–127.

However, the precise formulation of a type of cause which is an
"instrument through which" (ὄργανον δι' οὗ) something happens does not
occur in any of these three authors. That formulation, however, does occur
in Albinus, although in a somewhat different context. In Albinus the context
is epistemological rather than cosmological.

> Therefore as there is a faculty of judgment (τὸ κρῖνον) as well as an object of
> judgment (τὸ κρινόμενον), so too there is that which is the result of these, that
> which is called the judgment itself (ἡ κρίσις). This should properly be called the
> criterion of judgment (τὸ κριτήριον), although it is also commonly referred to
> as the faculty of judgment (τὸ κρῖνον). This criterion is twofold: first it is that
> by which (τὸ ὑφ' οὗ) the object of judgment is judged; second it is that through
> which (τὸ δι' οὗ) the object of judgment is judged. The former is our mind (ὁ ἐν
> ὑμῖν νοῦς), the latter is that instrument working through nature (ὄργανον
> φυσικόν) used in judging primarily things that are true and secondarily things
> that are false. The second is nothing other than that reasoning activity working
> through nature (λόγος φυσικός).
> . . . This reasoning activity (λόγος) is also twofold: the first is entirely beyond
> our comprehension and certain; the second is incapable of being deceived con-

---

[37] Seneca is a good example of this development:
Accordingly, there are five causes, as Plato says: the material (*id ex quo*), the agent (*id a
quo*), the make-up (*id in quo*), the model (*in ad quod*), and the end in view (*id propter
quod*) . . . The agent (*faciens*) is God; the source (*id ex quo*), matter; the forms (*forma*),
the shape and the arrangement of the visible world. The pattern (*exemplar*) is doubtless
the model according to which (*ad quod*) God has made this great and most beautiful
creation. The purpose is his object in so doing. Do you ask what God's purpose is? It is
goodness. (*Ep.* 65.8–10.)

[38] Theiler, *Die Vorbereitung des Neuplatonismus*, 37–38.

[39] The basic structure of this "metaphysics of prepositions" is Peripatetic, that is, based
on the four Aristotelian causes (formal, material, efficient, and final). But this scheme was
altered to include the role of the ideas as a cause. Seneca, Aetius, and this section from Philo
attest to its popularity among Middle Platonists. Dörrie ("Die Erneuerung des Platonismus im
ersten Jahrhundert vor Christus," *Platonica Minora*, 157-58) thinks that this scheme should be
derived from the *Timaeus* itself.

cerning the knowledge of objects and events. Of these the former is possible only for God and not for human beings, the latter however is possible also for human beings. (Albinus, *Didaskalikos*, IV, p. 154, 8–22.)

The primary concern of this passage is the way in which a judgment is made. The meaning of the phrase λόγος φυσικός is not entirely clear. Dillon translates it as "an activity of the mind working through nature."[40] For our purposes, what is important is that the *logos* is an "instrument through which" (ὄργανον δι' οὗ) something is done and, as is indicated by the contrast with the phrase "by which" (ὑφ' οὗ) something is done, it is part of a philosophical reflection through the use of prepositions. Also important for our analysis of Philo is the fact that this passage from Albinus, while primarily epistemological, does have a metaphysical bent to it. Albinus goes on to indicate that there is a mental activity, a type of *logos*, that is proper to God alone and quite beyond the reach of human beings. While not the same as the *Logos* figure in these passages from Philo, it is quite easy to see how the "epistemology of prepositions" in Albinus could have become a "metaphysics of prepositions" such as we find in Philo.

That may seem to be reversing things but, as I pointed out above, there is good reason to think that at least parts of Albinus' *Didaskalikos* are a reworking of a treatise of the first century B.C. Alexandrian philosopher Arius Didymus. This section from Albinus points in the same direction. It is a parallel Platonic formulation of a position taken by another Alexandrian philosopher of the first century B.C., Potamon of Alexandria. Potamon's formulation, however, is more Stoic in character.[41] A fragment that described Potamon's position is found in Diogenes Laertius.

> One word more: not long ago an Eclectic school was introduced by Potamon of Alexandria, who made a selection from the tenets of all the existing sects. As he himself states in his *Elements of Philosophy*, he takes as criteria (κριτήρια) of truth (1) that by which (τὸ ὑφ' οὗ) the judgment is formed, namely the ruling principle (τὸ ἡγεμονικόν); (2) the instrument used (τὸ δι' οὗ), for instance the

Tim. 28a and 28c; ὑπ' αἰτίου τινός
Tim. 28a and 28c; πρὸς τὸ παράδειγμα
Tim. 31b and 32c; ἐκ τοῦ πυρὸς καὶ ἀέρος κτλ.
Tim. 29d: δι' ἥντινα αἰτίαν
However, Aristotle's schematization of causality is so clear and prominent that it was an obvious model for further developments. Dörrie may be right, however, to maintain that these passages from the *Timaeus* contributed to the alteration of the structure and use of the scheme. For instance, the οὗ ἕνεκα of Aristotle becomes the δι' οὗ of Philo, and the paradigm is added as a cause distinct from Aristotle's formal cause.

[40] Dillon, *The Middle Platonists*, 273.

[41] The Suda places Potamon as a contemporary of Augustus and so also a contemporary of Arius Didymus (H. Diels, *Doxographi Graeci*, 81).

most accurate perception (ἡ ἀκριβεστάτη φαντασία). His universal principles
are matter and the active principle (τὸ ποιοῦν), qualities and place; for that out
of which (ἐξ οὗ) and that by which (ὑφ' οὗ) a thing is made, as well as
that through which (δι' οὗ) and the place in which (ἐν ᾧ) it is made, are principles. The end to which (ἐφ' ὅ) he refers all actions is life made perfect in all
virtue, natural advantages of body and environment being indispensable to its
attainment. (D. L. 1.21.)[42]

Potamon was quite clearly eclectic in that the principles he describes are a
mixture of Stoic and Peripatetic positions. The criteria of truth, which are
the ones of most interest to us, are Stoic. He, like Varro, Aetius, and Seneca,
witnesses to the popularity of the "metaphysics of prepositions." But also, as
in the passage from Albinus, he is interested in the "epistemology of prepositions." He uses the same prepositions (τὸ ὑφ' οὗ, τὸ δι' οὗ) to describe the
criteria of truth as does the passage from Albinus. The parallelism is so close
that one suspects that the two passages were written roughly around the
same period and were formulated as alternative solutions to the same question, only from two very different points of view, one Stoic and the other
Platonic. Both of the terms of Potamon's solution, the ἡγεμονικόν of the
soul and the ἀκριβεστάτη σαντασία (which seems to be identical with the
φαντασία καταληπτική) are quite clearly Stoic.[43] The solution proposed in
the passage from Albinus, however, is much more Platonic. The agent (τὸ
ὑφ' οὗ) is the mind, which in the *Didaskalikos* clearly transcends the material; and the instrument (τὸ δι' οὗ) is the "activity of the mind working
through nature" (ὁ φυσικὸς λόγος), an activity one type of which is predi-
cated only of God, who in the *Didaskalikos* also transcends the material
world. The antithetical parallelism of this passage from Albinus with the
fragment of Potamon strengthens the suspicion that, at this point, Albinus'
Didaskalikos is a reworking of Arius Didymus' *On the Doctrines of Plato.*
The passages in Philo then represent in a metaphysical form the "epistemology of prepositions" probably held by Arius Didymus. From both the
passage from Albinus and that from Potamon, we know that such a transformation was an easy one. These passages from Philo in which the
Logos figure is understood through this medium of prepositions would
fit well into the Middle Platonic philosophical developments in the second

---

[42] Diogenes Laertius must be quoting an earlier writer who could have correctly said "not
long ago . . ." In the text of Diogenes Laertius, the phrase "that through which (δι' οὗ) a thing is
made" is an emendation from ποίᾳ. As Dillon (*The Middle Platonists*, 138) points out, the ποίᾳ
is anomalous and probably represents a gloss on ποιότητα (qualities) which occurs two lines
earlier. The gloss then crowded out the proper reading.

[43] D. L. 7.54; Aetius *apud* Stobaeus, *Dox. Graec.* 393–94.

half of the first century B.C. If the figures of both Potamon and Arius Didymus are any indication, Alexandria would also be an appropriate place for such a development.

The final characteristic of the *Logos* figure is that it is an intermediate figure between God and the world. Such a figure also appears in the Middle Platonism of Alexandria in the second half of the first century B.C. Such an intermediate figure (in this case, the Monad) appears in the fragment of Eudorus of Alexandria which was quoted in Chapter I (p. 14). Both the fragment from Eudorus and these interpretations of Gen 1:27 found in Philo indicate that the development of such an intermediate figure between God and the sensible world was a part of the philosophical milieu of Alexandria in the second half of the first century B.C.[44]

Two other documents, however, offer the most important parallels to these passages on the *Logos* in Philo. The first of these is "Timaeus Locrus'" *On the Nature of the World and of the Soul*.[45] As I indicated in Chapter I (p. 16), it purports to be the teaching of Timaeus Locrus, the main figure in Plato's *Timaeus* and claims to be the teaching on which Plato based his dialogue. In reality the *Timaeus Locrus* is dependent on Plato's *Timaeus* and reflects the viewpoints of Middle Platonism, probably those of the circle of Eudorus.

Once again, it is the beginning of the treatise (93a–94c) that is of most interest for us:

Timaeus the Locrian said the following: There are two causes of all things, Mind (νόος) for everything that happens according to reason (κατὰ λόγον) and Necessity (ἀνάγκα) for that which happens by force (βίᾳ) according to the powers of bodies. Of these the one has the nature of the good and is called God and the principle (ἀρχά) of the best things, while the others, being secondary and contributory causes, are to be subsumed under Necessity. The totality of things is threefold: Idea, Matter, and the Sense Perceptible which is the off-spring of the other two. The Idea is eternal, unchanging and immovable, indivisible and of the nature of the Same, intelligible, and a paradigm of things which are made and which are in flux. Thus must one speak of and contemplate the Idea. Matter is the impression (ἐκμαγεῖον), the mother and nurse, and the one who brings forth the third kind of being. When Matter has taken to itself the likeness and, as it were, has been stamped by them, it produced those things

---

[44] An intermediate figure also appears in Albinus, *Didaskalikos* X, p. 164, 16–27. If, as seems plausible, the *Didaskalikos* is really a "new edition" of Arius Didymus' *On the Doctrines of Plato*, then the intermediate figure found in the *Didaskalikos* is another example of the kind of philosophical speculation that was taking place in first-century B.C. Alexandria.

[45] See the excellent commentary of M. Baltes, *Timaios Lokros: Über die Natur des Kosmos und der Seele*.

which have been made. He (Timaeus) said that Matter was eternal but not immovable, of itself formless and patternless but receiving every form. Because of its relationship to bodies it is divisible and of the nature of the Different. Matter is called place and space. These two then are principles, of which the Form (τὸ εἶδος) has the character of the male and father while Matter has that of the female and mother. The third (the Sense Perceptible) is the offspring of these two. Because they are three they are apprehended in three different ways: the Idea by mind (νόος) through scientific knowledge, Matter by a kind of spurious reasoning since it cannot be known directly but only by analogy, and what is begotten from these by sense perception and opinion.

Before the heaven, according to this account, came into being, the Idea and Matter already existed, as well as God, the maker of the better. Because the elder is better than the younger and the ordered than the disordered, when God who is good saw that Matter received the Idea and was changed in all kinds of ways but not in an orderly fashion, he wanted to order it and to bring it from an indefinite to a defined pattern of change, so that the differentiations of bodies might be proportional and Matter would no longer be changed arbitrarily. (*Timaeus Locrus*, 93a–94c.)[46]

There are two causes (αἰτίαι) for the existence of all things, Mind (νόος) and Necessity (ἀνάγκα). Mind is also called God and the Maker of the Better (δαμιουργὸς τῷ βελτίονος). Three other causes are then mentioned, the Idea (ἰδέα), Matter (ὕλα), and the Sense Perceptible (τὸ αἰσθητόν) which is the result of the mixture of the previous two causes, the Idea and Matter. At first it seems as if there are four basic causes. Yet it soon becomes apparent that the author of the *Timaeus Locrus* identifies Matter with Necessity. Necessity is mentioned only in the first sentence of the treatise and is thereafter replaced by Matter.[47] When the author begins to describe the ordering of the world, he refers only to the Idea, Matter, and God, the Maker of the Better. In this three tiered conception of reality, the Idea plays the intermediate role. As in the passages from Philo, the sensible world is created according to the Idea as a paradigm. The Idea in the *Timaeus Locrus* is also in the singular; nowhere in the treatise does the author refer to the "ideas" in the plural. On the contrary, the Idea is an intelligible reality that includes in itself all intelligible beings. The Idea is not simply a convenient way of referring to the Platonic ideas.[48] Rather the Idea is very similar to the *Logos* in that, like the

[46] The translation of the first half of the passage is from Dillon (*The Middle Platonists*, 126–27).

[47] This identification was fairly common in Middle Platonism. See Baltes, *Timaios Lokros*, 47.

[48] Baltes (*Timaios Lokros*, 35–36) underestimates the importance of the *Idea* in place of the *ideas*. As is clear from the fragment of Arius Didymus (Eusebius, *Praep. Evang.* 11.23), the unification of the ideas under the Idea is an important element in the development of the intermediate figure so characteristic of Middle Platonism.

Logos, it unites within itself the world of ideas and as a single intermediate figure serves as the paradigm for the sensible world.[49]

The second document is Plutarch's *De Iside et Osiride*, a work from the early part of the second century A.D. Here a *Logos* figure appears and functions in ways very similar to the *Logos* in the passages from Philo.

Thus Isis is the female principle in nature and that which receives all procreation, and so she is called by Plato (*Tim.* 49a, 51a) the Nurse and the All-receiving, while most people call her the Myriad-named because she is transformed by Reason (ὑπὸ τοῦ λόγου) and receives all forms and ideas (μορφὰς καὶ ἰδέας). Imbued in her she has a love of the foremost and most sovereign thing of all, which is the same as the Good, and this she longs for and pursues. The lot which lies with evil she shuns and rejects; for both she is indeed a possible sphere and material, but she leans ever of herself to what is better, offering herself to it for reproduction and for the fructifying in herself of effluxes and likenesses. In these she rejoices, and she is glad when she is pregnant with them and teems with procreations. For procreation in matter is an image of being (εἰκὼν οὐσίας), and what comes into being is an imitation of what is (μίμημα τοῦ ὄντος).

It is not therefore without reason that they relate in their myth that the soul of Osiris is eternal and indestructible, but that his body is frequently dismembered and destroyed by Typhon, whereupon Isis in her wanderings searches for it and puts it together again. For what is and is spiritually intelligible (νοητόν) and is good prevails over destruction and change; but the images (εἰκόνας) which the perceptible and corporeal nature (τὸ αἰσθητὸν καὶ σωματικόν) fashions from it, and the ideas, forms and likenesses (λόγοι καὶ εἴδη καὶ ὁμοιότητες) which this nature assumes, are like figures stamped on wax in that they do not endure forever. They are seized by the element of disorder and confusion which is driven here from the region above and fights against Horus, whom Isis brings forth as an image (εἰκόνα) of what is spiritually intelligible (τοῦ νοητοῦ), since he is the perceptible world (κόσμος αἰσθητός). This is why he is said to be charged with illegitimacy by Typhon as one who is neither pure nor genuine like his father, who is himself and in himself the unmixed and dispassionate Reason (λόγος), but is made spurious by matter through the corporeal element. He (Horus) overcomes and wins the day since Hermes, that is, Reason (λόγος), is a witness for him and points out that nature produces the world after being remodelled in accordance with what is spiritually intelligible (τὸ νοητόν). For the procreation of Apollo by Isis and Osiris, which occurred when the gods were still in the womb of Rhea, suggests symbolically that before this world became manifest and was completed by Reason (λόγος), matter, being shown by its nature to be incapable of itself, brought forth the first creation. For this reason they declare that god to have been born maimed in the darkness and they call

---

[49] Cf. *Timaeus Locrus* 95a; Arius Didymus *apud* Eusebius, *Praep. Evang.* 11.23; *Op.* 24–25.

him the elder Horus; for he was not the world, but only a picture and a vision of
the world to come. (Plutarch, *De Is. et Os.* 53–54.)[50]

These paragraphs represent one of several interpretations of the figures
of Isis and Osiris.[51] In this particular interpretation, Isis is taken to be the
female principle of nature who is explicitly identified with the "receptacle"
(ὑποδοχή) of Plato's *Timaeus*. What comes to be in nature, that is, in Isis, is
an image of being (εἰκὼν οὐσίας) and a copy of that which is (μίμημα τοῦ
ὄντος). Horus, whom Isis has brought forth, is the sensible world (κόσμος
αἰσθητός), which is an image of the intelligible world (κόσμος νοητός).
Once again the metaphor occurs in which the relationship of the intelligible
world to the sensible world is that of images stamped on wax.[52] In this
scheme both Hermes and Osiris are described as the *Logos*. Hermes is the
Logos in that he witnesses to the fact that the sensible world is modelled on
what is in the intelligible world. Osiris on the other hand, is the creative
Logos by whom the sensible world was completed and made manifest. This
doubling of the *Logos* probably reflects the complexity of the history of that
figure as used by Plutarch in this treatise.[53]

For our purposes it is the figure of Osiris as the creative *Logos* that is of
interest to us. The soul of Osiris is eternal and indestructible because it is of
the realm of the intelligible and good (νοητὸν καὶ ἀγαθόν) while his body is
frequently destroyed because it is part of the sensible and corporeal world
(αἰσθητὸν καὶ σωματικόν). The corporeal world contains the images, forms,
and ideas and likenesses of the intelligible world, but in the corporeal world
these images, etc., can only be temporary as are seals in wax. Osiris, then, in
addition to being the creative *Logos* by whom the sensible world was completed and made manifest, is also the *Logos* who serves as the paradigm who
stamps the sensible world with the images of the intelligible world. These are
basically the two roles played by the *Logos* in the passages that we analyzed
from Philo. Although the functions of the *Logos* figure (that is as paradigm
and as instrument of creation) in this treatise are quite similar to those found
in the passages from Philo, there is one significant difference. Osiris does not

[50] Translation by J. G. Griffiths, *Plutarch's De Iside et Osiride* (Cardiff: University of
Wales Press, 1970) 202–05 (slightly revised).

[51] In other interpretations Isis is the earth, Osiris the Nile, and Typhon the salt sea (32); or
Isis again is the earth, but Osiris is moisture and Typhon drought (33). These interpretations are
rather Stoic in that the gods are allegorized into elements in nature.

[52] See footnote 34.

[53] The role played by Hermes/Thoth as *Logos* in this interpretation of the myth is so
unclear that one hesitates to say anything about the figure. Wlosok (*Laktanz und die philosophische Gnosis*, 56) is probably right when she maintains that Plutarch has given us only scraps
of a larger interpretation.

seem to be an intermediate figure. He and Isis are themselves the two basic structural elements of reality.[54] In that sense the figure of Osiris as the *Logos* is quite different from that of the *Logos* in Philo. Nevertheless the similarities between the two are quite striking.

In attempting to understand the passages in Philo concerned with the *Logos*, this passage from Plutarch is important in several other ways. In the first place it witnesses to the use of much of the same vocabulary (εἰκών, μίμημα, σφραγίς, κόσμος νοητός, κόσμος αἰσθητός, λόγος) found in these passages from Philo. Secondly both the vocabulary and the conceptual framework of this passage from Plutarch are explicitly placed in the context of Plato's *Timaeus*. The roots of both the passages from Philo and that from Plutarch are the same. Thirdly both interpretations may well have arisen in Alexandria around the same time. In his commentary on *De Iside et Osiride*, J. Gwyn Griffiths points out that the form of the myth described by Plutarch, the information about the cult that he gives, and the sources that he used are all to be located in Egypt rather than in any of the Greek cult sites where Osiris is hardly mentioned at all.[55] In addition, his sources seem to end around the end of the first century B.C. or the early first century A.D.[56]

Far less certain is the question whether the interpretations of the myth, as distinct from the myth itself, are Plutarch's own or whether here too he has drawn on Alexandrian sources. The latter seems to be the more likely alternative for two reasons. In the first place, the figure of the *Logos* as a transcendent figure does not appear in Plutarch outside of the *De Iside et Osiride* and so does not seem to be a specific part of Plutarch's own viewpoint.[57] Secondly this Middle Platonic interpretation is only one of several interpretations of the myth, a fact which suggests that, in addition to having Egyptian sources for the myth itself, Plutarch also used sources for his

[54] Dillon (*The Middle Platonists*, 200–01) tries to integrate Osiris/*Logos* into Plutarch's overall philosophical position. He compares the figure of the *Logos* to that of Eros, the intelligible archetype of the sun, who leads one up toward the intelligible world (*Amat.* 764b–765c). But the *Logos* as such is not mentioned in this passage. The fact remains that the *Logos* in *De Iside et Osiride* is not as such an intermediate figure, even thought its functions are elsewhere (e.g., in Philo) connected with such a figure. Wlosok (*Laktanz und die philosophische Gnosis*, 56) makes the same mistake in assuming that the *Logos* in this section from Plutarch is an intermediate figure. However, the model for the interpretation in Plutarch is found in *Tim.* 47e–52d (especially 50a–52d). There is no intermediate figure in *Tim.* 47e–52d and so there is no intermediate figure in this section of *De Iside et Osiride*.

[55] Griffiths, *Plutarch's De Iside et Osiride*, 41–48.

[56] Ibid., 75–85.

[57] The term *logos* appears elsewhere in Plutarch. However, the closest it ever comes to having the meaning that it has in *De Iside et Osiride* is that of the "universe as ordered or structured" (*De def. or.* 25, 47–48; *Quaest. conv.* 8.2.3; *Compend. arg. Stoic. Absurd. poet. dic.* 48).

various interpretations. There is obviously no way to date those interpretations, but the close resemblance of this one interpretation to the passages
from Philo certainly suggests the second half of the first century B.C. as a
likely period.[58] Finally it is important to remember that both the passage
from Plutarch and the passages from Philo have similar goals, that is, they
are philosophical *interpretationes graecae* of non-Greek religious texts, and,
more specifically, Platonically oriented *interpretationes graecae.*[59]

All of this may seem like a poorly written detective story. Unfortunately
the history of Middle Platonic philosophy is so fragmentary that it is very
much like a detective story. The difference is that in a detective story the
clues, when properly understood, clearly establish that the butler did it. But
in the study of the various strands of Middle Platonism, no such clarity
emerges. The clues do not point unmistakably to one author as the originator of any given position: there is no butler. The same is true in the case of
these passages on Gen 1:27 from Philo. Their relationship to the religious
and intellectual environment is not very clear. The best that can be said is
that all of the "clues" point, although not clearly, to Alexandria at the end of
the first century B.C. as the proper environment for these passages. They fit
into the philosophical and interpretative patterns of that period and of that
city. They represent the attempt of Alexandrian Jewish writers of the late
first century B.C. to interpret their religious texts in conjunction with the
development of the Middle Platonism of the same period.[60]

When we compare this interpretation of Gen 1:27 with the anti-
anthropomorphic interpretations which were discussed in the previous chapter, the development is probably analogous to the development that is taking
place in the interpretation of Plato's *Timaeus.* The earlier anti-anthropomorphic interpretations of Gen 1:26–27 lack the intermediate figure so
important for the development of Middle Platonism (i. e., *Op.* 69–71). On
the other hand those anti-anthropomorphic interpretations maintain a much
closer relationship to the account of the creation of man in the *Timaeus*
(41a–44d). The interpretation of the phrase "let *us* make man" in *Op.* 72–75
is very close indeed to that of the *Timaeus.* What comes between these
anti-anthropomorphic interpretations and the passages from Philo discussed

---

[58] This applies only to the interpretation found in 53–54. Other interpretations may be
from different periods, probably earlier.

[59] On the surface at least, there is another major difference: Plutarch was not committed
to the cult of Isis and Osiris in the same way that Philo was commited to Judaism. But if
Plutarch was using a source for this interpretation, that source may have been an initiate in that
cult. Obviously there is no way to tell, but the interpretation on 53–54 may not have been by an
"outsider."

[60] See footnote 4.

in this chapter are the developments within Middle Platonism.[61] This dialogue is not an isolated phenomenon but is a constant factor within the exegetical traditions which Philo draws on. If the interpretation of Isis and Osiris mentioned earlier is any indication, then this dialogue with Middle Platonism is not restricted to Judaism but also involves the intellectual energies of adherents of other religious traditions as well.

B. *The Interpretation of Gen 2:7*

The interpretation of Gen 2:7 is more difficult to follow than is the interpretation of Gen 1:27 because it is more fragmentary. The interpretation of the creation of man as a double creation is usually introduced at this point in Philo's text (*Op.* 134–135; *L. A.* 1.31–32) and so the earlier interpretations of Gen 2:7 are pushed into the background. Although somewhat fragmentary, this earlier interpretation of Gen 2:7 is still visible in five passages (*L. A.* 1.39–40; *Spec.* 4.123; *L. A.* 3.161; *Som.* 1.33–34; *Q. G.* 2.59).

The most extended of these passages is found in *L. A.* 1.39–40 and is an interpretation of the phrase "into the face" of Gen 2:7:

> As the face is the dominant element in the body, so is the mind the dominant element of the soul: into this only does God breathe, whereas he does not see fit to do so with the other parts, whether senses or organs of utterance and of reproduction; for they are secondary in capacity.
>
> By what, then, were these also inspired? By the mind, evidently. For the mind imparts to the portion of the soul that is devoid of reason a share of that which it has received from God, so that the mind was be-souled by God, but the unreasoning part by the mind.

The interpretation is based on a comparison. Just as the face is the dominant part (τὸ ἡγεμονικόν) of the body, so the mind (νοῦς) is the dominant part (τὸ ἡγεμονικόν) of the soul (ψυχή). In this way the phrase "into the face" is taken to mean "into the mind." It is also clear from the verbs used (ἐμπνεῖν and ἐμπνεύειν) that what is inbreathed is "spirit" (πνεῦμα). This is stated explicitly in two other passages (*Spec.* 4.123; *L. A.* 1.161). This same comparison between the face as the dominant part of the body and the mind as the dominant part of the soul occurs in *Spec.* 4.123.

> For the essence of that other soul (the intelligent and reasonable soul) is a divine spirit (πνεῦμα θεῖον), a truth vouched for by Moses especially, who in his story of the creation says that God breathed a breath of life (πνοὴ ζωῆς) upon the first man, the founder of our race, into the most dominant part (ἡγεμονικώτατον) of

---

[61] The anti-anthropomorphic interpretations represent a Jewish appropriation of the early revival of the interpretation of the *Timaeus* while the level of interpretation discussed in this section represents the developments of the second half of the first century B.C.

his body, the face, where the senses are stationed like bodyguards to the great king, the mind. And clearly what was thus breathed was ethereal spirit (αἰθέριον πνεῦμα), or something if such there be better than ethereal spirit, even an effulgence (ἀπαύγασμα) of the blessed, thrice blessed nature of the Godhead.[62]

Again this interpretation of Gen 2:7 rests on the meaning of the phrase "into the face," a meaning arrived at by comparison of the face as the dominant part of the body with the mind as the dominant part of the soul.

Two phrases found in *Spec.* 4.123 help us to locate the provenance of this interpretation of Gen 2:7. The two phrases are "ethereal spirit"(αἰθέριον πνεῦμα) and "effulgence" (ἀπαύγασμα). The first of these phrases (αἰθέριον πνεῦμα) is to be taken with the phrase "divine spirit" (πνεῦμα θεῖον) which occurs earlier in the same passage. The second phrase "effulgence" (ἀπαύγασμα) is an expression parallel to ἀπόσπασμα (fragment) which is found in several other passages dealing with Gen 2:7.

> Every man, in respect of his mind, is allied to the divine Reason (θεῖος λόγος), having come into being as a copy or fragment (ἀπόσπασμα) or effulgence (ἀπαύγασμα) of that blessed nature, but in the structure of his body he is allied to all the world. (*Op.* 146.)[63]

In fact the term ἀπόσπασμα is primary while the term ἀπαύγασμα is a parallel, secondary formulation.[64] This is clear from three other passages dealing with Gen 2:7.

> The body, then, has been formed out of earth, but the soul is of the aether (αἰθήρ), a divine fragment (ἀπόσπασμα θεῖον) "for God breathed into his face a breath of life, and man became a living soul." (*L. A.* 3.161.)[65]

---

[62] The LXX uses πνοὴ ζωῆς to translate the Hebrew חיים נשמת. In seven of the nine places where he quotes Gen 2:7, Philo also uses πνοή (*Op.* 134; *L. A.* 1.31, 42; *Plant.* 19; *Her.* 56; *Som.* 1.34; *Spec.* 4.123); twice he uses the term πνεῦμα (*L. A.* 3.161; *Det.* 80). In none of the cases are there manuscript variants. In the two cases where πνεῦμα is used, the interpretation (πνεῦμα) has been introduced into the quotation (πνοή). The interpretation of πνοή as πνεῦμα was an obvious one for anyone who wanted to interpret the passage by means of Stoic concepts. P. Katz (*Philo's Bible* [Cambridge: University Press, 1950]) does not take this as one of his aberrant texts.

[63] Both this passage (*Op.* 146) and *Det.* 90 are passages that combine the interpretation of Gen 2:7 with that of Gen 1:27. They will be treated more fully in the next section of this chapter. They are introduced here simply to clarify the use of the term "fragment."

[64] As I shall suggest below, the term ἀπαύγασμα was probably used by Philo to replace ἀπόσπασμα.

[65] The MSS read ἀπόπλασμα rather than ἀπόσπασμα. Cohn emends the text to ἀπόσπασμα. Cohn's emendation seems correct for two reasons. First, the term ἀπόπλασμα is a hapaxlegomenon; it appears nowhere else in Philo or in any other Greek writer. Secondly, the context of *L. A.* 3.161 calls for ἀπόσπασμα.

Among created things, that which is holy is, in the universe, the heavens, in which natures imperishable and enduring through long ages have their orbits; in man it is mind, a divine fragment (ἀπόσπασμα θεῖον) as the words of Moses in particular bear witness, "He breathed into his face a breath of life, and man became a living soul" (Gen 2:7). (*Som.* 1.34.)

How, then, was it likely that the mind of man being so small, contained in such small bulks as a brain or a heart, should have room for all the vastness of sky and universe, had it not been an inseparable fragment (ἀπόσπασμα) of that divine and blessed soul? (*Det.* 90.)

In addition to the notion of the soul as a "divine fragment," we also find in the first of these three passages again the notion that soul is part of the aether (*L. A.* 3.161). The interpretation of Gen 2:7 which is found in bits and pieces in various passages in Philo is based on a comparison of the "face" as the dominant part of the body to the mind as the dominant part of the soul. Based on this comparison, Gen 2:7 is taken to mean that God breathed into the human mind a divine spirit (πνεῦμα θεῖον), a spirit that is part of the aether (αἰθέριον πνεῦμα), a divine fragment (ἀπόσπασμα θεῖον).[66]

These passages are in harmony with the Stoically oriented interpretation of *L. A.* 1.36–38, an anti-anthropomorphic passage dealt with in the preceding chapter. However, these passages are not anti-anthropomorphic. In addition, they represent a more developed interpretation of Gen 2:7. The introduction of the notions of aether and of the human mind as a "divine fragment" move considerably beyond the anti-anthropomorphic viewpoint of *L. A.* 1.36–38. Both formally and conceptually these passages represent a new level of interpretation when compared to *L. A.* 1.36–38.

This notion of the human soul reflects Stoic conceptions of man and the universe. A number of concepts found in these passages are also found in Diogenes Laertius' explanation of Stoic cosmology.

The world, they hold (i.e., the Stoics), comes into being when its substance has first been converted from fire through air into moisture and then the coarser part of the moisture has condensed as earth, while that whose particles are fine has been turned into air, and this process of rarefaction goes on increasingly till it generates fire. Thereupon out of these elements animals and plants and all other natural kinds are formed by their mixture. . . . The doctrine that the world is a living being, rational, animate and intelligent (λογικὸν καὶ ἔμψυχον καὶ νοερόν), is laid down by Chrysippus in the first book of his treatise *On Providence*, by Apollodorus in his *Physics*, and by Posidonius. It is a living

---

[66] In addition, *Op.* 83–88, 136–38, 140–41, 147 should be included under the Stoically oriented interpretations of Gen 2:7. However, these passages do not provide much help in either clarifying or in locating this type of interpretation.

thing in the sense of an animate substance endowed with sensation; for animal is better than non-animal, and nothing is better than the world, ergo, the world is a living being. It is endowed with soul as is clear from our several souls being each a fragment (ἀπόσπασμα) of it. (D. L. 7.142–143.)

For the Stoics, the world was of a piece, a living, rational, intelligent being and the human soul was a "fragment" of that living being. Yet the world is not an undifferentiated whole. Mind or reason (νοῦς) pervades the whole but some parts have more than others. In addition, for several Stoics, aether (αἰθήρ) is the ruling part (ἡγεμονικόν) of the world.

The world, in their (i.e., the Stoics') view, is ordered by reason and providence— so says Chrysippus in the fifth book of his treatise *On Providence* and Posidonius in his work *On the Gods*, Book III—inasmuch as mind (νοῦς) pervades every part of it, just as does the soul (ψυχή) in us. Only there is a difference of degree: in some parts there is more of it, in others less. For through some parts it passes as a cohesive force (ἕξις), as is the case with our bones and sinews: while through others it passes as mind (νοῦς), as in the ruling part of the soul. Thus, then, the whole world is a living being, endowed with soul and reason, and having *aether* (αἰθήρ) for its ruling principle (ἡγεμονικόν)—so says Antipater of Tyre in the eighth book of his treatise *On the Cosmos*. Chrysippus in his first book of his work *On Providence* and Posidonius in his book *On the Gods* say that the heaven, but Cleanthes that the sun, is the ruling part of the world. Chrysippus, however, in the course of the same work gives a somewhat different account, namely, that it is *the purer part of the aether* (τὸ καθαρώτερον τοῦ αἰθέρος); the same which they declare to be pre-eminently God and always to have, as it were in sensible fashion, pervaded all that is in the air, all animals and plants, and also the earth itself, as a principle of cohesion. (D. L. 7.138–139.)

Aether, at least for Antipater and Chrysippus, is understood as mind *par excellence* and is the ruling principle of the world.[67] In this way, just as the human soul is a fragment of the soul of the universe (D. L. 7.143), so too the human mind is a fragment of the aether, the ruling principle of the world. This aether, the ruling principle of the world, is defined as fire (D. L. 7.137), and fire is in turn identified with spirit (D. L. 7.156). From Chrysippus onward, "spirit" is also understood as a mixture of fire and air.[68] The

---

[67] The notion that aether was the ruling part of the cosmos was not the most common Stoic position. "Spirit" (πνεῦμα) as the ruling part of the world was certainly more common (see Long, *Hellenistic Philosophy*, 155). Yet it was an acceptable Stoic position, and, from Arius Didymus, we know that philosophers in first-century B.C. Alexandria were probably aware of it (Arius Didymus *apud* Eusebius, *Praep. Evang.* 15.15, 7–8).

[68] *SVF* 2.144–146.

combination of these two (fire and spirit) is also used by the Stoics to describe the soul.

> Nature in their view is an artistically working fire (πῦρ τεχνικόν), going on its way to create; which is equivalent to a fiery, creative breath (πνεῦμα πυροειδὲς καὶ τεχνοειδές). And the soul is a nature capable of perception. And they regard it as the spirit (πνεῦμα) congenital with us; from which they infer first that it is a body and secondly that is survives death. Yet it is perishable, though the soul of the universe, of which the individual souls of animals are parts (μέρη), is indestructible. Zeno of Citium and Antipater, in their treatises *On the Soul*, and Posidonius define the soul as a warm breath (πνεῦμα ἔνθερμον). (D. L. 7.156–157.)

From the Stoic texts just cited, it is clear that the interpretations of Gen 2:7 which we have been considering are rooted in concepts drawn from Stoic cosmology and psychology. The concept that the human mind is a divine spirit (πνεῦμα θεῖον), a spirit that is part of the aether, a divine fragment (ἀπόσπασμα θεῖον) is perfectly acceptable within a Stoic worldview.[69]

If the interpretation of Gen 2:7 found in these passages is Stoic, it is also clear that this interpretation is not Philo's own and that he subtly reinterprets it. Such a reinterpretation is found in *Her.* 281–283. This passage is an interpretation of Gen 15:15 in which God says to Abram, "You shall depart to your fathers nourished with peace, in a goodly old age."

> *Others* again have surmised that by "fathers" are meant the four first principles and powers, from which the world has been framed, earth, water, air, and fire. For into these, *they say*, each thing that has come into being is duly resolved.
>
> Just as nouns and verbs and all parts of speech which are composed of the "elements" in the grammatical sense are finally resolved into the same, so too each of us is composed of the four elements, borrowing small particles (μορία) from the substance of each, and this debt he repays when the appointed time-cycles are completed, rendering the dry in him to earth, the wet to water, the cold to air, and the warm to fire.
>
> These all belong to the body (σωματικά), but the soul whose nature is intellectual and celestial (νοερὸν καὶ οὐράνιον) will depart to find a father in aether (αἰθήρ), the purest of substances. For one may suppose that, as the men of old declared (ὁ τῶν ἀρχαίων λόγος), there is a fifth substance, moving in a circle, differing by its superior quality from the four. Out of this it was thought the

---

[69] Although locating the intelligent part of the soul in the head rather than in the heart is associated with Plato (*Tim.* 44d, 73c) rather than with the Stoics, nevertheless some Stoics placed the ruling part of the soul (τὸ ἡγεμονικόν) in the head (Philodemus, *De pietate* 15; *SVF* 3.217, 18–19). There is no reason then to think that locating the ruling part of the soul in the head (*L. A.* 1.39–40) could not also be Stoic. The rest of the vocabulary is clearly Stoic.

stars and the whole of heaven had been made and it was deduced as a natural consequence that the human soul also was a fragment (ἀπόσπασμα) thereof.

In many ways this passage reflects the same Stoic concepts found both in the other interpretations of Gen 2:7 and in the quotations from Diogenes Laertius. The human mind is a fragment of the aether. At the same time, however, Philo reinterprets that Stoic exegesis of Gen 15:15 in a way that is quite un-Stoic. This un-Stoic reinterpretation occurs in *Her.* 283. The human mind is still a fragment of the aether but the aether is no longer the subtle fire of Stoicism but the fifth substance of Aristotle.[70]

Her. 283 is probably Philo's own reinterpretation of an already existing Stoic interpretation of Gen 15:15. First of all, *Her.* 281–282 are clearly pre-Philonic since Philo indicates twice in *Her.* 281 that the interpretation that follows is not his own but the work of some unnamed "others" (τίνες . . . φασίν). In this way Philo both distances himself from that interpretation and sets the stage for *Her.* 283, a reinterpretation that seems to be the work of Philo himself.[71] *Her.* 283 clashes with *Her.* 281–282 in the sense that *Her.* 281–282 leaves no room for a fifth substance. The "fathers" of *Her.* 281–282 are the *four* elements of earth, water, air, and fire (281) of which human beings are composed and into which they are resolved at death (282). There is no room in this interpretation for aether as a fifth substance, for in Stoicism aether is either a heavenly fire or a mixture of fire and air, but not a fifth substance. Yet what emerges in *Her.* 283 is an interpretation in which the soul is no longer a fragment of one of the four elements but is a fragment of aether thought of as a fifth element, superior to the four elements of which the material world is composed. In this fashion Philo can maintain the immortality of the soul because it is a fragment of aether, a fifth substance which is not bodily (σωματικά) as are the other four substances, but intelligent and celestial (νοερὸν καὶ οὐράνιον). In other words *Her.* 283 is Philo's subtle critique of the Stoic viewpoint held by these unnamed "others" of *Her.* 281–282 This also indicates that all of the Stoic interpretations of Gen 2:7 cited above are pre-Philonic, since the interpretation of Gen 15:15 found in *Her.* 281–282 itself rests on the identification of the

---

[70] Philo seems to accept the notion of a fifth substance in four texts (*Q. G.* 3.6; 4.8; *Q. E.* 2.73, 85). In none of these texts is the fifth substance associated with the immaterial as it is in this text. It is associated simply with the heavens.

[71] Bousset (*Jüdisch-christlicher Schulbetrieb in Alexandria und Rom*, 11–14) also thought that *Her.* 283 was Philo's reinterpretation of the Stoic interpretation found in *Her.* 281–82. Bousset thought that the un-Stoic reinterpretation might have been Neopythagorean in character. However, the passages from Cicero make such a suggestion unlikely (see below).

human soul with the πνεῦμα/αἰθήρ, an identification made possible through the interpretation

Originally the position that aether was a fifth substance superior to the other four was Aristotelian. The notion that aether was to be associated with the heavenly bodies and their circular motions was also Aristotelian (Aristotle, *Cael.* 1.2–3). Given Philo's Platonic tendencies, the interpretation found in *Her.* 283, with its notion of aether as a fifth substance, may suggest that *Her.* 283 was not Philo's own reinterpretation but that of some other interpreter who was influenced by this Aristotelian notion. However, in the first century B.C., the notion of aether as a fifth substance seems to have become an acceptable position in Middle Platonic circles. In that case, the interpretation found in *Her.* 283 would be consistent with Philo's own philosophical tendencies.Several texts found in Cicero suggest that Philo was not alone or the first to interpret aether in a rather un-Stoic fashion. In Cicero's *Academica Posteriora*, Varro seems to imply that Antiochus of Ascalon (ca. 130–68 B.C.) may have accepted aether as a fifth substance. The passage is one in which Varro describes Antiochus' physics.[73]

> Well then, those qualities are of two sorts, primary and derivative. Things of primary quality are homogeneous and simple; those derived from them are varied and "multiform." Accordingly air (this word also we now use in Latin) and fire and water and earth are primary; while their derivatives are the species of living creatures and of things that grow out of the earth. Therefore those things are termed first principles and (to translate from the Greek) elements; and among them air and fire have motive and efficient force, and the remaining divisions, I mean water and earth, receptive and "passive" capacity. Aristotle deemed that there existed a certain fifth sort of element, in a class by itself and unlike the four that I have mentioned above, which was the source of the stars and of minds (*astra mentesque*). (*Acad. Post.* 26.)

Although Varro does not explicitly attribute this view to Antiochus, he certainly seems to imply that it is Antiochus' view as well as Aristotle's. This

---

[72] The number of times that Philo reinterprets the Stoic exegesis of Gen 2:7 (*Her.* 283; *Spec.* 4.123; *Plant.* 18; *Mut.* 223) is a further indication of the pre-Philonic character of the Stoic interpretation of Gen 2:7.

[73] Theiler (*Die Vorbereitung des Neuplatonismus*, 17–40) has overemphasized the contribution made by Antiochus of Ascalon to Middle Platonism. In the final analysis, Antiochus does not seem to have moved beyond the material realm; he stayed within the bounds of Stoic materialism. Nevertheless he did begin to combine some of those Platonic and Stoic elements which developed into Middle Platonism. One of those contributions was to begin to place "mind" in a class by itself, a class that was still material yet was beyond the usual four material elements of Stoicism (earth, air, fire, and water). See Dillon, *The Middle Platonists*, 81–84, 96–102.

suspicion is strengthened when later Varro tells how Antiochus describes Zeno's rejection of the fifth substance as a change from what Plato, the Old Academy, and Aristotle held and so what Antiochus himself wanted to hold.[74] The least that can be said is that Antiochus was open to such a formulation. Aristotle's fifth substance is also mentioned with great respect in Book I of the *Tusculan Disputations*.

> Aristotle, who far excels everyone—always with the exception of Plato—in genius and industry, after grasping the conception of the well-known four classes of elements which he held to be the origin of all things, considers that there is a special fifth nature from which comes mind (*mens*); for mind reflects and foresees and learns and teaches and makes discoveries and remembers and a multitude of other things. (*Tusc.* 1.22.)

The speaker in this passage was Cicero himself. Here the Aristotelian fifth substance is mentioned as only one possible interpretation of the relationship between body and soul. Yet one should note that several paragraphs earlier Zeno's notion that the soul is fire is passed over in one line (19). In other words, Aristotle's notion of aether as a fifth substance is treated with far more respect than is Zeno's more materialistic notion.[75]

In addition Philo's reinterpretation in *Her.* 283 has two other points of contact with these two quotations from Cicero. First of all Book I of the *Tusculan Disputations* is basically devoted to the question of the immortality of the soul, a question which is also the point of Philo's reinterpretation of *Her.* 281–282. Secondly, both *Tusc.* 1.22 and *Acad. Post.* 26 connect aether as a fifth substance with mind (*Tusc.* 1.22, *mens*; *Acad. Post.* 26, *mentes*). Philo makes the same point when he distinguishes the fifth substance, aether, from the other four substances which he characterizes as bodily (σωματικά). The human soul, as part of the aether, is intelligent and celestial (νοερὸν καὶ οὐράνιον). This second point is important because

---

[74] Another point of similarity between Antiochus and this text of Philo is the use of the term ἀρχαῖοι (ancients). Antiochus wanted to move back beyond the New Academy to the teachings of the "ancients." By these he meant Plato, Speusippus, Xenocrates, Polemon, Aristotle, and Theophrastus taken as a group (see Cicero, *Acad. Post.* 13, 22, 39). In addition to *Her.* 283, Philo also describes the concept of a fifth substance as the opinion of the "ancients" in *Q. G.* 3.6 (although strangely enough he associates it with the Pythagoreans in *Q. G.* 4.8 and with the "moderns" in *Q. E.* 2.73). One can hardly build an argument on such uses of a term, but it is worth noting when taken in conjunction with other similarities (see Dillon, *The Middle Platonists*, 55).

[75] Luck (*Der Akademiker Antiochus*, 30–40) has tried to show that Cicero's *Somnium Scipionis* can be traced back to Antiochus of Ascalon. Given the state of our knowledge of the origin of Middle Platonism, such specificity seems over-optimistic. Both the *Somnium Scipionis* and *Tusculan Disputations* I, however, do represent points of view that are fairly common in Middle Platonism.

Aristotle himself did not claim that aether was itself mind but only that it was a substance purer than the other four (*Cael.* 1.2–3). The association of aether as a fifth substance with mind seems to have been popular in circles represented by these texts from Cicero and Philo. The concepts involved in Philo's reinterpretation then were not something original with him but were part of the development of the Middle Platonism of the first century B.C.[76]

The particular reinterpretation of Stoic positions found in *Her.* 281–282 through the addition of *Her.* 283 clearly, from the point of view of a literary analysis, is the work of Philo. Philo has taken an already existing Stoic interpretation of Gen 2:7 and reinterpreted the concept of aether in such a way that the human soul is something distinct from and superior to the four basic elements of the material universe, although he may well not have been alone in reinterpreting Stoic concepts in this un-Stoic way.

This same technique of subtle reinterpretation also allows us to understand better the use of ἀπαύγασμα instead of ἀπόσπασμα in *Spec.* 4.123 which was quoted above (p. 77–78). After identifying the "divine spirit" (πνεῦμα θεῖον) that was breathed into man with "ethereal spirit" (αἰθέριον πνεῦμα), Philo then adds, "or something, if such there be, better than ethereal spirit, even an effulgence (ἀπαύγασμα) of the blessed, thrice blessed nature of the Godhead" (*Spec.* 4.123). While using a different technique, the result is the same: the soul of man is raised above the level of the elements of the material universe, specifically above aether which is here taken in its Stoic sense. In addition he substitutes the term "effulgence" (ἀπαύγασμα) for the Stoic term "fragment" (ἀπόσπασμα) because the term ἀπαύγασμα "effulgence" is less materialistically oriented.[77] Metaphors based on light and its shining forth were common ways of pointing to the immaterial aspects of reality.

The term ἀπαύγασμα also occurs in the Wisdom of Solomon.

> For in her (Wisdom) is a spirit intelligent (πνεῦμα νοερόν) and holy,
> unique of its kind yet manifold, subtle . . .
> and pervading all spirits,
> intelligent, pure, and most subtle.
> For Wisdom is more mobile than any motion,

[76] The origins of the association of aether as a fifth substance with mind are controversial. The association probably is not to be traced to a lost work of Aristotle (*De philosophia*). It may go back to the fourth century Platonist, Heraclides Ponticus (frgs. 98, 99, Wehrli). The further connection of this substance with the immortality of the soul is what may be the peculiar development represented in these passages from Cicero and Philo. For a full discussion of the problem, see P. Moraux, *Aristotle: Du Ciel* (Paris: Société d'édition "Les Belles Lettres," 1965) li–lx.

[77] These two terms appear together in *Op.* 146. The purpose is the same, to reinterpret the term "fragment."

she pervades and permeates all things by reason of her pureness.
She is an exhalation from the power of God,
a pure effluence from the glory of the Almighty;
therefore nothing tainted insinuates itself into her.
She is an *effulgence* (ἀπαύγασμα) of everlasting light,
an unblemished mirror of the active power of God,
and an image (εἰκών) of his goodness. (Wis 7:22–26.)[78]

This description of Wisdom as an "effulgence" of everlasting light and as
having an "intelligent spirit" that pervades all things is consistent with
Philo's use of the term in *Spec.* 4.123. While there is no indication that Philo
was specifically aware of the Wisdom of Solomon, he certainly was aware of
the uses of the figure of Wisdom. The attributes associated with the figure
of Wisdom may have provided him with the term, ἀπαύγασμα, that would have
run counter to the more materialistic notions represented by the Stoic notion
of "fragment."[79] Finally, Philo seems to use the authority of Moses to support his reinterpretation of "divine spirit" as an effulgence of the Godhead,
an effulgence beyond the ethereal spirit. This is the same procedure that
Philo uses elsewhere to reinterpret otherwise unacceptable concepts.[80]

The reason for Philo's reinterpretation is not hard to find. The monism
and materialism of Stoicism simply did not fit with Philo's more Platonic
notion of God and of the human mind as being beyond the realm of the
material. Philo used the notion of aether as a fifth substance and the substitution of "effulgence" for "fragment" to move to a more non-materialistic
notion of the nature of the human soul.

Because of the significant difference of outlook between the interpretations of Gen 1:27 and Gen 2:7 (one Platonic, the other Stoic), the origins of
the two interpretations were distinct. The Stoic interpretations of Gen 2:7
are in continuity not only with the anti-anthropomorphic interpretation of
L. A. 1.36–38 but also with the Stoic interpretations found in Aristobulus.
In terms of thought patterns these Stoic interpretations of Gen 2:7 are much
closer to the interpretations of Aristobulus than are the Platonic interpreta-

---

[78] The translation is from D. Winston, *The Wisdom of Solomon* (AB 43; Garden City:
Doubleday, 1979) 178, 184. As Winston points out (59–63), Philo and the Wisdom of Solomon
have a good number of ideas in common. However, the specific exegetical traditions about the
creation of man which we are dealing with have practically no parallels with the Wisdom of
Solomon and certainly no close parallels. It is impossible to establish literary dependence in
either direction.

[79] For a fuller treatment of Philo's use of the figure of Wisdom, see Mack, *Logos und
Sophia.*

[80] Cf. *Plant.* 18; *Mut.* 223. In these two cases the reinterpretation is achieved through the
use of Gen 1:27 as a corrective to the Stoic interpretation of Gen 2:7. These passages will be
dealt with in the next section.

tions of Gen 1:27. Given the fact that the tradition of interpretation that is available to us from Philo is a Platonizing one, these Stoic interpretations of Gen 2:7 probably represent interpretations prior to the appropriation of Middle Platonism by Jewish interpreters. Finally, while Philo felt that he had to distance himself from these Stoic interpretations and to reinterpret them, nevertheless he also felt a certain obligation to respect them, even if only partially.

C. *The Combination of Gen 1:27 and Gen 2:7*

Although the interpretations of Gen 1:27 and Gen 2:7 are so different (i.e., one Platonic and the other Stoic) that they had distinct origins, nevertheless they were combined and interpreted as complementary formulations of the same act of creation. A kind of *communicatio idiomatum* developed in which concepts or terms that originated in the interpretation of one of the two verses were applied to the interpretation of the other verse. The two major witnesses to this combination are *Det.* 79–90 and *Plant.* 18–22. At the same time, this combination of the interpretations of Gen 1:27 and Gen 2:7 offered Philo another way of subtly revising the Stoic interpretation of Gen 2:7. The combination itself, however, of the interpretations of the two verses preceded Philo's own interpretation. As I indicted in Chapter II, the interpretations of Gen 1:27 and Gen 2:7 as a description of a double creation of man (a pre-Philonic interpretation) seems to assume the existence of the combination of the Platonic interpretation of Gen 1:27 and the Stoic interpretation of Gen 2:7.[81] The two passages mentioned above (*Det.* 79–90 and *Plant.* 18–22) point in the same direction. An analysis of them will allow us to see both the pre-Philonic combination of these two interpretations and also Philo's attempt subtly to modify the balance between them in favor of the Platonic interpretation of Gen 1:27.

The first of these large sections, *Det.* 79–90, is prompted by the apparent contradiction that results from placing Gen 2:7 next to such verses as Lev 17:11, "For the life of all flesh is the blood." What then is the life-principle? Is it blood (Lev 17:11) or is it breath (πνεῦμα) (Gen 2:7)? The answer is that there are two life-principles, one in so far as we are living creatures (ζῷα) and that is blood and the other in so far as we are rational (λογικοί) and that is breath or spirit (πνεῦμα).

> What then are we to say? Each one of us, according to the primary analysis, is two in number, an animal (ζῷον) and a man. To each of these has been allotted an inner power akin to the qualities of their respective life-principles, to one the power of vitality, in virtue of which we are alive, to the other the power of

---

[81] See Chapter II, 25–29.

reasoning (ἡ λογική), in virtue of which we are reasoning beings (λογικοί). Of the power of vitality the irrational creatures partake with us; of the power of reasoning God is, not indeed partaker, but originator, being the Fountain of eldest Reason (ἡ τοῦ πρεσβυτάτου λόγου πηγή).

To the faculty which we have in common with the irrational creatures blood has been given as its essence; but of the faculty which streams forth from the fountain of Reason breath (τὸ πνεῦμα) has been assigned; not moving air (οὐκ ἀέρα κινούμενον), but, as it were, an impression and stamp (τύπον τινὰ καὶ χαρακτῆρα) of the divine power, to which Moses gives the appropriate title of "image" (εἰκών), thus indicating that God is the Archetype of rational existence, while man is a copy (μίμημα) and representation (ἀπεικόνισμα). (*Det.* 82-83.)

The basic distinctions of λογικοί/ἄλογα and πνεῦμα/αἷμα are Stoic and so quite consistent with the Stoic interpretation of Gen 2:7.[82] Breath or spirit, however, is interpreted in this passage in conjunction with concepts taken from the interpretation of Gen 1:27. This breath is a copy or representation of the Archetype of rational existence, God. The place of the *Logos* in this particular scheme is not altogether clear, that is, whether it is a distinct entity or whether it is only another way of speaking of God. Because the term πρεσβύτατος λόγος (*Det.* 82) is used elsewhere to refer to a distinct entity, the *Logos*, it probably also does so in this case.[83] But because the role of the *Logos* is not at issue in this section, it is passed over quickly and the notion of man's mind as a copy or representation is the point of emphasis. But what is important in this section is that the term "breath," taken from Gen 2:7, is interpreted in conjunction with Gen 1:27.

This section of *Quod Deterius Potiori Insidiari Soleat* also develops an image associated with both the interpretation of Gen 1:27 and Gen 2:7, the flight of the soul through the heavens toward God. It combines both the Platonic notion of going beyond the material (*Det.* 87-89a) with the philosophical commonplace of the ascent to contemplate the heavens and the cosmos (*Det.* 90).[84] In addition, this section draws on an image found at the end of Plato's *Timaeus* (90a-91e). It is the image of man as a "heavenly

---

[82] Λογικοί/ἄλογα: *SVF* 1.55.15-17; 86.37-87.2; 2.40.7-8; 43.18; 74.1-7. Πνεῦμα/αἷμα: *SVF* 1.38.30-33.

[83] Cf. *L. A.* 3.175; *Det.* 118; *Conf.* 146; *Her.* 205.

[84] The two metaphors are well integrated. It is only in *Det.* 87-89a when compared with *Det.* 90 that one can notice the combination of the two. The ascent in *Det.* 87-89a goes beyond the mortal to the immortal (87) and beyond the cosmos to God (89) and so is Platonic. On the other hand, *Det.* 90 assumes that the ascent is within the cosmos and does not go beyond it; this is the commonplace form of the metaphor which fits in well with the Stoic character of *Det.* 90. For a description of the different uses of the metaphor of the ascent of the soul, see Jones, "Posidonius and the Flight of the Mind Through the Universe," 97-113.

plant" (φυτὸν οὐράνιον) which, unlike other creatures whose roots are in the earth or whose head is pointed toward the earth, has its "roots" in the heavens. This is symbolized by the fact that man stands upright and can raise his eyes heavenward (*Det.* 84–85). The explanation of this fact combines the interpretations of both Gen 1:27 and Gen 2:7.

> The creator wrought for the body no soul capable by itself of seeing its Maker, but, accounting that it would be greatly to the advantage of the thing wrought should it obtain a conception of him who wrought it, since this is what determines happiness and blessedness, he breathed (ἐνέπνει) into him from above of his own Deity (τῆς ἰδίου θειότητος). The invisible Deity stamped on the invisible soul the impresses (τύπους) of Itself, to the end that not even the terrestrial region should be without a share in the image of God. . . . Having been struck in accord with the Pattern, it entertained ideas not now mortal but immortal. . . . How then, was it likely that the mind of man, being so small, contained in such small bulks as a brain or a heart, should have room for all the vastness of sky and universe, had it not been an inseparable fragment (ἀπόσπασμα) of that divine and blessed soul? For no part of that which is divine cuts itself off and becomes separate, but does but extend itself. (*Det.* 86–87, 90.)

The human soul is an inseparable fragment of the divine soul, a fragment into which has been breathed something of the divine itself (Gen 2:7); but it is also an impress (τύπος) of the divine, struck (τυπωθεῖσα) in accord with the divine Paradigm (Gen 1:27). The metaphor of man as a "heavenly plant" is integrated into this combination of Gen 1:27 and Gen 2:7. Man is a "heavenly plant" whose roots are in the world above because he is both a fragment of the divine and struck in accord with the divine Paradigm.

For the most part, neither the Platonic interpretation of Gen 1:27 nor the Stoic interpretation of Gen 2:7 predominates in *Det.* 79–90. The two interpretations are interwoven in such a way that they become two complementary formulations of the same act of creation. This complementary pattern of interpretation appears also in *Op.* 139, *Virt.* 203–205, *Her.* 55–57, and *Spec.* 1.171.[85] In these passages the interpretations of Gen 1:27 and Gen 2:7 are complementary formulations of the same act of creation. In addition, the last three passages, like *Det.* 79–90, establish that the basic pattern is a complementary one in which neither Gen 1:27 nor Gen 2:7 predominates.

At one point, however, in *Det.* 79–90, Philo's editorial hand is detectible. This occurs in *Det.* 83, a section mentioned above:

> To the faculty which we have in common with the irrational creatures blood had been given as its essence: but to the faculty which streams forth from the foun-

---

[85] In these passages the mixture is quite thorough and seemingly unselfconscious.

tain of Reason breath (πνεῦμα) has been assigned; not moving air (οὐκ ἀέρα κινούμενον) but, as it were, an impression and stamp (τύπον τινὰ καὶ χαρακτῆρα) of the divine power, to which Moses gives the appropriate title of "image" (εἰκών), thus indicating that God is the Archetype of rational existence, while man is a copy (μίμημα) and representation (ἀπεικόνισμα).

The phrase "not moving air" (οὐκ ἀέρα κινούμενον) points to Philo's editorial work. Philo is denying that the breath or spirit (πνεῦμα) that man has received is "moving air" and claims, on the authority of Moses, that man's rational faculty is an image of the Archetype of rational existence. This amounts to a denial of the Stoic notion of "spirit" which was defined by a Stoic such as Chrysippus as "moving air."[86] Yet the term "spirit" itself is not abandoned but reinterpreted in the light of the language of the Platonic interpretation of Gen 1:27, that is, as an image, a copy, a representation, an impression and a stamp.

There are two reasons for thinking that *Det.* 83 has been reworked by Philo. First of all, as I indicated earlier in this section, nowhere else in this passage (*Det.* 79–90) is there any indication that the interpretations of Gen 1:27 and Gen 2:7 are anything but complementary. The rest of the passage follows the pattern found in *Op.* 139, *Her.* 55–57, *Virt.* 203–205, and *Spec.* 1.171. The interpretations of Gen 1:27 and Gen 2:7 are also combined in *Det.* 86–87, 90 with no indication that Gen 2:7 is to be interpreted in the light of Gen 1:27. As a matter of fact, *Det.* 90 remains quite clearly Stoic.The second reason which indicates that Philo has reworked *Det.* 83 is the use of Moses as an authority. Philo used the same technique in *Spec.* 4.123 mentioned in the previous section and in *Plant.* 18 and *Mut.* 223, both of which will be treated later.[87] In these passages Philo used the authority of Moses to revise the Stoic interpretation of Gen 2:7 in a less materialistic and monistic direction. He uses the same technique in *Det.* 83 to revise the Stoic interpretation of Gen 2:7 in the light of the Platonic concepts used in the interpretation of Gen 1:27. It is important to note that in *Det.* 83 Philo has revised the *combination* of the interpretations of Gen 1:27 and Gen 2:7 so that the Platonic interpretation of Gen 1:27 predominates. He did *not*, however, revise the interpretation of Gen 2:7 *by combining it* with the interpretation of Gen 1:27. The combination itself was pre-Philonic; Philo's revision was to alter the balance of the combination in favor of the Platonic interpretation of Gen 1:27.

The editorial hand of Philo emerges much more clearly in the second large section in which the interpretations of Gen 1:27 and Gen 2:7 are com-

---

[86] *SVF* 2.152.31–35.
[87] See Chapter IV, 91–93.

bined (*Plant.* 18–22). Like *Det.* 79–90, *Plant.* 18–22 is an interpretation that combines Gen 1:27 and Gen 2:7 and that draws on both the metaphor of the flight of the soul from *Phaedrus* 246a–249d and the metaphor of man as a "heavenly plant" from *Timaeus* 90a–91e. *Plant.* 18–22 is in turn part of a larger discussion of the world as a "cosmic plant" (*Plant.* 1–27), a metaphor also derived from Plato (*Tim.* 30d, 69b-d) and further developed by the Stoics.[88] The combination of the two plant metaphors, however, in the interpretation of Genesis is secondary. This becomes quite clear when one compares the role of the *Logos* figure in each of the metaphors. In the metaphor of the world as a plant, the *Logos* is the bond (ὁ δεσμός) that holds the world together (*Plant.* 9). In the metaphor of man as a heavenly plant, however, the *Logos* is the image and archetype for the creation of man (*Plant.* 20). These roles are not mixed; the *Logos* is never the bond that holds man together nor is it ever the archetype for the "cosmic plant." This indicates that the two plant metaphors were originally distinct interpretations and only secondarily were they combined, perhaps by Philo himself.[89]

In the middle of this extended metaphor of man as a "heavenly plant," a combined interpretation of Gen 1:27 and Gen 2:7 appears that is clearly critical of the Stoic conceptual framework used to interpret Gen 2:7 and that tries to interpret Gen 2:7 in the light of Gen 1:27.

> Now while others, by asserting that our human mind is a portion (μοῖρα) of the ethereal nature (αἰθέριος φύσις), have claimed for man a kinship with the aether: our great Moses likened the form of the reasonable soul to no created thing, but averred it to be a genuine coinage (δόκιμον νόμισμα) of that dread Spirit, the Divine and Invisible One, signed and impressed by the seal of God, the stamp of which is the Eternal *Logos*.
>
> His words are "God in-breathed into his face a breath of life" (Gen 2:7); so that it cannot but be that he that receives is made in the likeness (ἀπεικονίσθαι) of him who sends forth the breath. Accordingly we also read that man has been made after the Image (εἰκών) of God (Gen 1:27), not however after the image of anything created.
>
> It followed then, as a natural consequence of man's soul having been made after the image of the Archetype, the *Logos* of the First Cause, that his body was made erect, and could lift up its eyes to heaven, the purest portion of our universe, that by means of that which he could see man might clearly apprehend that which he could not see. (*Plant.* 18–20.)

---

[88] See Früchtel, *Die kosmologischen Vorstellungen*, 53–61.

[89] Früchtel (*Die kosmologischen Vorstellungen*, 63–68) thinks that the two metaphors of the world as a "cosmic plant" and man as a "heavenly plant" were always together. But the very different roles played by the central figure of the *Logos* in each of the two metaphors indicates that the combination of these two metaphors in the interpretation of Genesis is secondary.

The use of the term "portion" (μοῖρα) instead of "fragment" (ἀπόσπασμα) cannot disguise the fact that what the "others" are asserting is the Stoic interpretation of Gen 2:7 in which man's rational soul is a "fragment" or, in this case, a "portion" of the aether.[90] In contrast to these "others," Philo claims, again on the authority of Moses, that man's rational soul is to be associated with no created thing (and here he means the Stoic aether) but rather is the seal or the impress of the eternal *Logos* who is the image of God.[91] In this way, the materialistic notion of Stoicism that the human mind is a fragment or portion of the aether is overcome by interpreting Gen 2:7 in the light of the Platonic interpretation of Gen 1:27.

A revision of the combination of Gen 1:27 and Gen 2:7 is also found in a shorter passage, *Op.* 146. In this passage Philo draws on two of the same techniques used in *Spec.* 4.123 and *Her.* 283:

> Every man, in respect of his mind, is allied to the divine *Logos* (λόγος θεῖος), having come into being as a cast (ἐκμαγεῖον) or fragment (ἀπόσπασμα) or effulgence (ἀπαύγασμα) of that blessed nature, but in the structure of his body he is allied to all the world, for he is compounded of the same things, earth, water, air, and fire, each of the elements having contributed the share that falls to each, to complete a material absolutely sufficient in itself for the Creator to take in order to fashion this visible image (ἡ ὁρατὴ εἰκών).

In *Op.* 146 a twofold reinterpretation has taken place. The first is the introduction of "effulgence" (ἀπαύγασμα) as a parallel to "fragment" (ἀπόσπασμα). As we saw in the analysis of *Spec.* 4.123, the term "effulgence" was introduced to express a less materialistic notion of the relationship of the human mind to God than was possible with the Stoic concept of "fragment." It serves the same purpose here. The term "fragment" is interpreted in the light of the two parallel terms, "cast" derived from the interpretation of Gen 1:27 and "effulgence" as it is used in *Spec.* 4.123. The second reinterpretation is very similar to that found in *Her.* 283. As in *Her.* 283, the four primary elements of Stoicism (earth, air, fire, and water) are said to pertain only to man's body while man's mind is fashioned as the visible image (ἡ ὁρατὴ εἰκών) of the divine *Logos*.

---

[90] Cf. *L. A.* 1.36–38, 39–40; *L. A.* 3.161; *Her.* 281–82; *Som.* 1.33–34; *Spec.* 4.123. The reason for the substitution of "portion" for "fragment" is not clear. *Plant.* 18–20 is the passage that is most openly critical of the Stoic interpretation of Gen 2:7. This passage comes closest to a denial of that Stoic interpretation. Given the fact that Philo tends to subtly revise rather than openly deny an interpretation that is questionable for him, he may have substituted "portion" for "fragment" in order to avoid a direct rejection of the Stoic interpretation of Gen 2:7 that made use of the term.

[91] Cf. *Spec.* 4.123; *Det.* 83; *Plant.* 18; *Mut.* 223.

Stoic monism, of course, also created a problem of a different sort. If all was in some basic sense one, then man and God must also be one and so the notion that the human mind is a divine fragment (ἀπόσπασμα θεῖον) must be very nearly literally true. This came perilously close to pantheism. Philo himself is aware of the problem and tries to deal with it in much the same way that he did in *Plant.* 18–22. He claims in the name of Moses that the notion of man as a faithful image (Gen 1:27) is a better interpretation than is the notion of the human mind as a fragment of the Deity.

> Now "reasoning" as a name is but a little word, but as a fact it is something most perfect and most divine, a fragment of the soul of the universe (τῆς τοῦ παντὸς ψυχῆς ἀπόαπασμα), or, as it might be put more reverently following the philosophy of Moses, a faithful cast of the divine image (εἰκόνος θείας ἐκμαγεῖον ἐμφερές). (*Mut.* 223.)

In this passage Philo's uneasiness seems to be less with the materialism of Stoicism than with its monism, the risk of turning the human mind into a part or piece of God. Philo avoids this Stoic notion by giving primacy to the Platonic interpretation of Gen 1:27, an interpretation that, at a conceptual level, better preserves the transcendence of God.

From our analysis of these passages (*Mut.* 223, *Plant.* 18–20, *Op.* 146, *Her.* 283, *Det.* 83, *Op.* 139, *Her.* 55–57, *Virt.* 203–205, and *Spec.* 1.171), it is clear that Philo is reinterpreting an already existing combination of the interpretations of Gen 1:27 and Gen 2:7. Those reinterpretations consistently move away from the materialism and monism connected with the Stoicizing interpretation of Gen 2:7 and in the direction of the more Middle Platonic interpretation of Gen 1:27.

All of the interpretations that cluster around Gen 2:7 and the combination of Gen 1:27 and Gen 2:7 are valuable both because they reveal levels of interpretation prior to Philo and also because they give us a glimpse into how Philo used the exegetical traditions available to him. On the one hand, he feels an obligation to carry on these traditions even though they represent an outlook quite different from his own. In some of the pasages cited above (i.e., *Op.* 139, *Her.* 55–57, *Virt.* 203–205, *Spec.* 1.171), Philo gives no indication that he is uneasy with the way in which Stoic concepts are used to interpret Gen 2:7. On the other hand, Philo's uneasiness with these interpretations emerges in the reinterpretations found in *Mut.* 223, *Plant.* 18–20, *Op.* 146, *Her.* 283, and *Det.* 83. It emerges, however, not as a direct rejection of the prior interpretation but as a reinterpretation.

D. *Methods of Interpretation*

Up until now we have been analyzing the content of these pre-Philonic interpretations of the creation of man because the content has offered the clearest way of differentiating the various levels of tradition. We must now look at the ways by which these interpretations were arrived at. Not all of the texts are of equal value for this purpose. Most of them do not contain the formal grounds for the interpretation given in them; most of them simply give the interpretation without any indication of how that interpretation was arrived at. Up until now that has not been of great importance because we were analyzing their content to see if they represented a fairly constant interpretation and what that interpretation was. However, to understand the way in which such interpretations were arrived at, we must restrict ourselves, for the most part, to those interpretations in which the reason for the interpretation is given. Only in such places can we get some notion of the "how" of the interpretation and not simply of the "what." The texts that give no reason for the interpretation can provide helpful supplements, but they cannot be the center of attention. The attempt to understand the "how" of these interpretations is more than a minor matter. To understand the way in which these Jewish exegetes arrived at their interpretations is also to understand something of how they saw the process of interpretation itself.

The basic interpretation of Gen 2:7 has been provided by the anti-anthropomorphic interpretation found in *L. A.* 1.36–38. The term "breath" (πνοή) is taken to be synonymous with the term "spirit" (πνεῦμα). "Spirit" is substituted for its synonym "breath" because "spirit" is the term used by the Stoics. Once this synonymous substitution has taken place, all of the nuances of the term can then be applied to the interpretation of the verse.

The result of this process is expanded in the interpretations of Gen 2:7 discussed in this chapter. *L. A.* 1.39–40 contains the most detailed justification of this interpretation, an interpretation that revolves around the meaning of the phrase "into the face" (εἰς τὸ πρόσωπον):

> The breathing "into the face" is to be understood both physically (φυσικῶς) and ethically (ἠθικῶς): physically, because it is in the face that he set the senses; for this part of the body is beyond other parts endowed with soul; but ethically on this wise. As the face is the dominant element in the body, so is the mind (ὁ νοῦς) the dominant element (τὸ ἡγεμονικόν) of the soul (ψυχῆς): into this only does God breathe, whereas he does not see fit to do so with the other parts, whether senses or organs of utterance and of reproduction; for these are secondary in capacity. By what, then, were these also inspired? By the mind evidently. For the mind imparts to the portion of the soul that is devoid of reason a share of that which it has received from God, so that the mind was be-souled by God, but the unreasoning part by the mind. For the mind, is so to speak, God of the unreasoning part.

The distinction between "ethically" (ἠθικῶς) and "physically" (φυσικῶς) is between that which deals with the specifically human and that which deals with man in so far as he is also part of the animal world. This particular contrast is peculiar, since "physical" usually refers to the study of nature or the universe, including man, while "ethical" refers to virtues, vices, and the nature of the good.[92] In the usual contrast between the two, both of these interpretations would fall under the rubric of "physical," since neither is concerned with virtue or vice. In addition, neither of the terms appears in the corresponding interpretation found in *Q. G.* 1.5. One suspects, then, that these two terms were not part of the original interpretations.

The first, "physical," interpretation claims that God put the senses in the face because the face, more than other parts of the body, is what has "soul" (ψυχή). By "soul" the interpreter means the Stoic faculty by which man has sense perception, a faculty that he has in common with other animals.[93] At this point he does not mean "mind." This interpretation is expressed more clearly in *Q. G.* 1.5.

> (Gen 2:7) Why is he said to have breathed life into his face?
>
> First of all, because the face is the principal part of the body. For the rest (of the body) was made like a pedestal, while the face, like a bust, is firmly placed above it. And sense perception is the principal part of the animal species, and sense perception is in the face.
>
> In the second place, man is admitted to be part not only of the animal order but also of that of rational animals, and the head is the temple of the mind, as some have said. (*Q. G.* 1.5.)

The interpretation is based on an analogy. As the face is the principal part of the body, so sense perception is the principal part of the animal species. Therefore, sense perception, the principal part of the animal species, should be located in the face, the principal part of the body. What is breathed into man's face, in this interpretation, is the power of sense perception. The analogy permits the interpreter to build a bridge between the text and a more philosophically oriented outlook.

A similar analogy is at work in the second, "ethical" interpretation (*L. A.* 1.39b–40; *Q. G.* 1.5b). As the face is the dominant part (τὸ ἡγεμονικόν) of the body, so the mind (νοῦς) is the dominant part (τὸ ἡγεμονικόν) of the soul (ψυχή). Therefore, by analogy, when the text of

---

[92] See *SVF* 2.15–17; Long, *Hellenistic Philosophy*, 147–209. The use of these two terms by Philo in their common meanings is found in *L. A.* 2.11–13. Philo is quite aware of the usual division of philosophy into logic, physics, and ethics (e.g., *L. A.* 1.57; *Agr.* 14–15; *Mut.* 74–75, 220; *Prob.* 74, 80). At least from *Q. G.* 1.5, one can say that the use of the terms "physical" and "ethical" is secondary and the work of Philo. But it is not quite clear why he uses the term "ethical" in such a peculiar sense in *L. A.* 1.39–40.

[93] Cf. *L. A.* 2.22–24; *SVF* 2.149–50.

Gen 2:7 says that God breathed into man's "face," this must mean that God breathed into the dominant part of man's soul, that is, into his mind. Therefore it is only into this dominant part, that is, into the mind, that God breathes. Once again the analogy serves as a bridge between the language of the text and the philosophical language of Stoicism. This second interpretation is the more adequate of the two because "spirit" (πνεῦμα) in Stoicism is identified with rationality rather than with sense perception as such.[94] In this way the initial interpretation of a crucial phrase in the text and the formal reason for that interpretation become a fulcrum on which the interpretation of the whole verse rests. Once the analogy is drawn, once the bridge between the two "languages" is built, then other concepts associated with the philosophical language can be applied to the text. In this case, Stoic concepts of the relationship of mind to soul and to body can then be applied to the interpretation of Gen 2:7.

This process is also at work in a number of the other passages which contain an interpretation of Gen 2:7 but give no formal grounds for the interpretation. Once the analogy of "breath" to "spirit" is accepted, the "spirit" can then be described as the "divine spirit" (*Spec.* 4.123), as part of the aether (*Spec.* 4.123; *L. A.* 3.161) and as a "fragment of the Deity" (*Som.* 1.34). All of these concepts are derived from Stoicism but are applied to Gen 2:7 through the fact that "breath" is synonymous with "spirit."

The interpretation of Gen 1:27 works in much the same way. The clearest justification for interpreting the phrase "after the image" in Gen 1:27 to mean "according to the pattern of the *Logos*" is found in *Her.* 230–231:

> Having said what was fitting on these matters, Moses continues, "the birds he did not divide" (Gen 15:10). He gives the name of birds to the two words (δύο λόγους), both of which are winged and of a soaring nature. One is the archetypal one above us, the other the copy of it which we possess. Moses calls the first the "image of God," the second the cast of that image. For God, he says, made man not "the image of God" but "according to the image" (Gen 1:27). And thus the mind in each of us, which in the true and full sense is the "man," is an expression at third hand from the Maker, while between them is the *Logos* which serves as model for our reason, but itself is the representation of God.

This interpretation of Gen 1:27 is embedded in a larger, allegorical interpretation of Gen 15:10. That larger interpretation is secondary; that is, the interpretation of Gen 1:27 is used as a basis for a second interpretation, that is, of Gen 15:10. For our purposes that second interpretation is not important; what interests us is the interpretation of Gen 1:27. God created man not as the "image of God" but "*according* to the image of God" (κατ' εἰκόνα).

---

[94] See Long, *Hellenistic Philosophy*, 155–58.

The interpreter draws on a crucial detail of the text (in this case, the interpretation of the preposition κατά as meaning "according to" rather than "as") and concludes that God's image must be a *tertium quid* between God and man. The image, of course, is his *Logos* (*Her.* 230). In the case of Gen 1:27 the formal grounds for interpretation are arrived at not by an analogy but through the interpretation of a crucial word in the text. Once again the interpretation of a crucial element in the text becomes a fulcrum on which the interpretation of the whole verse rests.

Once the interpretation has created a bridge between the text and the philosophical language connected with the *Logos*, all of that language can then be brought to bear on the interpretation of Gen 1:27. In this case it is the language not of Stoicism but of the Platonic paradigms and representations (*Her.* 231). This language occurs throughout the other passages which interpret Gen 1:27.[95] The introduction of Platonic language and thought structure is made much easier, of course, by the fact that the term "image" is itself of good Platonic pedigree.

This interpretation of Gen 1:27 also illustrates the way in which the interpretation of one verse can affect the interpretation of other verses. As I indicated earlier in this chapter, the *Logos* was probably introduced into the interpretation of the creation of man in Gen 1:27 from the interpretation of the creation of the world. There is an attempt to interpret consistently a larger text and not simply occasional problematic phrases or verses. This attempt goes beyond the earlier, anti-anthropomorphic interpretations of isolated verses. It also seems to go beyond the Stoic interpretation of Gen 2:7 such as is found in *L. A.* 1.39–40. While there were certainly Stoic interpretations of individual verses of the creation story, there is no indication that those interpretations were part of an effort to construct an overall interpretation of the creation of the world and of man.[96] That effort seems to have coincided with the Platonizing interpretation of the story of creation.

This same procedure also appears in the Platonic interpretation of the six days of creation. Here the interpretation of one phrase affects the meaning of a whole chapter. This is the case with the phrase "day one" in contrast

---

[95] Cf. *Op.* 24–25; *L. A.* 3.95–96; *Spec.* 1.80–81; *Spec.* 3.83.

[96] See *Op.* 42–44, 45–46. It is difficult to argue simply from an absence of evidence to a negative conclusion. In this case, however, there is a reasonable expectation that, if such evidence did exist, it would have shown up in Philo's interpretations of the creation of the world. Philo certainly includes a great deal of material that is not consistent with his own viewpoint and which is even at variance with other pre-Philonic interpretations found in Philo. Had the Stoic interpretation of the creation of the world an overall structure to it, evidence of that structure probably would have appeared somewhere in Philo's interpretation. No such evidence, however, can be found.

to the other five days of creation (Gen 1:5). The interpreter of Gen 1:5 claimed that "day one" pointed to the creation of the intelligible world. He based his claim on the fact that in Gen 1:5 the cardinal rather than the ordinal number was used to identify the first day of creation. "Day one," then, must indicate a kind of creation different from that of the other five days; that difference is the distinction between the creation of the intelligible world and the creation of the sensible world (*Op.* 15–16). That one interpretation then affects the interpretation of the whole of Genesis 1. All of the rest of Genesis 1 is the creation of the sensible world according to the paradigms of the intelligible world created on "day one."

There is nothing additional to say, in terms of method, about the process of interpretation involved in the combination of Gen 1:27 and Gen 2:7, except to note that it too illustrates the tendency to move beyond the interpretations of isolated verses. When one assumes that the creation of man described in each of the two verses refers to the same event, then there is no exegetical reason why the two interpretations (i.e., of Gen 1:27 and Gen 2:7) cannot be combined. The problems that arise are at the philosophical level, that is, in the very different philosophical backgrounds of the two interpretations. Eventually this fact led Philo to modify the combination by making the interpretation of Gen 1:27 the primary interpretation in the light of which the interpretation of Gen 2:7 was to be seen.

Two further points must be made about the process of interpretation found in these two verses. First of all, these interpretations, like the earlier anti-anthropomorphic interpretations, are not seen by the interpreters as allegorical. They contain none of the technical vocabulary of allegory (e.g., ἀλληγορεῖν, ὑπόνοια, συμβολικῶς). In addition, there is neither the internalization of the meaning of the text nor the awareness of multiple levels of interpretation, both of which characterize the Philonic allegory of the soul.

Secondly, the interpretations of Gen 1:27 and Gen 2:7 are procedurally very similar. In both interpretations one begins by clarifying the meaning of a crucial phrase. This clarification has a twofold result. From the side of the text, it establishes the way in which the whole verse is interpreted; from the side of the interpretation, it forms the bridge by means of which various philosophical concepts can be utilized. The categories which are introduced may be very different (i.e., Platonic or Stoic) but the procedure is basically the same.

This procedure is also quite similar to that used by Heraclitus in his interpretation of the wrath of Apollo in Book One of the *Iliad.*

> How indeed does one explain why Apollo, who has been eager to shoot his arrow,

"then sat down apart from the ships and let fly a shaft;
terrible was the twang of the silver bow" (*Il.* 1.48–49).
For if he (Apollo) were shooting in anger, the archer would have had to stand
near those whom he wounded. But as he (Homer) wants to speak allegorically
(ἀλληγορῶν) of the sun, he quite fittingly supposes that its cargo of plague-
ridden rays comes from afar. (*Quaes. Hom.* 13.4–5.)

The fact that Apollo shoots his arrows from afar, rather than from near his
victims, indicates that Apollo should be taken not literally but allegorically
as the sun whose intense rays can cause a plague. Once such an interpretation is made, Heraclitus can go on to interpret the rest of the story according
to the pattern established by this interpretation, an interpretation which is
heavily Stoic.[97] The interpretations of both Gen 1:27 in *Her.* 230–231 and
Gen 2:7 in *L. A.* 1.39–40 are closer in terms of technique to this interpretation of Homer than were the anti-anthropomorphic interpretations
discussed in the previous chapter. The interpretations in Heraclitus, in
Her. 230–231, and in *L. A.* 1.39–40 all try to offer some textual justification
for their interpretations, which was not for the most part the case with the
anti-anthropomorphic interpretations.[98] What distinguishes these passages
in Philo from Heraclitus' interpretation is not technique but the way in
which the interpretations are conceived of. The interpretations in Philo
claim to represent the one, real meaning of the text; they do not desert the
literal level for another, allegorical level of meaning as does the interpretation of Heraclitus. The techniques of interpretation are similar, but the way
in which each understands the interpretation given is quite different.

E. *Summary and Conclusion*

The interpretations analyzed in this chapter represent a significant
development over the earlier anti-anthropomorphic interpretations. Many
are no longer interpretations of isolated verses, but are attempts to interpret
consistently a text of considerable length, the creation account in Genesis
1–2. There is also an attempt to ground the interpretations textually; the
justification is no longer simply a matter of appropriateness. The bridge to
philosophical patterns of thought is constructed with care, based on the
interpretation of a crucial word or phrase in the text.

However, the most obvious characteristic of the interpretations analyzed in this chapter is the Platonizing trend of the tradition. The Platonic

[97] Heraclitus, *Quaes. Hom.* 15–16.

[98] In *Op.* 72–75 (*et par.*), the interpretation starts from a textual observation on the
phrase "Let *us* make man . . ."; but there is no formal reason given for interpreting the "us" as
God's "powers." The *consistent* attempt at textual justification of an interpretation comes at a
level beyond that of the anti-anthropomorphic interpretation.

interpretation of Gen 1:27 now forms part of an overall Platonic interpretation of both the creation of man and the creation of the world. On the other hand, the Stoic interpretation of Gen 2:7, while it develops beyond the anti-anthropomorphic interpretation found in *L. A.* 1.36–38, never becomes part of a general Stoic interpretation of the creation account. Rather, it is integrated into a larger Platonic interpretation of the creation account in Genesis simply by being combined with the Platonic interpretation of Gen 1:27. Even though these two interpretations (Gen 1:27 and Gen 2:7) were seen as complementary accounts of the same act of creation, nevertheless the fact that the overall interpretation of the creation of the world and of man was Platonic meant that the Stoic interpretation of Gen 2:7 was now only a Stoic fragment in a larger Platonic whole.

The Platonic interpretation of Gen 1:27 and the larger Platonic interpretation of the creation of the world is paralleled by developments in the Middle Platonism found in the second half of the first century B.C. in Alexandria. This is most obvious in the development of the intermediate *Logos* figure similar to figures found in Eudorus of Alexandria and in the *Timaeus Locrus*. These developments in the interpretation of the creation of man in Genesis took place in conjunction with similar developments in the interpretation of Plato, especially of his *Timaeus*. The work of these Jewish interpreters then was by no means an isolated phenomenon. In fact, the Platonic sections of Plutarch's *De Iside et Osiride* (53–54) indicate that still another religious tradition, that of Isis, was also involved in a similar process of interpretation. In each case the result was somewhat different. The patterns of interpretation are similar but never identical. Jewish interpreters gladly appropriated the philosophical developments of their environment but they always turned them to their own purposes and interpreted them in their own way.

Although the Stoic interpretations of Gen 2:7 are closer to the material found in Aristobulus than are the Platonic interpretations of Gen 1:27, it is impossible to discover the relationship between the authors of the Stoic interpretation of Gen 2:7 and those of the Platonic interpretation of Gen 1:27. One cannot say whether they represented stages with a single interpretative tradition or whether they were part of two distinct traditions. One can say, however, that in the course of the first century B.C. the Platonic tradition became the predominant one and that certain traditional, Stoic interpretations (e.g., the Stoic interpretation of Gen 2:7) were integrated into it. In addition, one can say that the ideology of the Platonic tradition was one of continuity. As was the case with most of the ancient world, previous interpretations were to be prized. Previous interpretations were something to which they felt a responsibility, something which therefore could not be easily or openly rejected. Their patterns of thought were rooted in continuity. Because of this, the shift from the Stoic interpretation of the creation of man to a Platonic one was exactly that, a shift and not a break. The Stoic interpretation of Gen 2:7 was not rejected but integrated into and finally reinterpreted in the light of the Platonic interpretation of Gen 1:27. Change was always seen within a larger context of continuity.

CHAPTER V

THE DOUBLE CREATION OF MAN

In the previous chapter I described how two rather different interpretations, one Platonic, the other Stoic, developed and were combined so that they were seen as complementary formulations of the one creation of man. I also pointed out the ways in which Philo subtly reinterpreted the Stoic interpretation of Gen 2:7 so that the more Platonic interpretation of Gen 1:27 became dominant. Now, however, it is necessary to deal with a third level of interpretation, one in which Gen 1:27 and Gen 2:7 are no longer interpreted as complementary formulations but in which Gen 1:27 is interpreted as the creation of a "heavenly man" and Gen 2:7 is interpreted as the creation of an "earthly man."[1] Once again, as Philo himself indicates in *Q. G.* 1.8, we are dealing with a pre-Philonic interpretation.[2]

A. *The State of the Question*

Unlike the two previous levels of interpretation, a great deal has been written about the origins of the distinction between the heavenly man and the earthly man and about the identity of the heavenly man from the point of view of the history of religions. The reason for the quantity of research on these questions is due to the fact that the figure of the heavenly man or Primal Man appears in a number of Gnostic, Mandean, and Manichean texts. Indeed, in most of the research, the primary interest has been directed toward the figure as it appears in these texts rather than as it appears in Philo. This may seem strange since the figure of the heavenly man first appears in Philo, but it is due largely to the fact that until recently the origins

---

[1] This contrast is found in *L. A.* 1.32 and in *L. A.* 1.90. Although other terms are also used to contrast these two figures, I have consistently used the terms "heavenly" and "earthly" to distinguish between them.

[2] *Q. G.* 1.8a:

(Gen 2:8) Why does he place the molded man in Paradise, but not the man who was made in His Image?

Some, believing Paradise to be a garden, have said that since the molded man is sense-perceptible, he therefore rightly goes to a sense-perceptible place. But the man made in His Image is intelligible and invisible, and is in the class of incorporeal species.

of the figure have been sought in Iranian sources thought to be much earlier than Philo. Philo was then used as a subordinate witness to the influence of those sources.

It would be impossible to go into all of the past research on this question.[3] I will simply point out the work of two scholars whose viewpoint on the origins of the figure has been the dominant one until recently. Then I will indicate the criticisms of that position by more recent scholarship, criticisms upon which I hope to build a better understanding of the origins of the figure of the heavenly man by examining that figure as it appears in Philo.

Wilhelm Bousset, in his book *Hauptprobleme der Gnosis*, tried to trace the figure of the Primal Man back to an ancient Aryan or at least Indo-Iranian myth "in which it was related that the world came into existence through the sacrifice of the Primal Man and was constructed out of his body."[4] Bousset found traces of this original myth in Indian religion and in Persian speculation about the figure of the Gayomart. When this myth came into contact with Greek thought, a change took place; instead of the creation of the world through the sacrifice of the Primal Man, the Primal Man became the First Man, the first born of the highest God, the δεύτερος θεός, "who in the beginning of the world sinks down into matter or is imprisoned in matter and so provides the impulse for the development of the world."[5] Bousset associated figures such as the Platonic World Soul and the Demiurge with this stage of the development of the myth of the Primal Man.[6] At a still later stage the myth underwent another change. In a text such as the *Poimandres*, the Primal Man figure becomes almost exclusively anthropological rather than cosmological. It was no longer the whole world that developed from this figure but only other men.[7]

It is at this stage of development that Bousset situated the figure of the heavenly man found in Philo. For Bousset, Philo was an early example for the kind of figure that was found much more clearly in the story of the fall of the Primal Man in the *Poimandres*.[8] Although Bousset was firmly convinced of the widespread development and use of the Primal Man myth, nevertheless, he felt forced to concede that Philo himself devoted very little attention

---

[3] Both the history of the research in this area and a critique of that research are found in C. Colpe, *Die religionsgeschichtliche Schule* (Göttingen: Vandenhoeck & Ruprecht, 1961) and in H.-M. Schenke, *Der Gott "Mensch" in der Gnosis.*

[4] W. Bousset, *Hauptprobleme der Gnosis* (Göttingen: Vandenhoeck & Ruprecht, 1907).

[5] Ibid., 216.

[6] Ibid., 216.

[7] Ibid., 216.

[8] Ibid., 193–94.

to the explanation of the heavenly man, at least in a way that Bousset found helpful for his own inquiry.[9]

The single most influential writer in tracing the figure of the Primal Man to Iranian influences has been Richard Reitzenstein. Reitzenstein's own position on the subject was a changing one. In his first work on the subject, *Poimandres*, published in 1904, he was somewhat ambiguous about the origins of the figure.[10] In one place he seemed to point to an Egyptian origin, while in other places he seemed to maintain a Mesopotamian origin.[11] In any case, his study of the then newly discovered *Turfan Fragment M7* convinced him that the latter was the proper place of origin for the figure of the Primal Man. His final position then appeared in *Das iranische Erlösungsmysterium* (1912).[12] Put simply, his thesis was that there existed on Iranian soil well before the time of Christ a belief that conceived of the soul or the inner man as a divine being that was sent from the world of light into matter but was later freed from matter and returned to the world of light. In such a conception the World Soul and the individual soul, the Primal Man and the individual man were mixed together.[13] This "man" is the one who is the bearer of divine power and of divine revelation. In addition, he is the redeemer of the whole human race. Yet he is first of all the one who is redeemed, who himself must return to the world of light.[14] This belief was then mixed at a very early period with Babylonian myths and speculations.[15] It is out of this that the Gnostic Primal Man developed, especially in Mandeism and Manicheism.

But it was not only the Gnostics who were thus influenced. For Reitzenstein the influence of this myth was widespread in post-exilic Judaism and included the figure of the "Man" or the "Son of Man" that appears in Daniel, *4 Ezra*, and *1 Enoch*.[16] In addition, Reitzenstein thought that the development of Christianity could be understood only when the influence of this myth was taken into consideration.[17] According to him, Philo was also heavily influenced by this Iranian belief. Reitzenstein thought that it was impossible to derive the figure of the heavenly man found in Philo from the

---

[9] Ibid., 195.

[10] R. Reitzenstein, *Poimandres* (Leipzig: Teubner, 1904).

[11] Ibid., 68, 109.

[12] R. Reitzenstein, *Das iranische Erlösungsmysterium* (Bonn: Marcus & Weber, 1921).

[13] Ibid., v, 56.

[14] Ibid., 116.

[15] Ibid., v.

[16] R. Reitzenstein, *Das mandäische Buch des Herrn der Grosse und die Evangelienüberlieferung* (Sitzungsberichte der Heidelberger Akademie der Wissenschaften 12: Heidelberg, 1919) 45–46.

[17] Reitzenstein, *Das iranische Erlösungsmysterium*, 116.

juxtaposition of Plato and the early chapters of Genesis.[18] To understand the figure of the heavenly man, one had to turn to Iranian influences for a clarification of the two types of man found in Philo.

The criticism of Reitzenstein, Bousset, and others who held similar positions has come from two directions.[20] One concerns their use of source material, especially the Mandean and Manichean texts; the other amounts to an alternative explanation of the origins of the Primal Man. In this area, the criticisms of Reitzenstein's work are the most important and the most illustrative.[21]

The evaluation of Reitzenstein's use of the *Turfan Fragment M7* exemplifies the first type of criticism. Reitzenstein himself admitted that, until he was able to analyze this fragment, his hypothesis about the Iranian origins of the Primal Man figure were suspicions rather than real demonstrations.[22] Therefore, if his analysis of the *Turfan Fragment M7* was wrong, his whole case would be substantially damaged. The fragment is in Parthian and in its present form it is a Manichean hymn. Reitzenstein, however, felt that the mention of the name of Zarathustra indicated that this part of the hymn was pre-Manichean and represented a Persian text that came from a circle of believers in Zarathustra.[23] In this part of the fragment Zarathustra plays the role of redeemer, and therefore Reitzenstein thought that this fragment indicated the existence of a pre-Christian Iranian myth that became the basis not only of Gnosticism but also of much of post-exilic Judaism and early Christianity. Later research, however, has shown that it is no such thing. Both Carsten Colpe and Hans-Martin Schenke have pointed out that the text is a thoroughly Manichean document in which Zarathustra is mentioned as a forerunner of Mani, just as in other Manichean texts Buddha and Jesus are also mentioned as forerunners of Mani. *Turfan Fragment M7*, then, does not lead us back to any pre-Christian Iranian myth, since the mention of Mani's predecessors does not at all mean that the text is pre-Manichean.[24]

---

[18] R. Reitzenstein and H. H. Schaeder, *Studien zum antiken Synkretismus aus Iran und Griechenland* (Leipzig: Teubner, 1926) 24–25.

[19] Reitzenstein, *Das iranische Erlösungsmysterium*, 104–11.

[20] Similar positions are found in C. H. Kraeling, *Anthropos and the Son of Man* (New York: Columbia University Press, 1927); A. Olerud, *L'idée de macrocosmos et de microcosmos dans le Timée de Platon*; G. Widengren, *The Gnostic Attitude* (Santa Barbara: University of California at Santa Barbara, 1973).

[21] Specific criticism of the other authors is found in Schenke, *Der Gott "Mensch" in der Gnosis*, 9–68.

[22] Reitzenstein, *Das iranische Erlösungsmysterium*, v.

[23] Ibid., 4.

[24] Schenke, *Der Gott "Mensch" in der Gnosis*, 21–23; Colpe, *Die religionsgeschichtliche Schule*, 69.

Schenke has also pointed out a more general methodological objection to the work of Reitzenstein. Reitzenstein tended to argue that, because the figure of the Primal Man appeared most fully and clearly on Iranian soil (i.e., in Manicheism), the concept then must have been of Iranian origin. That kind of argument has turned out to be untenable. The origins of a religious tradition and its fullest development need not occur in the same place.[25] This has led scholars to suggest an alternative theory for the origins of the Primal Man.

What has become more and more apparent is the fact that those documents in which one finds the figure of the heavenly man or the Primal Man are all more or less interpretations of Genesis 1–3. This suggests that the origins of the figure are to be found not in Persian circles but in some form, perhaps heterodox, of Judaism. Over forty years ago C. H. Dodd, in his book *The Bible and the Greeks*, suggested that the figure of the heavenly man in texts such as the *Poimandres* probably owed more to Jewish interpretations of the Genesis story than it did to the Iranian Gayomart figure.[26] More recently Gilles Quispel, in his article "Der gnostische Anthropos und die jüdische Tradition," maintained that the Gnostic teaching about the Primal Man was a development of heterodox Judaism, and in some cases of a Samaritan heterodoxy.[27] This development was also influenced by particular Hellenistic viewpoints, especially of a Platonic or Pythagorean character. For Quispel this influence was often by way of reaction and conflict and not simply a matter of easy acceptance.[28] Robert McL. Wilson has added several bits of evidence in which Christian interpretations of Gen 1:26–7 point in the same direction, that is, to Jewish sources.[29] In any case, Quispel denied the necessity or the plausibility of turning to Iranian sources for the origins of the figure of the Primal Man.[30]

The strongest and most detailed case for seeing the origins of the figure of the Primal Man in successive interpretations of Genesis 1–3 has been made by Hans-Martin Schenke in his book, *Der Gott "Mensch" in der Gnosis*.[31] Like Quispel, Schenke maintains that the teaching about the God

---

[25] Schenke, *Der Gott "Mensch" in der Gnosis*, 23.

[26] C. H. Dodd, *The Bible and the Greeks* (London: Hodder and Stoughton, 1934) 146. M. Nilsson, *Geschichte der griechischen Religion* (3rd ed.; Munich: C. H. Beck, 1974), 2.606–07.

[27] G. Quispel, "Der gnostische Anthropos und die jüdische Tradition," *Eranos Jahrbuch* 22 (1953), 195–234.

[28] Ibid., 209, 210, 214, 219–223.

[29] R. McL. Wilson, "The Early History of the Exegesis of Gen 1:26," *Studia Patristica* I (ed. K. Aland and F. L. Cross; Berlin: Akademie Verlag, 1957) 420–37.

[30] Quispel, "Der gnostische Anthropos und die jüdische Tradition," 234.

[31] Schenke also deals with some of the material found at Nag Hammadi.

"Man" was the product of a Jewish, or perhaps, Samaritan Gnosis that was either pre-Christian or contemporary with Christianity.[32] Only in Manicheism and Mandeism are these interpretations influenced by the Iranian traditions about the Gayomart figure.[33] What is most valuable in Schenke's study is the detailed analysis of the texts in which the figure of the Primal Man appears, including two of the Coptic texts found at Nag Hammadi.[34] According to Schenke there are two types of Primal Man. In the first type God himself is the Primal Man and the earthly Primal Man, the ancestor of the human race, is made according to his image. In this pattern there are two Primal Men. This pattern is found in the *Apocryphon of John*.[35] The second and far more common pattern involves three Primal Men. Between the two figures already mentioned comes a third figure, the heavenly Primal Man. This third figure is in the image of God and is the pattern for the earthly Primal Man.[36] This pattern is found in the *Poimandres*, Zosimus, the report on the Naassenes in Hippolytus, and *The Hypostasis of the Archons* from Nag Hammadi.[37]

Schenke's treatment, however, of the figure of the heavenly man in Philo is less adequate. In a sense this is understandable since Schenke's focus is on those Gnostic texts in which the figure of the Primal Man is a god. In Philo the heavenly man is not really a god, certainly not in any sense that would compromise monotheism. Schenke points out that sometimes the man created in Gen 1:27 is an earthly man and sometimes a heavenly man.[38] When a distinction is made between the two, the heavenly man is identified with the figure of the *Logos* (*Conf.* 146).[39] In this way it is not the figure of the Primal Man that Philo introduces into the interpretation of Gen 1:27 but that of the *Logos*.[40] As we shall see, it is true that Philo did attempt to resolve the figure of the heavenly man into that of the *Logos*. But what is

---

[32] Schenke, *Der Gott "Mensch" in der Gnosis*, 71.

[33] Ibid., 155.

[34] Ibid., 34–63.

[35] Ibid., 34–43, 64–66. English translations of all of the Nag Hammadi texts are conveniently collected in *The Nag Hammadi Library* (ed. J. M. Robinson; New York: Harper and Row, 1977).

[36] Schenke, *Der Gott "Mensch" in der Gnosis*, 44–64, 65–68.

[37] See *Poimandres* in *Corpus Hermeticum* (ed. A. D. Nock and A. J. Festugière; Paris: Société d'édition "Les Belles Lettres," 1946), 1. 1–28; Zosimus of Panopolis, *On the Letter Omega* (ed. H. M. Jackson; Missoula: Scholars, 1978); the Naassene material in *Quellen zur Geschichte der christlichen Gnosis* (ed. W. Völker; Tübingen: J. C. B. Mohr, 1932) 11–26; *The Hypostasis of the Archons* (ed. R. Bullard and M. Krause; Berlin: de Gruyter, 1970).

[38] Schenke, *Der Gott "Mensch" in der Gnosis*, 122.

[39] Ibid., 123–24.

[40] Ibid., 140.

true of Philo is not true of the traditions on which he drew. In these traditions the heavenly man is not identified with the *Logos* but is a distinct figure. This emerges from an analysis of the levels of tradition found in Philo. Although an investigation of the possible relationship of the figure of the heavenly man in Philo to that figure in various Gnostic documents goes well beyond the bounds of this study, an analysis of that figure in Philo may eventually prove helpful in understanding the use of the figure of the Primal Man in Gnostic documents, since the traditions found in Philo contain our earliest attestations of the distinction between a heavenly man and an earthly man. After all, the figures found in Philo and in these Gnostic documents are both the result of interpretations of the same texts of Genesis. The Gnostic interpretations may represent further developments, or perversions, if you prefer, of the kinds of interpretations that appear in Philo.[41] In any case, the exegetical traditions found in Philo throw light on the process of interpretation that produced the contrast between a heavenly man and an earthly man and indicate that Hellenistic Judaism (and not simply "heterodox" or Samaritan Judaism) played a significant role in the development of a figure quite prominent in a number of Gnostic texts.

B. *The Double Creation of Man*

The double creation of man is an interpretation which tries to explain why the description of the creation of man occurs twice in Genesis. In such an interpretation this is taken to mean that two different "men" were created, the one heavenly and part of the intelligible world, the other earthly and part of the sensible world. The clearest example of this interpretation is found in *Op.* 134–135:

> After this he says that "God formed man by taking clay from the earth, and breathed into his face the breath of life" (Gen 2:7). By this also he shows very clearly that there is a vast difference between the man thus formed and the man that came into existence earlier after the image of God; for the man so formed is an object of sense perception, partaking already of such or such quality, consisting of body and soul, man or woman, by nature mortal; while he that was after the image was an idea (ἰδέα), or genus (γένος) or seal (σφραγίς), an object of thought, incorporeal, neither male nor female, by nature incorruptible.
>
> It says, however, that the formation of the individual man, the object of sense, is a composite one made up of earthly substance and of divine spirit; for it says that the body was made through the Artificer taking clay and molding out of it a

---

[41] One must be aware that, although many Gnostic documents interpreted Jewish texts (e.g., Genesis 1–3) and developed from Jewish interpretations of those texts, it does not follow that these Gnostic texts were written by Jews.

human form, but that the soul was originated from nothing created whatever, but from the Father and Ruler of all; for that which he breathed in was nothing else than a divine spirit that migrated hither from that blissful and happy existence for the benefit of our race, to the end that, even if it is mortal in respect of its visible part, it may in respect of the part that is invisible be rendered immortal. Hence it may with propriety be said that man is the borderland between mortal and immortal nature, partaking of each so far as is needful, and that he was created at once mortal and immortal, mortal in respect of the body, but in respect of the mind immortal.

The differences between the two become clearer when they are set off schematically against each other.

A. ὁ κατὰ τὴν εἰκόνα γεγονώς (Gen 1:27)	B. ὁ πλασθεὶς ἄνθρωπος (Gen 2:7)
1. νοητός	1. αἰσθητός
2. ἰδέα, γένος, σφραγίς	2. μετέχων ποιότητος
3. ἀσώματος	3. ἐκ σώματος καὶ ψυχῆς
4. οὔτε ἄρσεν οὔτε θῆλυ	4. ἀνὴρ ἢ γυνή
5. ἄφθαρτος φύσει	5. φύσει θνητός

Once the interpreter became aware of the two descriptions of the creation of man as a problem, he could look at the two descriptions of the creation of man for indications that would allow him to distinguish, on the basis of the text, between the two of them. When one looks at the table given above, two of the characteristics are obviously the result of interpretations of the two verses from Genesis (Gen 1:27 and Gen 2:7). Those characteristics are: (1) neither male nor female (Gen 1:27); and (2) composed of body and soul (Gen 2:7). The interpreter has made use of two details in the text (one from Gen 1:27 and the other from Gen 2:7) and has based his interpretation on them. The text of Gen 1:27 says that God made man "male *and* female" (ἄρσεν καὶ θῆλυ). The interpreter takes that to mean not that the first man was an androgyne but that he was *neither* male *nor* female and so prior to any sexual differentiation. This characteristic contrasts with what is said about the man created in Gen 2:7. In Gen 2:7 there is no indication that the man is "male and female." On the contrary, the creation of the man in Gen 2:7 is followed by the creation of woman (Gen 2.21–22) and so the man created in Gen 2:7 is sexually differentiated, is *either* male *or* female.[42]

---

[42] In Philo's allegory of the soul, woman is a symbol of sense perception (e.g., *Op.* 165–66; *L. A.* 2.19–26). As is clear from *Q. G.* 1.24–29, there were earlier, non-allegorical interpretations of the creation of woman. But these interpretations are disparate in character, and none of them reflects the exegetical developments which centered around the interpretation of Gen 1:27 and Gen 2:7. It is only at the level of the allegory of the soul that the figure of

The detail that is singled out in Gen 2:7 is the fact that "God formed man by taking from the *earth*, and breathed into his face the *breath of life*." The interpreter takes this to mean that the man created in Gen 2:7 was composed of *body* and *soul*, that is, he was a composite being. By contrast, there is no indication in the text of Gen 1:27 that the man created there was a being composed of body and soul. The interpretation of Gen 2:7 as indicating that the man created in Gen 2:7 was composed of body and soul (in contrast to the man created in Gen 1:27) was more important for the development of this interpretation than was the interpretation of Gen 1:27 in which God made man "male and female." Certainly this interpretation of Gen 2:7 plays the dominant role in both *Op.* 134–135 and *L. A.* 1.31–32. Once it was established that the man created in Gen 1:27 was *not* a composite being, then the interpretation of the phrase "male *and* female" as meaning "*neither* male *nor* female" would be more reasonable than taking it to mean that the man of Gen 1:27 was an androgyne (that is, *composed* of male and female). Expanding on these two details in the text, the interpreter could then go on to maintain that the man created in Gen 1:27, because simple and prior to any sexual distinction, must have belonged to the intelligible realm, to the realm of idea, genus, or seal. Conversely the man created in Gen 2:7 must belong to the sensible realm. The man created in Gen 1:27 is of the κόσμος νοητός while the man created in Gen 2:7 is of the κόσμος αἰσθητός.

As a result of this distinction between the two types of men, the concepts that were used as complementary formulations at an earlier level of interpretation are now distinguished and refer *either* to the intelligible man created in Gen 1:27 *or* to the sensible man created in Gen 2:7.[43] For instance, only the man of Gen 1:27, the man "after the image," can be referred to as a "seal" (*Op.* 134) or as something "stamped with the image of God" (κατ' εἰκόνα τετυπῶσθαι θεοῦ) (*L. A.* 1.31). On the other hand, it is the sensible man of Gen 2:7 who has the "divine spirit." That concept is familiar to us from the earlier, Stoic interpretations of Gen 2:7. The soul of the earthly man is a "divine spirit" sent from that blissful and happy nature for the benefit of the human race (*Op.* 135). Similar formulations appeared earlier in the interpretation of Gen 2:7 found in *Det.* 90, *Op.* 146, and *Spec.* 4.123.[44]

With regard to this level of interpretation, two further points must be kept in mind. The first concerns the relationship of the heavenly man to the

woman is integrated into a larger interpretative scheme. In this case, that turned out to be a dubious honor.

[43] These earlier interpretations were discussed in Chapter IV, and the explanation why the interpretations of the creation of man as a double creation depend on the interpretations of the creation of man as a single creation was given in Chapter II.

[44] See Chapter IV, 77–79, 87–92.

figure of the *Logos*. At an earlier stage of interpretation, the man created in Gen 1:27 was the man made according to the image of God and that image was the *Logos*. The man so created was an image in the *sensible* world of an idea, a paradigm from the intelligible world. The two figures were easily distinguishable: the *Logos* in the *intelligible* world was the paradigm for the man in the *sensible* world. However, when the man created in Gen 1:27 becomes the heavenly man, he is no longer part of the sensible world but, like the *Logos*, is part of the intelligible world (*L. A.* 1.31). This situation creates an uneasy relationship between the two figures. The heavenly man retains the characteristic of being formed "after the image of God" (*Op.* 134, *L. A.* 1.31), but at the same time he also takes on the characteristics of the *Logos* in that he too is now an idea, a seal, and belongs to the intelligible world (*Op.* 134). Some attempt seems to have been made to distinguish the two. For example, in *L. A.* 2.4 the "man after the image" longs for the "image" (i.e., the *Logos*) in the way in which every copy longs for that of which it is a copy. Yet functionally the two figures are very similar.[45]

The second point to keep in mind is that the earthly man of Gen 2:7 is made up of both body and soul. The composite character of the earthly man appears in both *Op.* 134–135 and in *L. A.* 1.31. At first reading *L. A.* 1.32 might suggest that Gen 2:7 is referring only to the earthly *mind* (νοῦς γεώδης):

> We must account that *man* made out of the earth to be a mind mingled with, but not completely blended with, body (εἰσκρινόμενον σώματι, οὔπω εἰσκεκριμένον). But this earthly mind is in reality also corruptible, were not God to breathe into it a power of real life; when he does so, it does not any more undergo molding, but becomes a soul, not an inefficient and imperfectly formed soul, but one endowed with mind and actually alive; for he says, "man becomes a living soul."

Yet a careful reading indicates that this passage is an interpretation of the relationship of the earthly mind to the body (a mind already mingled with, but not completely blended with, body) and not an interpretation of the earthly mind *by itself.* The earthly mind is connected with a body from the beginning. In addition, this passage goes on to emphasize that this corruptible mind (νοῦς φθαρτός) was in need of God's breathing power of real life into it. Gen 2:7, then, is not taken to refer to the earthly *mind alone* but to the whole earthly *man* composed of body and soul.[46]

---

[45] At the next level of interpretation this uneasy relationship will be resolved by the identification of the two figures (*Conf.* 41, 62, 146; *Deus* 31).

[46] This will become important when we consider, in Chapter VI, the interpretations of Gen 2:8, 15, 16–17 in which the creation of the earthly man is integrated into the allegory of the soul and so becomes earthly *mind* rather than earthly *man* (*L. A.* 1.55, 88, 90).

At this level of interpretation the concepts and the vocabulary of prior interpretations of Gen 1:27 and Gen 2:7 are both used and yet adapted to a quite new and distinctive interpretation of the relationship of Gen 1:27 to Gen 2:7. Gen 1:27 and Gen 2:7 are now taken to refer to the creation of two different men, one heavenly and part of the intelligible world and the other earthly and part of the sensible world.

C. *The Search for Consistency: The Paradigm of Man*

The interpretation of Gen 1:27 and Gen 2:7 as a double creation was an attempt to explain why the creation of man was described twice in Genesis. Yet the fact that the description of the creation of man occurs twice in Genesis is not a sufficient explanation for the form that the interpretation of the creation of man as a twofold creation takes. After all, the fact that man's creation was described twice in Genesis had not forced previous generations of interpreters to the conclusion that two different men had been created. They were able to take the descriptions of man's creation in Gen 1:27 and Gen 2:7 as complementary descriptions of the same event. Rather what seems to have moved the interpretation of the relationship of Gen 1:27 to Gen 2:7 in this direction was the combination of the fact that the creation of man was described twice in Genesis and the need to interpret consistently both the creation of man and the creation of the world in a way that was in keeping with the Middle Platonism of the period.

The starting point of that interpretation was that the sensible world (κόσμος αἰσθητός) was created as a copy of paradigms or models from the intelligible world (κόσμος νοητός). The most developed form of this outlook is found in the early sections of *De Opificio Mundi*.[47] These sections represent a pre-Philonic interpretation of the creation of the world which draws heavily on Plato's *Timaeus* (especially 27c–31b). In this interpretation "day one" of creation is devoted to the creation of the intelligible world which will in turn serve as a paradigm or model for the creation of the world of sense perception (*Op.* 16). The reason given for this is the same one given in Plato's *Timaeus* (28b–29d; 30c–31a), that is, a beautiful copy can be made only through the use of a beautiful pattern (*Op.* 15–16). The creation of the sensible world begins only on the second day (*Op.* 36). Within such a structure the man who is made "after the image" of Gen 1:27 is the single man who is created as an image of the *Logos*.

---

[47] *Op.* 15–36. Some of the interpretations in Philo of the second through the sixth days give no indication that the distinction of "day one" from the other five days is present (e.g., *Op.* 42–44, 45–46). These passages are Stoic in orientation. These interpretations, like the Stoically oriented interpretations of the creation of man, give no indication that they are part of a larger interpretative scheme. They seem to be piecemeal interpretations.

Should a man desire to use words in a more simple and direct way, he would say that the world discerned only by the intellect (νοητὸν κόσμον) is nothing else than the *Logos* of God when he was already engaged in the act of creation. For the city discernible by the intellect alone is nothing else than the reasoning faculty of the architect in the act of planning to found the city.

It is Moses who lays down this, not I. Witness his express acknowledgement in the sequel, when setting on record the creation of man, that he was molded after the image of God (Gen 1:27). Now if the part is an image (εἰκών) of an image, it is manifest that the whole is too, and if the whole creation, this entire world perceived by our senses (αἰσθητὸς κόσμος) (seeing that it is greater than any human image) is a copy of the Divine image (μίμημα θείας εἰκόνος), it is manifest that the archetypal seal also, which we aver to be the world described by the mind, would be the very *Logos* of God (ὁ θεοῦ λόγος). (*Op.* 24–25.)

When one looks at this interpretation closely (i.e., *Op.* 15–31), a certain lack of consistency emerges. The intelligible world is created on the first day, and the sensible world during the next five days. On the last of these five days man is created according to the Image of God, that is, according to the *Logos*. The intelligible world created on "day one" is based on the interpretation of Gen 1:1–3 (LXX):

In the beginning God made the heaven and the earth. The earth was invisible (ἀόρατος) and without form (ἀκατασκεύαστος), and darkness was over the abyss, and the spirit of God was over the waters. And God said, "Let there be light," and there was light.

The various elements of these verses from Genesis are then interpreted in the following way (*Op.* 29–31):

Element	Interpretation
1. heaven	incorporeal heaven
2. earth	invisible earth
3. darkenss	the idea of air
4. the abyss	the idea of the world
5. water	the incorporeal essence of water
6. spirit	the incorporeal essence of spirit
7. light	the incorporeal essence of light

The intelligible world created on "day one" consists entirely of *cosmological* elements. There is no mention of the creation of the model or paradigm of man, only of the models for everything else. This creates a certain lack of consistency, for, while the intelligible paradigms for everything else were created on "day one," the creation of the paradigm for man went unmentioned.

This lack of consistency is very Platonic in the sense that Plato did not mention the use of a paradigm when he described the creation of man in the *Timaeus* (40d–47e). Yet, at least by the latter part of the first century B.C., the notion of a model or paradigm for man was a philosophical common-place. In the extant fragment of Arius Didymus' *On the Doctrines of Plato*, we find the following explanation of the Platonic ideas.

> He (Plato) says that the ideas (ἰδέας) are certain patterns (τινὰ παραδείγματα) arranged class by class (κατὰ γένος) of the things which are by nature sensible (τῶν αἰσθητῶν), and that these are the sources of the different sciences and definitions. For besides all individual men there is a certain conception of man; and besides all horses, of a horse; and generally besides the animals, a conception of an animal uncreated and imperishable (ἀγένητον καὶ ἄφθαρτον).
>
> And in the same way as many impressions (ἐκμαγεῖα) are made of one seal (σφραγίς), and many images (εἰκόνες) of one man, so from each single idea of the objects of sense a multitude of individual natures are formed, from the idea of man all men, and in like manner in the case of all other things in nature. Also the idea is an eternal essence (ἀΐδιον οὐσίαν), cause, and principle, making each thing to be of a character such as its own. (Eusebius, *Praep. Evang.* 11.23.)[48]

Arius Didymus is giving here what must have been an interpretation of the Platonic ideas fairly common in the latter half of the first century B.C. Prominent among these ideas is the idea or paradigm of man, a paradigm that is uncreated and imperishable (ἀγένητον καὶ ἄφθαρτον) and that serves as a seal (σφραγίς) for the creation of particular men who are then images (εἰκόνες) of that one seal. It is a viewpoint of this sort which, when combined with the recognition that the creation of man was described twice in Genesis, would have led in the direction of the interpretations found in *Op.* 134–135 and *L. A.* 1.31–32.

However, the "idea of man" in this fragment of Arius Didymus is purely paradigmatic. It is in no sense a real figure as is the "heavenly man" in these passages from Philo. Yet the figure of the heavenly man probably did not appear immediately in its fully developed form. There was an intermediate stage, recognizable only in fragments, that was closer to the viewpoint found in Arius Didymus than was *Op.* 134–135. In this intermediate stage the "heavenly man" of Gen 1:27 was less a real figure and more a pure paradigm and so closer to the "paradigm" found in Arius Didymus. This prior stage was based on the distinction between genus (γένος) and species (εἶδος).

---

[48] Translation by E. H. Gifford, *Eusebii Pamphili Evangelicae Praeparationis Libri* XV, 3/2, 589. Aristotle (*Metaph.* 1.9.1–15, 991ab) indicates that Plato had an "idea" of man but that notion is not found clearly in the Platonic texts themselves. The "idea" of man as a standard example became popular in the Platonic tradition only later.

And when Moses had called the genus (τὸ γένος) "man," quite admirably did he distinguish its species (τὰ εἴδη), adding that it had been created "male *and* female" (Gen 1:27), and this though its individual members had not yet taken shape. For the primary species are in the genus to begin with and reveal themselves as in a mirror to those who have the faculty of keen vision. (*Op.* 76.)

Equality, too, divided the human being into man and woman, two sections unequal in strength, but quite equal as regards what was nature's urgent purpose, the reproduction of themselves in a third person. "God made man," he says, "made him after the image of God. Male and female he made"—not now "him" but "them" (Gen 1:27). He concludes with the plural, thus connecting with the genus (τῷ γένει) mankind the species (τὰ εἴδη). (*Her.* 163–164.)

The two terms (γένος, εἶδος) are only apparently used in the Aristotelian sense of modes of classification. Their real meaning is the distinction of the ideal world from the sensible world.[49] The use of these two terms in this way appears a number of times in Philo.[50] Much of the terminology in Philo used to characterize a genus is the same as that used in the passage from Arius Didymus.

Arius Didymus	*Philo*
ἰδέα	*Det.* 77–78
ἄφθαρτος	*Sac.* 6–8; *Post.* 105; *Mut.* 78–80; *Cher.* 5–8
σφραγίς	*Mut.* 78–80
ἀρχέτυπον	*Det.* 77–78; *Her.* 126–127[51]

Although the passage from Arius Didymus does not refer to the ideas precisely as a genus, he nevertheless does refer to the idea as "patterns arranged *by class* of things which are by nature sensible" (τῶν κατὰ φύσιν αἰσθητῶν κατὰ γένος ὡρισμένα τινὰ παραδείγματα).

A closer parallel to the use of the γένος /εἶδος distinction in Philo is found in Seneca's *Epistulae Morales*. In *Ep.* 58 Seneca discusses the six ways in which Plato divided all existing things. What interests us are the first, third, and fourth classes of being. In this section from Seneca the concepts of genus, idea, and species are of central importance.

---

[49] Undoubtedly Middle Platonists looked to Plato for the justification of this distinction. In Plato the two terms γένος and εἶδος can mean the same thing (e.g. *Sph.* 253b) and exist apart from the sensible world. The term εἶδος is far more common in this meaning while γένος can also come close to the meaning of "type" (*Tht.* 228e and *Sph.* 253d). For the notion of ideas immanent in matter, they may well have looked to *Phd.* 103b–104b or to *Tim.* 50c–51a. Whether either of these texts really refers to forms or ideas immanent in matter is disputable, but later Platonists probably understood them in that sense.

[50] *Det.* 77–78; *Sac.* 6–8; *Post.* 105; *Deus* 119–20; *Mut.* 77–80; *Her.* 126–27; *Cher.* 5–8.

[51] Most of these passages were quite allegorical, while neither *Op.* 76 or *Her.* 163–64 are allegorical in the sense in which we have been using the term. The distinction obviously proved helpful at that level of interpretation, although it was certainly not confined to that level.

The first class of "that which exists" cannot be grasped by the sight or by the touch, or by any of the senses; but it can be grasped by thought. Any generic conception (*quod generaliter est*), such as generic man (*tamquam homo generalis*), does not come within the range of the eyes; but "man" in particular (*specialis*) does; as, for example, Cicero, Cato. The term "animal" is not seen; it is grasped by thought alone. A particular man (*species eius*), however, is seen, for example, a horse, a dog. . . .

The third class is made up of those things which exist in the proper sense of the term; they are countless in number, but are situated beyond our sight. "What are these?" you ask. They are Plato's own furniture, so to speak; he calls them "ideas," and from them all visible things are created, and according to their pattern all things are fashioned. They are immortal, unchangeable, inviolable (*hae immortales, immutabiles, inviolabiles sunt*). And this idea, or rather, Plato's conception of it, is as follows: "The 'idea' is the everlasting pattern (*exemplar aeternum*) of those things which are created by nature." I shall explain this definition, in order to set the subject before you in a clearer light: Suppose that I wish to make a likeness (*imaginem*) of you; I possess in your person the pattern (*exemplar*) of this picture, wherefrom my mind receives a certain outline, which it is to embody in its own handiwork. That outward appearance, then, which gives me instruction and guidance, this pattern for me to imitate, is the "idea." Such patterns, therefore, nature possesses in infinite number,—of men, fish, trees, according to whose model everything that nature has to create is worked out.

In the fourth place we shall put "form" (*idos*). And if you would know what "form" means, you must pay close attention, calling Plato, and not me, to account for the difficulty of the subject. However, we cannot make fine distinctions without encountering difficulties. A moment ago I made use of the artist as an illustration. When the artist desired to reproduce Virgil in colours he would gaze upon Virgil himself. The "idea" was Virgil's outward appearance, and this was the pattern (*exemplar*) of the intended work. That which the artist draws from this "idea" and has embodied in his own work, is the "form." Do you ask me where the difference lies? The former is the pattern (*exemplar*); while the latter is the shape (*forma*) taken from the pattern and embodied in the work. . . . If you desire a further distinction, I will say that the "form" is in the artist's work, the "idea" outside his work, and not only outside it, but prior to it. (Seneca, *Ep.* 58, 16, 18–21.)[52]

How the thought of this passage from Seneca develops is not completely clear. The cause of this lack of clarity is that the distinction of genus and species in the first class of "things which exist" seems to be the same as that found in the third and fourth classes between idea (*idea*) and form (*idos*).

---

[52] Translation by R. M. Gummere (Seneca, *Ad Lucilium Epistulae Morales* [Cambridge: Harvard University Press, 1917], 1.396–400).

Seneca may have taken what was intended as alternative formulations to be separate classes of being. His purpose may have been to emphasize the *genus/species* distinction, since this was the rubric under which he discusses these six "Platonic" distinctions.[53] The distinction of *genus/species* seems, then, to be parallel to the distinction between *idea* and *idos*. Both the *genus* and the *idea* are part of the intelligible world and serve as patterns for the *species* or *idos*, that is, for the individuals in the sensible world. The conceptual structure of this passage from Seneca's *Epistle* 58 and the fragment from Arius Didymus are of a piece. This suggests that the framework found in Seneca, including the *genus/species* distinction, goes back to the latter part of the first century B.C.[54]

This suggestion is strengthened by several passages in Albinus' *Didaskalikos*, which, as I indicated earlier, may well be a reworking of Arius Didymus' *On the Doctrines of Plato*.[55] In Chapter Four Albinus distinguishes between the primary intelligibles (τὰ πρῶτα νοητά) and the secondary intelligibles (τὰ δεύτερα νοητά). The primary intelligibles are the ideas (ἰδέαι) and these are transcendent. The secondary intelligibles are the "forms" (εἴδη) and these are in matter and are inseparable from matter (τὰ ἐπὶ τῇ ὕλη ἀχώριστα ὄντα τῆς ὕλης).[56] The same distinction appears in Chapter Ten, this time in connection with a demonstration that God is incorporeal.

> From these things it appears that he (God) is also incorporeal. This can be demonstrated by the following reasons. For if God is a body he would be composed of matter and form (εἶδος) because every body is some sort of combination of matter and form joined to it (τοῦ σὺν αὐτῇ εἴδους), a form which bears a likeness (ἐξομοιοῦται) to the ideas (ταῖς ἰδέαις) and participates in them in a way that is hard to describe. Therefore it is absurd that God would be made up of matter and form. (Albinus, *Didaskalikos*, X, pp. 165.37–166.6.)

Here the distinction is between ἰδέα and εἶδος. This fact supports the notion that the distinctions *genus/species* and *idea/idos* in Seneca's *Epistle* 58 are really synonymous distinctions. *Species* is simply the Latin equivalent of the Greek εἶδος, and *genus* and *idea* (ἰδέα) are interchangeable terms for the patterns of the intelligible world. The parallelism is indicted in the following table:

---

[53] See Seneca, *Ep.* 58. 5–18.

[54] Dillon (*The Middle Platonists,* 137) suggests that Arius Didymus may have been the source for Seneca. Certainly the outlook common to Seneca, the *Didaskalikos* (see below), and Arius Didymus points to the first century B.C. even if the passages in Seneca are not directly derived from Arius Didymus.

[55] See Chapter IV, 65–66, 68–69.

[56] Albinus, *Didaskalikos* IV, p. 155,33–35.

	Philo	*Seneca*	*Albinus* (Arius Didymus)
Intelligible world:	γένος	genus-idea	ἰδέα
Sensible world:	εἶδος	species-idos	εἶδος

The position taken in the *Didaskalikos* that the ideas are transcendent and that the "forms" (*species*/εἴδη) are in matter and inseparable from it is the same position taken at the end of the passage from Seneca. The thought patterns of these passages from Arius Didymus, Seneca, and the *Didaskalikos* are all of a piece and all probably go back to the latter part of the first century B.C.

What is important for our purposes, of course, is that these passages are also of a piece with *Op.* 76 and *Her.* 163–164. In *Op.* 76 and *Her.* 163–164, the genus (γένος) is of the ideal world, immortal and recognizable only by the mind, while the species (εἶδος) is part of the sensible world. In addition, as in Seneca and the fragment from Arius Didymus, the emphasis is on individual man as made according to the pattern of "man" in the intelligible world. The interpretation found in *Op.* 76 and *Her.* 163–164 takes up this outlook from Middle Platonism and applies it to the double description of the creation of man in Genesis. The Jewish interpreter explains the relationship of the man created in Gen 1:27 to the man created in Gen 2:7 in a way that establishes the parallelism between the patterns of the intelligible world and the pattern or idea of "man" and between the objects of the sensible world and the sensible man. This parallelism, although absent from the *Timaeus*, was a philosophical commonplace by the end of the first century B.C. This also explains why the "generic man" of *Op.* 76 and *Her.* 163–164 is more of a paradigm than a real figure. These two passages in Philo follow the pattern found in Seneca and Arius Didymus, and in that pattern the "generic man" is the *paradigm* for the "specific man" but not a real figure.

All of this process was made much easier, of course, for a Jewish interpreter since, as a matter of fact, the creation of man was described twice in Genesis. The man created in Gen 1:27 was the heavenly paradigm while the man created in Gen 2:7 was the cast or image of that man in the sensible world. Yet because the man created in Gen 1:27 was a real figure and not a paradigm and because he was interpreted as a real figure in prior interpretations (e.g., *Op.* 24–25; *L. A.* 3.95–96; *Her.* 230–231), the description of the creation of the heavenly man in *Op.* 134–135, *L. A.* 1.31–32, and *L. A.* 2.4 has its own peculiar character. This peculiar character is most prominent in *L. A.* 2.4:

> It is not good that any man should be alone. For there are two races of men, the one made after the Image, and the one molded out of the earth. For the man made after the Image it is not good to be alone, because he yearns after the Image. For the Image of God is a pattern of which copies are made, and every

copy longs for that of which it is a copy, and its station is at its side. Far less is it good for the man molded of the earth to be alone. Nay, it is impossible. For with the mind so formed, linked to it in closest fellowship, are senses, passions, vices, ten thousand other presences.

The heavenly man is more than an eternal paradigm; he is a real figure capable of "yearning after the Image," that is, after the *Logos*. Jewish interpreters were conditioned to treat the "heavenly man" as a real figure and not just as a paradigm both because of the text of Gen 1:27, which describes the creation of a real man, and because previous levels of interpretation whose concepts and vocabulary these interpreters used also thought that Gen 1:27 described the creation of a real man and not a paradigm.

D. *The Search for Consistency: The Intelligible and Sensible Worlds*

Although the interpretation of Gen 1:27 and Gen 2:7 as two separate creations remedied the lack of consistency caused by the fact that there was no mention of the creation of an "intelligible man" as a paradigm for the man of the sensible world in Gen 1:1–3, it created another kind of anomaly. If the distinction between the ideal world and the sensible world is the distinction between "day one" (Gen 1:1–5) and the other five days, then the fact that the heavenly man is created on the *sixth* day, a day otherwise devoted to the creation of creatures of the *sensible* world, is anomalous. As we have seen in previous interpretations of Gen 1:27, there was an attempt to coordinate the interpretation of the creation of the world and the interpretation of the creation of man. This attempt to be consistent can be seen in the introduction of the figure of the *Logos* from the interpretation of the creation of the world into the interpretation of the creation of man so that the two interpretations are parallel.[57] It can also be seen in the interpretation of Gen 1:27 as the creation of an ideal, paradigmatic man so that both the world *and* man are created according to intelligible paradigms.[58] It was important in this exegetical tradition that the interpretation of the creation of the world and the interpretation of the creation of man be consistent with each other. Once Gen 1:27 was interpreted as the creation of the intelligible, heavenly man, then, to be consistent, the line of demarcation between the intelligible world and the sensible world had to fall somewhere between Gen 1:27 and Gen 2:7 so that the intelligible man created in Gen 1:27 was created with the intelligible world and the sensible man created in Gen 2:7 was created along with the rest of the sensible world.

[57] See Chapter IV, section A.
[58] See Chapter IV, sections B and C.

It is precisely this sort of shift that emerges in *L. A.* 2.11–13, and again it is connected with the distinction between man as γένος and man as εἶδος. This section in the *Legum Allegoriae* is an interpretation of Gen 2:19 ("And God molded *moreover* out of the earth all the wild beasts of the field") and its relationship to Gen 1:24 ("Let the earth bring forth living soul *after its kind*, four-footed animals and creeping things and wild beasts."):

> The addition of "moreover" (ἔτι) to "molded" is by no means otiose. How do we see this? Because above also he mentions the molding of the wild beasts before the creation of man, as we see from these words referring to the sixth day: and he said, "Let the earth bring forth the living soul *after its kind* (κατὰ γένος), four-footed animals and creeping things and wild beasts" (Gen 1:24).

> How comes he, then, to mold other wild beasts now, and not to be satisfied with those former ones? From the ethical point of view (ἠθικῶς) what we must say is this. In the realm of created things the class of wickedness is abundant. It follows that in this the worst things are ever being produced. From the philosophical point of view (φυσικῶς) our answer must be, that on the former occasion (Gen 1:24), when engaged in the Work of the six days, he wrought the genera (γένη) and the originals (ἰδέας) of the passions, whereas now he is fashioning the species as well.

> This is why he says, "He molded *moreover*." That what were created in the first instance were genera, is evident from the words employed, "Let the earth bring forth the living soul," not according to species (κατ' εἶδος) but according to genus (κατὰ γένος). And we find in him every instance working in this way. Before the species he completes the genera. He does so in the case of man. Having first fashioned man as a genus, in which the prophet says that there is "the male and the female" genus, he afterwards makes Adam, the species.

The first thing to note about this passage is that two very different kinds of interpretations are set side by side. One is the "ethical" (ἠθικῶς) interpretation in which the creation of the wild beasts is described twice because in the world of becoming (ἐν τῷ γενητῷ) evils are always being produced (ἀεὶ γεννᾶσθαι). Whatever the origins of this interpretation may have been, it is clearly separate from the interpretation that follows, since it in no way involves a distinction between the intelligible world and the sensible world. It simply talks about the abundance of evil in the world of becoming.[59]

---

[59] The "ethical" interpretation which is concerned with the abundance of evils probably depends on the allegorical interpretation of the animals as symbols of the passions. This is because, for Philo, evil is rooted in the passions. This interpretation, like the interpretation to be discussed below of the animals as symbols of the passions, is part of the Philonic allegory of the soul. The use of the terms ἠθικῶς and φυσικῶς to characterize these interpretations is also probably the work of Philo. When used by Philo in such a context, the term φυσικῶς no longer

The second, more "physically" oriented interpretation (φυσικῶς) takes the creation of the wild beasts in Gen 1:24 as the creation of the genera or the types of the passions (τὰ γένη καὶ τὰς ἰδέας τῶν παθῶν) and the creation of the wild beasts in Gen 2:19 as the creation of the species (τὰ εἴδη). The basis of this interpretation is twofold: (1) in Gen 1:24 the earth is said to bring forth animals κατὰ γένος, which is taken to mean not "according to kind" but "generically"; and (2) in Gen 2:19 the text reads "and God molded moreover (ἔτι)" which means that he had molded animals before this.

The second interpretation is itself a combination of two levels. The first level is one in which there is a distinction drawn between the generic and the specific creation of the *animals*. This interpretation is represented by *L. A.* 2.11b, 13. In this interpretation, the wild animals are not symbols of the passions; they are the intelligible paradigms of the animals (Gen 1:24) and the animals themselves (Gen 2:19). The interpretation found in *L. A.* 2.11b refers only to the creation of the animals (θηρία), and not to the creation of the passions. This becomes even clearer when one examines the analogy made with the creation of man at the end of the passage (*L. A.* 2.13). Just as there was a generic and a specific creation of *man*, so too there was a generic and a specific creation of the *animals*. The analogy involves only the distinction of the generic creation of the animals and man from the specific creation of the animals and man. The interpretation in *L. A.* 2.13 does not involve a further level of interpretation in which these two would represent, for example, the generic and the specific "mind" (νοῦς) or the generic and the specific passions (πάθη).[60] This indicates that the interpretation of the creation of the animals as symbols of the passions is a second, additional level of interpretation.

The reason for such an addition is quite clear. In *L. A.* 2.9–11a the wild animals are interpreted allegorically as the soul's passions, that is, as part of the allegory of the soul, a mode of interpretation that forms the framework for Philo's own interpretation. In order to integrate the interpretation of *L. A.* 2.11b, 13 into the allegory of the soul, Philo has added a second level of interpretation (that is, the wild beasts as symbols of the passions) to the

---

refers to the interpretation of a verse that is "in accord with reality" but to an interpretation that is "physical" rather than "ethical." The meaning of the term differs, then, from the way Aristobulus used it and from the way it was used in previous levels of interpretation of the creation of man.

[60] In the developments to be described in Chapter VI, the man created in Gen 2:7 does become a symbol for the human mind (*Plant.* 44–46; *L. A.* 1.53–55, 88–89, 90–96). But this is not the case in *L. A.* 2.13 where we are talking about the whole man, Adam, and not about a symbol for the mind. That indicates that the interpretation of the wild animals as symbols for the passions is a secondary interpretation by Philo himself.

pre-Philonic distinction of the generic and the specific creations of the animals. An even clearer indication of the secondary character of the wild animals as symbols of the passions comes from *Q. G.* 1.19, which is also an interpretation of Gen 1:24 and Gen 2:19:

> Why are beasts and birds now again created, when their creation was announced earlier in the six-day (creation story)?
> Perhaps those things which (were created) in the six days were incorporeal and were symbolically typical types of beasts and birds. But now were produced in actuality their likenesses, sensible likenesses of the invisible things.

In this passage from the *Questions on Genesis*, there is no indication of the second level of interpretation found in *L. A.* 2.12. Rather the interpretation is the same as that found in *L. A.* 2.11b 13, the first level of interpretation. All of this clearly shows that the interpretation of the wild beasts as symbols of the passions is an addition by Philo, used to integrate *L. A.* 2.11b, 13 into his overall interpretation of Gen 2:19 as part of the allegory of the soul. Once again this layering of interpretation is important because it shows the way in which Philo organized the exegetical traditions available to him. The interpretation of the wild animals as symbols of the passions is introduced in *L. A.* 2.12 without rejecting or even explicitly altering the previous interpretation. A second level is subtly grafted onto the stem of the earlier interpretation.

It is the first, pre-Philonic interpretation that is of interest to us because it clarifies the effect that the interpretation of Gen 1:27 and Gen 2:7 as separate creations had on the interpretation of the story of the creation of the world. The division between the ideal, generic world and the sensible, specific world no longer comes between day one and the other six days. Now all of the creation described on these six days refers to the ideal, generic world (*L. A.* 2.11b). It is only in Genesis 2 (the seventh day) that one finds the creation of the sensible world. In this way the first creation of man in Gen 1:27 falls within the creation of the intelligible world while the second creation in Gen 2:7 falls within the creation of the sensible world.

The way in which *L. A.* 2.11b, 13 is constructed also strengthens the suggestion made earlier that, unlike the introduction of the *Logos* figure from the context of the creation of the world into the context of the creation of man, the direction of influence at this level of interpretation is reversed. The interpretation of Gen 1:27 and Gen 2:7 as a double creation of man is what causes the restructuring of the interpretation of the creation of the world. *L. A.* 2.13b is an appeal by analogy to the story of the double creation of man (ὥσπερ καὶ ἐπὶ τοῦ ἀνθρώπου). It is the double creation of man that serves as a support for this particular interpretation of the double creation of the world and not the other way around. This means that this particular interpretation of the double creation of the world is consequent on the double creation of man.

Finally, there is a passage that allows us to locate more precisely where this new line of demarcation between the creation of the intelligible world and the creation of the sensible world comes. It is just such a line of demarcation that emerges in *Op.* 129–130:

> In his concluding summary of the story of creation he says: "This is the book of the genesis of heaven and earth, when they came into being, in the day in which (ᾗ ἡμέρᾳ) God made the heaven and the earth and every herb of the field before it appeared upon the earth, and all grass of the field before it sprang up" (Gen 2:4–5). Is he not manifestly describing the incorporeal ideas present only to the mind (ἀσωμάτους καὶ νοητὰς ἰδέας), by which as by seals, the finished objects that meet our senses were molded? For before the earth put forth its young green shoots, young verdure was present, he tells us, in the nature of things without material shape, and before grass sprang up in the field, there was in existence an invisible grass.
>
> We must suppose that in the case of all other objects also, on which the sense pronounces judgment, the elder forms and measures (πρεσβύτερα εἴδη καὶ μέτρα), to which all things that come into being owe shape and size, subsisted before them; for even if he has not dealt with everything together *according to genus* (κατὰ γένος), aiming as he does at brevity in a high degree, nevertheless what he does say gives us a few indications of universal Nature, which brings forth no finished product in the world of sense without using an incorporeal pattern.[61]

In this interpretation Gen 2:4–5 serve as a summary of everything that has gone before. At first it seems as if the phrase "in the *day* in which" (ᾗ ἡμέρᾳ) (Gen 2:4) means that the line of demarcation between the creation of the intelligible world and the creation of the sensible world in *Op.* 129–130 is still between "day one" and the other five days, that is, that the intelligible paradigms of heaven, earth, herbs, and grass were all created on "*day* one."

---

[61] All of the manuscripts except M read κατὰ μέρος rather than κατὰ γένος. However to read κατὰ μέρος, one must, as Cohn did, emend the text by inserting ἀλλ᾽ between μέρος and ἀθρόα in order to establish the contrast between μέρος and ἀθρόα. If however one reads κατὰ γένος with manuscript M (which with manuscript V are the best) one need make no emendation. This also fits the context better because Philo is really saying that, although Moses has not mentioned everything according to genus but only the "herbs of the field" and the "grass of the field," nevertheless we can learn something universal about the nature of things. Philo is arguing from the exemplary to the general and not from the general to the particular. The contrast is between the ἀθρόα πάντα and the herbs and grass. The κατὰ γένος then refers to the τὰ πρεσβύτερα εἴδη καὶ μέτρα, the *original* forms and measures, that is, not those in matter but those in the ideal world, those κατὰ γένος. This basically preserves the γένος/εἶδος distinction as ideas/forms-in-matter.

Yet the interpretation of these two verses found in *Op.* 129–130 seems to bypass the phrase "in the day in which," since it is not mentioned in the interpretation of Gen 2:4–5. The phrase seems to be taken to mean nothing more precise than "at the time when." This becomes clear when one analyzes the phrases "according to genus" (κατὰ γένος) and the "elder forms" (τὰ πρεσβύτερα εἴδη) in *Op.* 130. The use of these phrases is based once again on the distinction of genus (γένος) as identical with "idea" or "intelligible paradigm" and form (εἶδος) as identical with form-in-matter. The term "*elder* forms" then is another way of referring to the "ideas" or "genera" since the forms are copies of pre-existent ideas which are therefore "elder" forms (*Op.* 130). In this way the terms "incorporeal ideas present only to the mind" (*Op.* 129), the "elder forms and measures" (*Op.* 130), and "genus" (*Op.* 130) are synonymous.

In addition, when the interpreter admits that Moses has not dealt with everything "according to genus," he is referring to those places in the creation account in Genesis 1 where Moses does recount the creation of plants on the third day (Gen 1:11), fish and birds on the fifth day (Gen 1:21), and land animals on the sixth day (Gen 1:24–25), all "according to genus" (κατὰ γένος). For the interpreter that means that all of these creations are part of the intelligible world. For the sake of brevity, however, Moses has not mentioned, either in Genesis 1 or in the summary of Gen 2:4–5, the creation of each thing "according to genus." Nevertheless, the interpreter claims, all sensible objects must have intellible paradigms which existed before them (*Op.* 130). This means that not only the plants, fish, birds, and land animals created in Genesis 1 but also everything else, including the sun, moon, stars, and the man created in Gen 1:27 must be part of the intelligible world of paradigms. The interpretation found in *Op.* 129–130 then is of a piece with *L. A.* 2.11b, 13 and *Q. G.* 1.2, 19 in which all of the creation account in Genesis 1 refers to the creation of the intelligible world, that is, "according to genus." The line of demarcation found in *Op.* 129–130, then, is set not at Gen 1:5 between "day one" and the other five days but at Gen 2:5 between what was created on the first six days and what was created on the seventh day (*Q. G.* 1.19). The same distinction between the first six days of the creation of the world and the seventh day is also parallel to the distinction between the creation of the heavenly man and that of the earthly man. According to *Q. G.* 2.56, the heavenly man was created on the sixth day and the earthly man was created on the seventh day.

The development of the interpretation of the creation of man as a double creation is an exegetical development, the impetus for which is the search for consistency. If the sensible *world* was created according to an ideal paradigm, so too was the sensible *man*. This search for consistency on the part of Jewish interpreters was paralleled in Middle Platonism.[62] Both Middle Platonists and these Jewish interpreters of Genesis sought to maintain the existence of a paradigm of man parallel to the paradigms for the rest of the sensible world. But because of the peculiar character of the text of Genesis and its prior interpretation, this search for consistency caused a double shift. First of all, the single creation of man in Gen 1:27 and Gen 2:7 became a double creation. Sensible man, like the sensible world, was created according to a paradigm in the intelligible world. That was easy enough, since the creation of man was described twice in Genesis. The second shift was more difficult since the creation of the world was not so clearly described twice. Yet the early verses of Genesis 2 seemed to take up again the creation of the world and so the line of demarcation between the intelligible world and the sensible world was shifted from Gen 1:5 to Gen 2:5. In this way the man of Gen 1:27 could be created with the rest of the intelligible world, and the man of Gen 2:7 could be created with the rest of the sensible world. The logic of these two shifts is of a piece in the sense that, to be consistent, the creation of the intelligible man in Gen 1:27 had to take place within the creation of the intelligible world. The interpretation of Gen 1:27 as the creation of the paradigm of man then forced the change of the line of demarcation between the creation of the intelligible world and the creation of the sensible world to be moved from Gen 1:5 to Gen 2:5. Because of this, these two shifts are not two distinct stages of interpretation; rather they are two sides of the same coin. The shift in the interpretation of the creation of man and the shift in the interpretation of the creation of the world are two aspects of a single interpretative development.

E. Methods of Interpretation

The methods of interpretation used in these passages are basically the same as those analyzed in the previous chapter. A crucial phrase in a verse is interpreted in such a way that it points the interpreter toward a certain set of philosophical concepts. Once that connection has been established, the philosophical concepts can then be used to interpret the whole passage. In addition this interpretation can then serve as a fulcrum that changes the balance, the interpretation, of a more extended text.

As I indicated earlier in this chapter, the interpretation of the creation of man as a double creation developed in two stages. In the first stage, the

---

[62] This is part of a larger endeavor to interpret Plato in a way that is internally consistent. Such a concern for consistency is reflected in the "metaphysics of prepositions" found in Seneca's descriptions of types of causality in *Ep.* 65, in the concern for categorization found in Seneca's *Ep.* 58, and in the appearance of handbooks on philosophy such as that of Arius Didymus' *On the Doctrines of Plato.*

distinction between the man created in Gen 1:27 and the man created in Gen 2:7 was between the generic man (Gen 1:27) and the specific or individual man (Gen 2:7).[63] In the second stage, the heavenly man emerged as a real figure rather than simply as a type or paradigm.[64] The transition from the first to the second stage was almost certainly quite rapid both because the text of Gen 1:27 describes the creation of a real man, not just a type or paradigm, and because the verse had been understood in that way in previous interpretations.[65] This development pushed the interpreter of Gen 1:27 in the direction of viewing the heavenly man as more than a type of "genus."

The first, intermediate, stage has survived only in fragments (i.e., *Op.* 76; *Her.* 163–164), and so the explicit grounds for the interpretation have been lost. It is, however, clear from *Op.* 76 and *Her.* 163–164 that the justification for the interpretation must have been based on the phrase in Gen 1:27, "male *and* female." In this interpretation, the generic man is "male *and* female" not because he is an androgyne but because the species (male and female) are inherent (ἐνυπάρχει) in the genus (*Op.* 76). A philosophical commonplace (the notion of inherence) is used to interpret the meaning of the crucial phrase in the text.[66]

A similar kind of justification is given for the second stage of the interpretation. This justification is found most clearly expressed in *Op.* 134–135. Since the interpretation involves the contrast between Gen 1:27 and Gen 2:7, the justification is meant to establish that contrast:

> After this he says that "God formed man by taking clay from the earth, and breathed into his face the breath of life" (Gen 2:7). By this also he shows very clearly that there is a vast difference between the man thus formed and the man that came into existence earlier after the image of God: for the man so formed is an object of sense perception, partaking already of such or such quality (ποι-ότης), consisting of body and soul, man or woman, by nature mortal; while he that was after the image was an idea (ἰδέα) or type (γένος) or seal (σφραγίς), an object of thought, incorporeal, neither male nor female, by nature incorruptible. It says, however, that the formation of the individual man, the object of sense, is a composite one (σύνθετον) made up of earthly substance and of divine spirit; for it says that the body was made through the Artificer taking clay and molding out of it a human form, but that the soul was originated from nothing created whatever, but from the Father and Ruler of all: for that which he breathed in was nothing else than a divine spirit that migrated hither from that blissful and

---

[63] Op. 76; *Her.* 163–64.

[64] *Op.* 134–35; *L. A.* 1.31–32.

[65] E.g., *Op.* 69–71; *L. A.* 3.95–96.

[66] Cf. Aristotle, *An. Post.* 1.4, 73b; *Ph.* 2.1, 193a; *Metaph.* 3.3, 998a; 5.18, 1022a; Plotinus 5.3.11; Julian, *Or.* 4.140c.

happy existence for the benefit of our race, to the end that, even if it is mortal in respect of its visible part, it may in respect of the part that is invisible be rendered immortal. Hence it may with propriety be said that man is the border-land between mortal and immortal nature, partaking of each so far as is needful, and that he was created at once mortal and immortal, mortal in respect of the body, but in respect of the mind immortal.

As I indicated earlier in this chapter, the interpretation is based on two particular phrases, one found in each of the two verses. The interpreter took this phrase to mean that the man created in Gen 1:27 was prior to any sexual distinction and so neither male nor female. This phrase, however, is not found in Gen 2:7. On the other hand, the man created in Gen 2:7 was made from earth and "divine spirit" (*Op.* 135). This means that the man was composite (σύνθετον). This concept, however, is not found in Gen 1:27, nor is there any mention of the fact that the man created in Gen 1:27 has a body. The contrast, then, is between a man who is not composite but incorporeal and is neither male nor female and a man who is composite, bodily, and either male or female. The interpreter then concludes that what is simple and incorporeal and prior to any sexual differentiation must also be immortal; conversely what is composite, bodily, and sexual must be mortal by nature. The conclusion is based on philosophical commonplaces which are given a Platonic twist: only that which is a composite (σύνθετον) can be dissolved and so be mortal by nature; the incorporeal is by nature immortal; sexuality is restricted to the realm of becoming.[67] The interpreter has understood the text in such a way that crucial phrases in the text reflect common, but Platonically interpreted, philosophical notions, and then draws a conclusion proper to those philosophical notions. Once again, the basic interpretation serves as a bridge to a different world of discourse. When that bridge had been completed, a set of concepts drawn from that other, philosophical world of discourse can then be applied to the text.

That application in turn forces a recasting, but *not* a rejection, of the previous interpretation of Gen 1:27 and Gen 2:7. Attributes which at a previous level of the interpretation of Gen 1:27 and Gen 2:7 were applied to the one man who was the result of a single act of creation must now be applied *either* to the heavenly man created in Gen 1:27 *or* to the earthly man created in Gen 2:7. Now only the heavenly man is an image, an idea, or a seal and only the earthly man receives the divine spirit. One has, then, not only

---

[67] None of these three commonplaces as such is exclusively Platonic. A Peripatetic could subscribe to all three of them. In addition to the overall structure, what gives the passage a Platonic coloring is the connection of "quality" (ποιότης) with "body" (*Op.* 134). This same peculiar connection is found in *Tim.* 49c–50a.

the reinterpretation of the text of Genesis; one also has the reinterpretation of a previous interpretation. This fact is by no means unimportant because it means that the interpreter saw himself not only as interpreting the text but also as interpreting that text within a tradition to which he felt a responsibility and so to which he had to pay attention. While the interpretation changed, a sense of continuity was still maintained.

There is one further pre-Philonic development in the interpretation of Gen 1:27 and Gen 2:7 that illustrates, in an anomalous way, the power of an interpretation that has become traditional. It involves the contrast of "spirit" (πνεῦμα) and "breath" (πνοή). This contrast appears in *L. A.* 1.42 and is reflected in *Plant.* 44:

> He uses the word "breath" not "spirit" (in Gen 2:7) implying a difference between them; for "spirit" is conceived of as connoting strength and vigour and power, while a "breath" is like an air or a peaceful and gentle vapour. The mind that was made after the image and original might be said to partake of spirit, for its reasoning faculty possesses robustness; but the mind that was made out of matter must be said to partake of the light and less substantial air, as of some exhalation, such as those that rise from spices; for if they are kept and not burned for incense there is still a sweet perfume from them. (*L. A.* 1.42.)

This interpretation has been reworked by Philo, since it refers to two kinds of "minds" rather than to two kinds of "men." But it is clear from *Plant.* 44 that there was a pre-Philonic interpretation that made the same distinction but about two "men" rather than about two "minds."[68] The justification for the interpretation is based on the fact that Gen 2:7 refers to "breath" and not to "spirit." "Spirit must therefore refer to the heavenly man of Gen 1:27. What is remarkable about this interpretation is that it completely overlooked the fact that "spirit" was introduced in the first place into the interpretation of the creation of man in Gen 2:7 because it was synonymous with "breath."[69] Yet the fact that the earthly man and not the heavenly man received the "divine spirit" must have seemed inappropriate, and so the "divine spirit" was transferred to the heavenly man. This interpretation is valuable because it gives another insight into the power of a traditional

---

[68] It is with deliberate care that the lawgiver says not of the man (ἄνθρωπος) made after the image but of the man fashioned out of earth, that he was introduced into the garden. For the man stamped with the spirit (πνεῦμα) which is after the image of God differs not a whit, as it appears to me, from the tree that bears the fruit of immortal life. (*Plant.* 44.)
It is clear from this passage that the term "spirit" was first transferred to the figure of the heavenly *man*. Only at the level of Philo's allegory of the soul do the two "men" become two "minds." This development will be discussed in the next chapter.

[69] The term "spirit" first occurs in connection with the Stoic interpretation of Gen 2:7 found in *L. A.* 1.36–38.

interpretation. The notion of a "divine spirit" involved in the creation of man had become almost "canonical" and so had to be accounted for, even when the original textual basis for that interpretation (i.e., the "breath" of Gen 2:7) was bypassed.

The techniques involved in the interpretation of Gen 1:27 and Gen 2:7 as a double creation are, therefore, the same as those discussed in the previous chapter. The interpretation of a crucial phrase links the verse to a more philosophical language, in this case Platonism. Once this link has been made, the structure of that philosophical language can then be introduced to clarify the meaning of the whole text.

In the previous chapter I indicated that the interpretation of a crucial phrase influenced the interpretation not only of the immediate context but also of much larger sections of the text. The same thing is true of these interpretations. Together they serve as a fulcrum on which rests the interpretation of much of Genesis 1–2. Once it is established that Gen 1:27 tells of the creation of the heavenly man and Gen 2:7 tells of the creation of the earthly man, then Gen 1:27 logically must fall within the creation of the intelligible world and Gen 2:7 must fall within the creation of the sensible world. But that was impossible within the previous interpretation of the creation of the world in which the line of demarcation between the creation of the two worlds fell between Gen 1:5 and Gen 1:6; the creation of both men would then fall within the creation of the sensible world. Because of that, a new line of demarcation had to be drawn, this time between Gen 2:5 and Gen 2:6.

> In his concluding summary of the story of creation he says: "This is the book of the genesis of heaven and earth, when they came into being, in the day in which God made the heaven and the earth and every herb of the field before it appeared (πρὸ τοῦ γενέσθαι) upon the earth, and all grass of the field before it sprang up" (Gen 2.4–5). Is he not manifestly describing the incorporeal ideas present only in the mind, by which as by seals, the finished objects that meet our senses were molded? For before the earth put forth its green shoots, young verdure was present, he tells, in the nature of things without material shape, and before grass sprang up in the field, there was in existence an invisible grass.
>
> We must suppose that in the case of all other objects also, on which the senses pronounce judgment, the elder forms and measures, to which all things that come into being owe shape and size, subsisted before them; for even if he has not dealt with everything together according to genus, aiming as he does at brevity in a high degree, nevertheless what he does say gives us a few indications of universal Nature, which brings forth no finished product in the world of sense without using an incorporeal pattern. (*Op.* 129–130.)

The interpreter has taken this rather difficult verse to mean that the creation of the heavens and the earth described in Gen 1:1–2:3 refers to the creation

of the intelligible world. The reason is that it took place before (πρό) herbs
or grass were on the *earth*, that is, before the creation of the sensible world.
Once again the interpretation rests on a crucial detail in the text. This detail,
however, allows the interpreter to realign the story of creation in such a way
that the creation of the heavenly man in Gen 1:27 can be a part of the creation
of the intelligible world and the creation of the earthly man can be a part of
the creation of the sensible world. This same interpretation is reflected in
L. A. 2.11b, 13.

The techniques used at this level of interpretation are the same, then, as
those used in the interpretations of Gen 1:27 and Gen 2:7 discussed in Chapter IV. Given the stability of those techniques, it may be worthwhile at this
point to highlight three basic assumptions on which these techniques rested.

When one compares the Stoic interpretations of Gen 2:7 with the Platonic interpretations of Gen 1:27, one is struck by the fact that the interpretations of Gen 1:27 are part of an overall interpretation of the creation of the
world and of man. There is a quite conscious attempt to coordinate the
interpretation of the creation of the world with the interpretation of the
creation of man. When the interpretation of one shifts, so does the interpretation of the other. The same cannot be said for the Stoic interpretation of
Gen 2:7. There is no indication that either the Stoic interpretation of Gen 2:7
or the Stoic interpretations of several verses in the creation of the world
(*Op.* 42–44, 45–46) were part of an overall Stoic interpretation of the creation of the world or of man. This difference is far more than a matter of
quantity. Rather it is a matter of how the biblical text of the creation account
was perceived. For the Stoic interpreters of Gen 2:7, the text represented a
series of discrete units, each of which was interpreted separately. The consistency in the interpretation was the consistency of the Stoic categories that
were used rather than the consistency of a unified, overall interpretation of
the text. The text of the creation story as a whole was not an object of
interpretation. The text of the creation story was perceived differently by the
interpreters of Gen 1:27. The text of the creation story as a whole had
become an object of interpretation. The text of the creation story was no
longer a series of disparate units but a complex whole whose interpretation
had to do justice to that complexity and that wholeness. The interpretation
of the text could be no less integral than the text of the creation story itself.
The Platonic interpretations of the creation account in Genesis reflect a quite
different perception of the nature of the text in Genesis.

A second assumption is imbedded in the process by which a crucial
phrase in the text of Genesis is interpreted in such a way that it allows a set of
philosophical concepts to be used in the interpretation of the text. This
technique assumes that there is a basic isomorphism between the text and
certain sets of philosophical concepts. It is assumed that what is said in the

text of the creation account in Genesis is congruent with, for the most part, Platonic philosophical concepts. Because of that congruence, these philosophical concepts can appropriately be used to interpret the text of Genesis. Included in this assumption is the belief that what is of value in these philosophical concepts was first maintained by Moses. This belief was a constant among Jewish interpreters from Aristobulus to Philo.[70] One must remember in this context that, while these Jewish interpreters were using what we call Middle Platonic concepts, they saw themselves as using concepts derived directly from Plato. These concepts had the authority of Plato. But more importantly, they had the authority of Moses on whom Plato indirectly depended. Therefore the use of Platonic concepts such as the distinction between the intelligible world and the sensible world to interpret either the creation of man or the creation of the world was not seen as the introduction of a foreign body into the explanation of the biblical text but as the reappropriation of that which was originally the thought of Moses. This is specifically stated by Philo when he interprets Plato's *Timaeus* as maintaining that the world is created (γενητός) but indestructible (ἄφθαρτος).

> Some think that the poet Hesiod is the father of this Platonic doctrine (that the world is created but indestructible) and suppose that he calls the world created and indestructible, created because he says
>
> > First Chaos was, and then broad–breasted earth
> > Safe dwelling–place for all for evermore (*Theogony* 116f),
>
> indestructible because he never declared that it will be dissolved or destroyed. Chaos in Aristotle's opinion is a space because a body must have something there already to hold it, but some of the Stoics suppose that it is water and that the name is derived from its diffusion (χύσις).
>
> But whichever of these is right, Hesiod very clearly states the view that the world is created, and long before Hesiod Moses the lawgiver of the Jews said in the Holy Books that it was created and imperishable. These books are five in number, to the first of which he gave the name of *Genesis*. In this he begins by saying "In the beginning God made the Heavens and the Earth and the Earth was invisible and without form." Then again he goes on to say in the sequel that "days and nights and seasons and years and the sun and moon whose natural function is to measure time are together with the whole heaven destined to immortality and continue indestructible." (*Aet.* 17–19.)

Under such circumstances the use of Platonic philosophical categories to interpret the text of Genesis was the most natural thing in the world. Moses and Plato (or Hesiod) were saying the same things and Moses had said them first.

---

[70] Aristobulus *apud* Eusebius, *Praep. Evang.* 13.12.1, 3; Philo, *Aet.* 19.

This quotation from *De Aeternitate Mundi* can also help to clarify a third and final assumption imbedded in these interpretations. That assumption is that the interpretation given is the one, real interpretation of the meaning of the text. Although the techniques used in the interpretations are similar to those used in Heraclitus' interpretations of Homer, interpretations that are explicitly described as "allegorical," these interpretations of Genesis are never characterized as "allegorical." In Chapter III I suggested that one reason for this was that Alexandria was the center of opposition to the Stoic allegorization of Homer. This quotation from *De Aeternitate Mundi* suggests a second reason. From *Aet.* 13–19 it is clear that Plato's *Timaeus* is seen as a text whose meaning does not depend on allegorization. The dispute described in *Aet.* 14 over whether Plato held that the world was created or uncreated is a dispute over the one real meaning of the text of the *Timaeus.* There is no question of allegorization. Jewish interpreters may have found it inappropriate then to describe their interpretation of the creation account in Genesis, their equivalent of the *Timaeus,* as an allegorical interpretation.

F. *Summary and Conclusion*

The purpose of this chapter has been to show that the appearance of the figure of the heavenly man was caused by an interpretation of the text of Genesis and not by alleged influence from Iranian traditions about a Primal Man. The appearance of the heavenly man was rooted in the necessity of reconciling two facts. The first fact was that the creation of man was described twice in Genesis. The second fact, the catalyst for the interpretation, was that in Middle Platonism it was a commonplace that man, like other sensible beings, was made according to an intelligible paradigm. The man created in Gen 1:27 became that heavenly paradigm while the man created in Gen 2:7 became the sensible, earthly man. The Greek philosophical texts that enabled us to explain the appearance of the *Logos* figure are basically the same texts that enable us to explain the appearance of the figure of the heavenly man. This fact suggests that the shifts in interpretation discussed in this chapter followed fairly closely on the heels of the Platonic interpretation of Gen 1:27 discussed in the previous chapter, that is, in the latter half of the first century B.C. or the very early part of the first century A.D.[71] The thought

---

[71] Another indication that points to the latter part of the first century B.C. is found in Paul. Rom 5:12–21 and 1 Cor 15:20–22, 44–50 know of the distinction between a heavenly man and an earthly man. From 1 Cor 15:44–50 it is clear that the distinction was made prior to Paul. If we assume, as seems reasonable, that some time was required for the distinction between the two to spread, then the origin of the distinction would be pushed back to the end of the first century B.C. See Brandenburger, *Adam und Christus*; Scroggs, *The Last Adam.*

patterns used in these interpretations of the creation account in Genesis are of a piece with the Middle Platonic interpretations of Plato, and especially of his *Timaeus*, from the latter half of the first century B.C. in Alexandria.

The similarity, however, goes beyond patterns of thought. The interpretation of Plato's *Timaeus* played an important role in the development of Middle Platonism. Eudorus of Alexandria commented on the *Timaeus*.[72] Thrasyllus (d. A.D 36), a native of Alexandria, commented on the works of Plato, although we do not know for certain that he commented specifically on the *Timaeus*.[73] Arius Didymus, again a native of Alexandria, wrote the treatise *On the Doctrines of Plato*, which, if we are to judge by Albinus' *Didaskalikos*, was heavily influenced by the *Timaeus*. Finally the *Timaeus Locrus* was really nothing more than an interpretation of Plato's *Timaeus*. Much of the Middle Platonism of this period was rooted in the interpretation of the *Timaeus*. The *process* by which much of Middle Platonism developed was the interpretation of an authoritative text. This process of interpretation is analogous to the process of interpretation of the creation account in Genesis. Both Middle Platonic and Jewish exegetes were interpreting texts which had to do with the creation of the world and of man. From *Aet.* 17–19 it is clear that this analogy was not lost on Jewish interpreters.[74] Plato's *Timaeus* was seen as the Greek philosophical equivalent of Moses' account of creation in Genesis. Moses' account, however, was the earlier and original version. As Middle Platonic cosmology was rooted in the interpretation of the *Timaeus*, so Jewish cosmology was rooted in the interpretation of the creation account in Genesis. Middle Platonic interpretations of Plato's *Timaeus* served as a ready foil for Jewish interpretations of Genesis.

The interpretations analyzed in this chapter, like those of the previous chapter, also show us how this tradition of interpretation developed. Once again the development took place by way of shifts rather than by the rejection of a previous interpretation. In the interpretation of creation discussed in the previous chapter, God made the sensible world and man through the medium of the *Logos* who served as both paradigm and instrument of creation. That basic interpretation is maintained but a shift takes place in which

---

[72] Plutarch, *De Anima Proc. in Tim.* 1013B, 1019E, 1020C.

[73] Porphyry, *Plot.* 20.

[74] *Aet.* 14, 17–18 also indicates that Jewish interpreters were aware of various interpretations of Plato's *Timaeus*, although one cannot tell from this passage which interpretations they were aware of. In addition, one must remember that the analogy between the Jewish interpretations of Genesis and the Middle Platonic interpretations of the *Timaeus* is in terms of the way in which philosophical reflection is carried on, that is, through the interpretation of authoritative texts. We do not know precisely what these interpretations of the *Timaeus* looked like, and so we do not know how closely they resembled the Jewish interpretations of Genesis.

the line of demarcation between the creation of the intelligible world and the creation of the sensible world changes. Instead of coming between the first and the second days of creation (Gen 1:5), that line now falls at Gen 2:5. In this way the creation of the heavenly man (Gen 1:27) falls within the creation of the intelligible world, and the creation of the earthly man (Gen 2:7) falls within the creation of the sensible world. Although significant details of the interpretation are changed, the shift takes place within a structure of interpretation that remains the same.

In this development the text is read not only directly but also through the lens of the previous level of interpretation. In this case the problem of the double description of the creation of man (Gen 1:27 and Gen 2:7) is viewed through the lens of an interpretation in which the creation of the intelligible world is distinguished from that of the sensible world. That previous interpretation establishes the structure within which the next level of interpretation takes place. Consequently the solution to the problem of the double description of the creation of man follows the structure established by the distinction between the intelligible and the sensible worlds.

The previous interpretation, however, not only sets the limits within which the solution must be found, it also creates part of the problem. This is because the line of demarcation between the intelligible world and the sensible world drawn at Gen 1:5 makes it impossible to place the creation of the heavenly man of Gen 1:27 in the intelligible world. In this way the solution at one level of interpretation becomes a problem for the next level of interpretation. The solution, then, must both respect the limits set by the previous interpretation and solve the problem that the previous interpretation created. The issue involves the delicate balance between continuity and change within a tradition of interpretation.

This search for balance characterizes a tradition of interpretation that feels itself responsible not only to the text but also to its predecessors. At the same time it is a tradition which is not satisfied with simply repeating what has been said but goes beyond the interpretations of the past to find solutions to what it perceives as real problems.

CHAPTER VI

PHILO AND THE ALLEGORY OF THE SOUL

Up until now we have been analyzing interpretations of the creation of man which have been the work of Philo's predecessors. We must now look at interpretations which are the work of Philo himself. Philo's interpretations are developments of the interpretation of the creation account as a creation of two men, one heavenly and the other earthly. Yet, as we shall see, several significant shifts take place which set Philo's interpretations off from those of his predecessors. An analysis of these Philonic interpretations will give a clearer sense not only of Philo's outlook but also of Philo's evaluation of the work of his predecessors, which, taken as a whole, shares certain characteristics. This will also give us an opportunity to say something about how these interpretations were passed on and what the institutional framework was in which they developed. This is possible because, when one comes to Philo himself, one is no longer dealing with small blocks of interpretation but with whole treatises in which one finds not only interpretations but indications of a theory of interpretation and hints about the institutional arrangements through which these interpretations may have been developed and passed on.

A. *Philo's Interpretation of the Creation of Man*

Philo's own interpretation of the creation of man is rooted not in an interpretation of Gen 1:27 and Gen 2:7 directly but in an interpretation of Gen 2:8, 15, 16–17, verses which describe the placing of man in the Garden of Paradise. At this level of interpretation the question of course is: which man was placed in the garden, the heavenly man of Gen 1:27 or the earthly man of Gen 2:7? Philo's interpretations indicate that the traditions on which he drew gave two different answers both of which he developed in the same direction.

The first of those answers is found in *Q. G.* 1.8:

8. (Gen 2:8) Why does He place the molded man in Paradise, but not the man who was made in his image?
Some, believing Paradise to be a garden, have said that since the molded man is sense-perceptible, he therefore rightly goes to a sense-perceptible place. But the man made in his image is intelligible and invisible, and is in the class of incorporeal species.

> *But I would say* that earth-formed man is a mixture, and consists of soul and body, and is in need of teaching and instruction, desiring, in accordance with the laws of philosophy, that he may be happy. But he who was made in his image is in need of nothing, but is self–hearing and self-taught and self-instructed by nature.

In this interpretation only the earthly, molded man of Gen 2:7 is placed in the garden, while the heavenly man who was made according to the image (Gen 1:27) is not. There are two different reasons given for this. First, since the garden is a sensible reality, only the earthly, sense-perceptible man could be placed there. Philo quite explicitly says that this is not his own interpretation but that of some unnamed "others." This interpretation is of a piece with those which were analyzed in Chapter V.[1] It continues the interpretation of Gen 1:27 and Gen 2:7 as the creation of two different men.

The second reason given for the fact that only the "molded man" is placed in Paradise is Philo's own, and it is that only the "molded man" is in need of teaching and instruction. From this section of *Q. G.* 1.8 alone, the reason why the molded man's need of instruction leads to his introduction into Paradise is not at all clear. It becomes somewhat clearer, however, in *Plant.* 44–46:

> It is with deliberate care that the lawgiver says not of the *man* made after God's image, but of the man fashioned out of earth, that he was introduced into the garden. For the man stamped with the spirit which is after the image of God differs not a whit, as it appears to me, from the tree that bears the fruit of immortal life; for both are imperishable and have been accounted worthy of the most central and most princely portion: for we are told that the tree of life is in the midst of the garden (Gen 2:9). Nor is there any difference between the man fashioned out of the earth and the earthly composite body. He has no part in a nature simple and uncompounded, whose house and courts only the self-trainer knows how to occupy, even Jacob who is put before us as a "plain man dwelling in a house" (Gen 25:27).
>
> The earthly man has a disposition of versatile subtlety, fashioned and concocted of elements of all sorts. It was to be expected, then, that God should plant and set in the garden, or the whole universe, the *middle mind* (τὸν μέσον νοῦν), played upon by forces drawing it in opposite directions and given the high calling to decide between them, that it might be moved to choose and to shun, to win fame and immortality should it welcome the better, and incur a dishonourable death should it choose the worse. Such then were the trees which He who alone is wise planted in *rational souls.*

Once again the "man made according to the image" is not placed in Paradise;

---

[1] Chapter V, section B.

only the "molded man" is. The man made according to the image, however, has the same characteristics as the tree of life, that is, both are imperishable and worthy of the most central and princely portion. The heavenly man, then, is assimilated to the figure of the tree of life. The tree of life in turn is a symbol of generic virtue (γενικωτάτη ἀρ :τή) (L. A. 1.58) and stands in the center of Paradise, the symbol of earthly wisdom, the imitation of heavenly Wisdom (L. A. 1.43).[2] In addition, both the figure of the heavenly man and the figure of the tree of life are connected with the virtues that bring the soul to happiness and immortality (Plant. 37). These are the virtues that the "middle mind" must choose or reject and so achieve immortality or be punished with a dishonorable death (Plant. 45).

In Plant. 44–46 the two distinct interpretations found in Q. G. 1.8 have been reworked by Philo into one interpretation. A first level of interpretation (corresponding to Q. G. 1.8a) in which the molded man is introduced into Paradise, that is, into the sensible world, has been overlaid with a second level of interpretation in which the middle mind (ὁ μέσος νοῦς) rather than the composite man must choose or reject the virtues represented by the tree of life and the other trees, virtues to which the man made according to the image has been assimilated.[3] Philo has taken over an earlier interpretation of the double creation of man and has transformed it to his own purposes. The crucial change is one in which the "molded man" of Gen 2:7 becomes a symbol for the human mind and the "man made according to the image" (Gen 1:27) becomes a symbol of virtue and wisdom.[4]

The second answer given by the traditional interpretations which Philo drew on was that both the heavenly man and the earthly man were placed in

---

[2] Moving beyond the immediate context of Plant. 44–46 to interpret that passage is justified in this case. Plant. 44–46 has the same concern as L. A. 1.43, 58, the acquisition of virtue; the same structure, the allegory of the soul; and the same basic allegorical equivalents, the garden and its trees as wisdom and the virtues.

[3] The term "middle mind" in this context simply means the human mind caught between choosing good and choosing evil. Philo uses the same term, "middle," to describe prudence, that virtue by which one distinguishes good from evil (Op. 154).

[4] Another change involves the fate of the "divine spirit" (πνεῦμα θεῖον). In previous interpretations the "breath" (πνοή) of Gen 2:7 was interpreted to mean "divine spirit" breathed into man at his creation. Even when the creation of the "heavenly man" was distinguished from the creation of the "earthly man," the "divine spirit" remained a characteristic of the "earthly man" (Op. 134–35). Yet it must have seemed anomalous that the earthly man should possess the "divine spirit" while the heavenly man did not. Because of this, the "divine spirit" was transferred to the heavenly man and the earthly man was left with only "breath." This change is reflected in Plant. 44 but is explicitly stated in L. A. 1.42. In Plant. 44 the "divine spirit" is an attribute of the heavenly man. This suggests that the transfer of the "divine spirit" from the man created in Gen 2:7 to the man created in Gen 1:27 took place prior to the introduction of the allegory of the soul, that is, it is pre-Philonic.

Paradise (*L. A.* 1.53–55, 88–89, 90–96). These three passages are based on a textual variant that is not represented in our manuscripts of the *LXX*. The *LXX* of Gen 2:15 reads:

> Καὶ ἔλαβεν κύριος ὁ θεὸς τὸν ἄνθρωπον, ὃν ἔπλασεν καὶ ἔθετο αὐτὸν ἐν τῷ παραδείσῳ, ἐργάζεσθαι αὐτὸν καὶ φυλάσσειν.
>
> And the Lord God took the man *whom he had molded* and placed him in Paradise to till it and to guard it.

The text, however, on which Philo's interpretations rest has ὃν ἐποίησεν (whom he *made*) in place of ὃν ἔπλασεν. This is then contrasted with Gen 2:8 where God placed in Paradise the man "whom he had molded" (ὃν ἔπλασεν).[5] Because this is the same contrast found between Gen 1:27 (" . . . and God *made* the man") and Gen 2:7 (" . . . and God *molded* the man"), Gen 2:15 is taken to refer to the "man made according to the image" and Gen 2:8 is taken to refer to the "molded man" of Gen 2:7. This interpretation is found in *L. A.* 1.53–55:

> Speaking here of the man whom God *molded* (ὃν ἔπλασεν), it merely says that he "placed him in the garden" (Gen 2:8). Who then is it of whom it says later on "The Lord God took the man whom he had *made*, and placed him in the garden to till it and to guard it" (Gen 2:15)? It would seem then that this is a different man, the one that was made after the image and archetype, so that two men are introduced into the garden, the one a molded being, the other "after the image." The one then that was made according to the original has his sphere not only in the planting of virtues but is also their tiller and guardian, and that means that he is mindful of all that he heard and practised in his training; but the "molded" one neither tills the virtues nor guards them, but is only introduced to the truths by the rich bounty of God, presently to be an exile from virtue.
>
> For this reason in describing the one whom God only places in the garden, Moses uses the word "molded" but of the one whom he appoints both tiller and guardian he speaks of not as "molded," but he says "whom he had *made*"; and the one he receives, and the other he casts out. And he confers on him whom he receives three gifts, which constitute natural ability, facility in apprehending, persistence in doing, tenacity in keeping. Facility in apprehending is the placing in the garden, persistence in doing is the practice of noble deeds, tenacity in keeping the guarding and retaining in the memory of the holy precepts. But the "molded" mind (ὁ πλαστὸς νοῦς) neither keeps in mind nor carries out in action the things that are noble, but has facility in apprehending them and no more than this. Accordingly after being placed in the garden he soon runs away and is cast out.

[5] Both the LXX and this interpretation in Philo assume a reading of Gen 2:15 that differs from the Masoretic text. The LXX assumes the reading את האדם אשר יצר; the interpretation in Philo assumes the reading את האדם אשר ברא or עשה. The Masoretic text has only את האדם.

In *L. A.* 1.53–55, unlike *Plant.* 44–46, the integration of the two levels of interpretation is more successful. The distinction between the man made according to the image of God and the molded man is in terms of practice and persistence in virtue. In *L. A.* 1.54–55, however, one becomes aware that it is the molded *mind* rather than the whole composite earthly *man* who is inconstant in virtue. This emphasis on the earthly mind rather than on the earthly man is also found in two other passages (*L. A.* 1.88–89, 90–96).[6] This shift, especially in the latter two passages, highlights the two levels of interpretation. The first of these levels did not involve the transformation of the molded man into the molded mind nor was it concerned with virtue (*L. A.* 1.53). In this respect it was similar to the pre–Philonic interpretation found in *Q. G.* 1.8a. The second level, which fits into Philo's allegorical scheme, reinterprets the text in such a way that it now refers to the human mind's acquisition of virtue. Once again, as in *Plant.* 44–46, the man made according to the image becomes closely associated with the complete and certain practice of virtue (*L. A.* 1.55, 89, 94). In both *Plant.* 44–46 and these passages from the *Legum Allegoriae*, the man made according to the image no longer plays the role of archetype or paradigm for the earthly man but becomes the personification of perfect virtue.

Philo himself then seems less interested in the figure of the "heavenly man" as such than he is in integrating interpretations of Gen 2:8, 15, 16–17 into his allegory of the soul in which the earthly man of Gen 2:7 becomes a symbol for the human mind that is striving after virtue, which is symbolized by the tree of life and secondarily by the heavenly man. In this development one must also be aware of the importance of the figure of Wisdom. The river that goes forth from Eden is generic virtue (*L. A.* 1.63). But Eden itself, the source of that river, is a symbol of the Wisdom of God (*L. A.* 1.64–66). In

---

[6] "And the Lord God took the man whom he had made, and placed him in the garden to till and to guard it" (Gen 2:15). "The man whom God made" differs, as I have said before, from the one that was molded; for the one that was molded is the more earthly *mind*, the one that was made the less material, having no part in perishable matter, endowed with a constitution of a purer and clearer kind. This pure *mind*, then, God takes, not suffering it to go outside of himself, and having taken it, sets it among the virtues that have roots and put forth shoots, that he may till them and guard them. (*L. A.* 1.88–89.)

"And the Lord God commanded Adam saying: 'From every tree that is in the garden thou shalt freely eat, but of the tree of knowing good and evil ye shall not eat of it; and the day ye eat of it ye shall surely die'" (Gen 2:16–17). We must raise the question *what* Adam he commands and who this is; for the writer has not mentioned him before, but has named him now for the first time. Perchance, then, he means to give us the name of the man that was molded. "Call him earth" he says, for that is the meaning of "Adam," so that when ye hear the word "Adam," you must make up your mind that it is the earthly and perishable *mind*; for the *mind* that was made after the image is not earthly but heavenly. (*L. A.* 1.90.)

addition, human prudence is a reflection of universal prudence which has its abode in the Wisdom of God (*L. A.* 1.78). In this way the figures of the heavenly man, the *Logos* and Wisdom are being assimilated to each other in Philo's interpretation of God's placing man in Paradise.[7]

The attempt to identify the figure of the "heavenly man" with other figures also occurs in three passages from *De Confusione Linguarum* (41, 62, 146). The attempt at integration is more successful here because Philo is not interpreting a specific text from Genesis 1–3 but is simply stating his own view in a more general way. In all three passages, the figure of the heavenly man is assimilated to that of the *Logos*.

And therefore when I hear those who say "We are all sons of one man (ἑνὸς ἀνθρώπου), we are peaceful" (Gen 42:11), I am filled with admiration for the harmonious concert which their words reveal. "Ah! my friends," I would say, "how should you not hate war and love peace—you who have enrolled yourselves as children of one and the same father, who is not mortal but immortal— God's *Man* (ἄνθρωπον θεοῦ), who being the *Logos* of the Eternal (τοῦ ἀϊδίου θεοῦ) must needs himself be imperishable?" (*Conf.* 40–41.)

I have heard also an oracle from the lips of one of the disciples of Moses, which runs thus: "Behold a man (ἄνθρωπος) whose name is the rising" (Zech 6:12), strangest of titles, surely, if you suppose that a being composed of soul and body is here described. But if you suppose that it is that Incorporeal One (τὸν ἀσώματον ἐκεῖνον), who differs not a whit from the divine image (θείας εἰκόνος), you will agree that the name of "rising" assigned to him quite truly describes him.

For that man is the eldest son, whom the Father of all raised up, and elsewhere calls his first born (πρωτόγονον), and indeed the Son thus begotten followed the ways of his Father, and shaped the different kinds, looking to the archetypal patterns which that Father supplied. (*Conf.* 62–63.)

But if there be any as yet unfit to be called a Son of God, let him press to take his place under God's First-born, the *Logos* (τὸν πρωτόγονον αὐτοῦ λόγον), who holds the highest rank among the angels, their ruler as it were. And many names are his, for he is called, "the Beginning," and the Name of God and his *Logos*, and the Man after his image, and "he that sees," that is Israel.

And therefore I was moved a few pages above to praise the virtues of those who say that "we are all sons of one man" (Gen 42:11). For if you have not yet

---

[7] Up until this point the figure of Wisdom has not been a part of the speculation about the *Logos*. The *Logos* has been understood in previous interpretations of the creation of man in Platonic terms, that is, as an archetype or paradigm, but not as Wisdom. But at this new level, the interpretations of the two figures affect each other significantly. Mack (*Logos und Sophia*, 20) rightly emphasizes the importance of Wisdom speculation for understanding the figure of the *Logos* in Philo; but that influence applies only to this later Philonic level of interpretation of the creation of the world and of man. It does not apply to the earlier exegetical traditions about the creation of man or to the Platonic model on which it rests.

become fit to be thought sons of God yet we may be sons of his invisible image, the most holy *Logos*. For the *Logos* is the highest born image of God (θεοῦ γὰρ εἰκὼν λόγος ὁ πρεσβύτατος). (*Conf.* 146–147.)

When one reads these three passages together, one is immediately struck by the fact that all are in the first person and so we are dealing here with the work of Philo himself. When one moves from the formal to the conceptual level, the first thing to note is that the figure of the heavenly man has been completely assimilated to the figure of the *Logos*. The heavenly man no longer has any separate existence of his own. Secondly, the figure of the *Logos* itself is described in a number of different ways: the Incorporeal One, the divine image, the highest of the angels, the archangel, the name of God, the beginning, the first-born, and the first-born son. This plethora of titles indicates that these passages represent a conflation of various speculative traditions about the figure of the *Logos*. It represents Philo's effort to draw together and to integrate, at least partially, interpretations of the *Logos* figure which come from a number of sources. In this conflation of interpretations, the relationship of either the *Logos* or the heavenly man to the Platonic paradigms or archetypes is minor (*Conf.* 63). The dominant concept is that of filiation. The *Logos* is the first-born son of the Father (*Conf.* 146) and human beings are in turn sons of that first-born son (*Conf.* 40–41, 146–147). The attribute, πρωτόγονος, as well as the notion that the *Logos* is the Son of God, indicates that the *Logos* has taken on characteristics similar to those of the figure of Wisdom, for in other passags from Philo Wisdom is referred to as the "first-born mother of all things" (*Q. G.* 4.97) and the "daughter of God" (*Q. G.* 4.97, 243; *Fug.* 50ff). In addition, the *Logos* is referred to as the "Beginning" (ἀρχή), again an important attribute of Wisdom (cf. Prov 8:22; *Ebr.* 30–32; *Virt.* 61–63). In turn the figure of Wisdom takes on some of the attributes of the *Logos* such as "image" and "vision of God" (*L. A.* 1.43). Once again one has the conflation of the figures of the heavenly man, the *Logos,* and Wisdom. This represents Philo's own work in which he tries to bring together disparate traditions. The assimilation of the heavenly man to the *Logos* and the identification of the *Logos* figure with Wisdom are examples of that process. The integration of these three figures fits in well with Philo's overall concern for man's striving after virtue, a striving that results in wisdom and immortality. In such an interpretation, figures such as the heavenly man and the *Logos* are not primarily archetypal but anagogic, that is, they are primarily the guiding divine power by which the human mind is enabled to ascend toward God.[8] In this sense they are

[8] See Mack, *Logos und Sophia,* 133–41; Wlosok, *Laktanz und die philosophische Gnosis,* 77–97.

functionally equivalent to the figure of Wisdom and so, in these Philonic interpretations, they are assimilated to that figure.

The interpretations of the creation of man analyzed in Chapters IV and V were coordinated with interpretations of the creation of the world.[9] This meant especially the proper positioning of the division between the creation of the intelligible world and the creation of the sensible world. At first this division was placed at Gen 1:5, between "day one" of creation and the other five days (e.g., *Op.* 29–35). With the appearance of the heavenly man, that division was moved to Gen 2:5, so that the creation of the heavenly man in Gen 1:27 could be part of the creation of the heavenly, intelligible world (*Op.* 129–130). This second division was based on an interpretation in which Gen 2:4–5 referred to the creation of incorporeal and intelligible ideas in Genesis 1, ideas which served as paradigms for the objects of the sensible world to be created later in Genesis 2.

The division between the creation of the intelligible world and the creation of the sensible world is kept at Gen 2:5 in the Philonic interpretation of the creation of the world. However, the interpretation of Gen 2:4–5 is different.

> "In the day in which God made the heaven and the earth and every green thing of the field before it appeared upon the earth and all grass of the field before it sprang up; for God had not sent rain on the earth, and there was no man to till the earth" (Gen 2:4–5). Above he has called this day a book, for he delineates the creation of heaven and earth as wrought in both, for by his own supremely manifest and far-shining *Logos* God makes both of them, both the *idea* of the mind, which in symbolic language he calls "heaven," and the *idea* of sense perception, to which by a figure he gave the name of "earth." (*L. A.* 1.21.)[10]

The basic structure of the previous level of interpretation of Gen 2:4–5 has been maintained, that is, the division between the intelligible world and the sensible world. But the interpretation of the specific contents of these two verses has changed. In Philo's interpretation of Gen 2:4–5, Genesis 1 is concerned with the creation of the idea (ἰδέα) of *mind* (heaven) and the idea (ἰδέα) of *sense perception* (earth). The Platonic structure of the world of ideas has been maintained, but the specific content of that world has been narrowed in such a way that it becomes consistent with the interpretation of the creation of man as "mind" and of woman as "sense perception." This shift in the interpretation of Gen 2:4–5 is clearly dependent on the shift in the interpretation of the creation of man from a creation of two "men" to a

---

[9] Chapter IV, 59–60; Chapter V, section D.

[10] This same interpretation is found in *L. A.* 1.1.

creation of two "minds." The notion that there is an "idea" of sense perception is very odd from a Platonic point of view.[11] It makes sense only when
one realizes that Philo is trying to interpret the creation of the world in a way
that is consistent with his allegory of the soul.[12]

An important question at this level of interpretation is why the two
"men" of Gen 1:27 and Gen 2:7 become two "minds." In a sense the answer is
obvious: in order to form a link with the story of the fall in which man is a
symbol of mind, woman of sense perception, and the serpent of pleasure.
This answer also reveals something less obvious. Unlike previous levels of
interpretation, the roots of this final level are not in the interpretation of the
creation account but in the allegorical account of the fall. The structure of
De Opificio Mundi indicates that the allegorical interpretation of the fall
begins with the description of Paradise in Gen 2:8. Op. 13–150 is the interpretation of the creation of the world and of man. It also includes an interpretation of man's naming the animals (Gen 2:19) (Op. 148–150). There is no
indication that the interpretations found in Op. 13–150 were thought of as
allegorical. There is no allegorical terminology. Op. 151–170a, on the other
hand, is a summary of the quite explicitly allegorical interpretation of the
fall.[13] This allegorical interpretation of the fall begins with an interpretation
of Paradise in Gen 2:8 as the ruling part of the soul in which various virtues
are planted (Op. 153–154). The description of the Garden of Paradise and
the placing of the man in the garden (Gen 2:8–20) are where the non-
allegorical and the allegorical interpretations most clearly overlap. The
interpretation of Gen 2:8, 15, 16–17 which refers to two *men* continues the
non-allegorical interpretation of Gen 1:27 and Gen 2:7, while the interpretation which refers to two *minds* is an attempt to develop an interpretation of
the creation of man that is consistent with Philo's allegorical interpretation
of the fall, an interpretation that begins in earnest only with the description

---

[11] In both Plato and Middle Platonism, sense perception (αἴσθησις) and the sensible
(αἰσθητόν) are by their very nature part of the material world and not part of the
intelligible world.

[12] This interpretation of Gen 2:4–5 in L. A. 1.21–27 also points to one of the puzzles in
the interpretation of Philo. It points toward an *allegorical* interpretation of the creation of the
world. The same is true of L. A. 1.1. Such an allegorical interpretation is not found in De
Opificio Mundi. The question then remains about whether Legum Allegoriae 1 really was the
beginning of the allegories on the law or whether there was an allegorical interpretation of the
creation of the world. In a sense the question is unanswerable, but L. A. 1.1, 21–27 point to the
intriguing possibility that such an interpretation existed.

[13] ἀλληγορία, Op. 157; ὑπόνοια, Op. 157; συμβολικός, Op. 154, 164; σύμβολον,
Op. 157.

of the Garden of Paradise in Gen 2:8.[14] In the same way the interpretation of
Gen 2:4–5 as a description of the creation of the ideas of mind and of sense
perception is an attempt to develop an interpretation of the creation of the
world that is consistent with the allegorical interpretation of the fall. These
two developments are quite different from previous levels of interpretation.
At these previous levels the center of attention was a consistent interpretation of the *creation* account. At the level of the allegory of the soul, the
center of attention is a consistent interpretation of the account of the *fall*.[15]

At the level of the allegory of the soul, the techniques of interpretation
also undergo a shift. Since the allegory of the soul is so pervasive in Philo, it
would be impossible in a study such as this to give an adequate account of all
of the techniques used in the allegory of the soul. But something can be said
about how these techniques are used in the passages that we have analyzed in
connection with the interpretation of the creation of man.

At previous levels of interpretation, certain details in a biblical verse
were seen as pointing to a philosophical concept that could then be used to
interpret the whole verse. The resulting interpretation was seen as the proper
interpretation of the verse. There was no awareness of levels of interpretation.[16] However, in the allegory of the soul, there is an awareness that the
allegorical interpretation is not simply a different interpretation but involves
a different *level* of interpretation. Because of this, particular details in the
biblical text serve two functions. First they point to a different, that is,
allegorical, level of interpretation and then, secondly, to a specific interpretation at that level. This development can best be illustrated by taking the
example of God's "planting" the Garden of Eden (Gen 2:8).

> This description is, I think intended symbolically (συμβολικῶς) rather than
> literally (κυρίως); for never yet have trees of life or of understanding appeared
> on earth, nor is it likely that they will appear hereafter. No, Moses evidently
> signifies (αἰνίττεται) by the garden the ruling power of the soul which is full of
> countless opinions, as it might be of plants; and by the tree of life he signifies
> reverence toward God, the greatest of the virtues by means of which the soul

---

[14] The allegory of the soul is mentioned in *L. A.* 1.42, which is an interpretation of Gen
2:7. This reflects Philo's attempt to introduce the allegory of the soul into the interpretation of
Gen 2:7 from his allegorical interpretation of the fall. *L. A.* 1.42 is one of the subordinate
interpretations of Gen 2:7; the main interpretation (*L. A.* 1.31–32) is not part of the allegory of
the soul.

[15] The description of the garden and of God's placing the man (or men) in the garden is
the area in which literal interpretations of the creation of man overlap with allegorical interpretations of the fall. That is why, at this point, one has Philo subtly moving from the literal to
the allegorical level of interpretation.

[16] Chapter III, 42–44; Chapter IV, section E; Chapter V, 129–32.

attains to immortality; while by the tree that is cognisant of good and evil things he signifies moral prudence. (*Op.* 154.)

The peculiar detail in Gen 2:8 that Philo found absurd was the description of the trees as "trees of life and understanding." This peculiarity first forces him to an allegorical level of interpretation, that is, one which is on the symbolic level (συμβολικῶς). The same peculiarity then leads him to say what specifically the trees are symbols of. He then suggests that Moses is signifying (αἰνίττεται) by the tree of life the virtue of reverence and by the tree of understanding the virtue of prudence. In this type of interpretation, the crucial detail in the text points not only to a specific interpretation but also to a level of interpretation that lies beneath the surface of the text. This same basic technique is used to justify the allegorical interpretation of both the serpent (*Op.* 157) and the woman (*L. A.* 2.19–25).

Philo twice refers to these textual details as "opportunities" or "invitations" (ἀφορμαί) to allegory (*Plant.* 36; *Conf.* 191). As Jean Pépin has pointed out, these invitations to allegory are of various sorts. Some are etymological (e.g., *Det.* 15–17); others are based on an "error" in the literal text (e.g., *Som.* 2.246); still others are based on paradoxical and absurd details in the text (e.g., *Agr.* 130–131).[17] In a sense these allegorical interpretations, since they make use of particular details in the biblical text, use techniques similar to those used in previous interpretations. The techniques, however, when used in an allegorical interpretation, are understood differently. They now point not only to a specific interpretation of a detail in the text but also to a different level of interpretation for the whole passage. The techniques are the same but they function differently.

B. *The Allegory of the Soul*

Philo's interpretation of the creation of man reflects two very significant shifts in interpretation. The first of these shifts is the introduction of the allegory of the soul. Up until this point in the history of the interpretation of the creation of man, the figures in the text of Genesis have been understood as figures in the external world. That world may have been either the heavenly, intelligible world or the earthly, sensible world, but it still was the external world. A qualitative change, however, takes place when the earthly composite *man* becomes the earthy *mind*. This becomes much clearer when one realizes that Adam, the earthly mind, is not alone. Eve, his wife, is interpreted as sense perception (*Op.* 165; *L. A.* 2.19–48), and the serpent is interpreted as pleasure (*Op.* 157; *L. A.* 1.71–77). In addition, the wild ani-

---

[17] Pépin, "Remarques sur la théorie de l'exégèse allégorique chez Philon," 162–67.

mals created in Gen 2:19 are interpreted as the passions (*L. A.* 2.9–13). Finally the Garden of Paradise and the tree of life become symbols of wisdom and virtue after which the earthly mind should strive. The story of the fall in Genesis 3 is interpreted as a struggle between mind (man) and pleasure (the serpent) in which sense perception (woman) is the medium through which pleasure is able to corrupt the mind (*Op.* 165–166).[18] The shift that has taken place is the internalization of the meaning of the text of Genesis. Adam, Eve, and the serpent are no longer understood as figures in the external world but become symbols for parts of each human being, parts which struggle against each other for supremacy.

This specific form of the allegory of the soul in which man is mind, woman sense perception, and the serpent pleasure is part of a much larger pattern of interpretation which dominates a number of Philo's treatises. The pattern is not uniform in the sense that this particular tripartite division appears in every interpretation. On the contrary, there is a great deal of variety in the allegorical interpretations of the biblical texts.[19] An examination of these patterns would take us well beyond the bounds of this study. But what seems constant in these patterns is the attempt to interpret the events of the external world described in the biblical text in terms of the conflicts within the human *soul* in its striving toward virtue and wisdom or in its corruption by vice.[20] This particular allegory of the soul also involves the sense of an almost mystical enlightenment of the soul by God through the medium of the *Logos* or of Wisdom.[21]

Philo himself is quite conscious of the fact that the allegory of the soul forms a distinct pattern of interpretation. In the interpretation of the crea-

---

[18] There is an earlier, pre-Philonic interpretation of the fall in which Adam and Eve were interpreted as figures of the external world. This interpretation appears in *Op.* 151–52, 156, 167–70a and in the literal interpretations of *Q. G.* 1.26–53. The "fall" results from the love, desire, and pleasure which characterize the relationship between the man and the woman.

[19] The variety within Philo's allegorical interpretations can be seen by simply looking through the index of names in *Philo* (LCL), 10.269–433. While Philo probably knew little if any Hebrew, he seems to have made use of an *onomastikon*, which contained a list of Hebrew proper names and their putative etymologies. See D. Rokeah, "A New Onomasticon Fragment from Oxyrhynchus and Philo's Etymologies," *JTS* (1968) 70–82; S. Sandmel, "Philo's Knowledge of Hebrew," *SP* (1978) 107–112.

[20] The centrality of the allegory of the soul for Philo has been emphasized by P. Boyancé, "Etudes philoniennes," *REG* 76 (1963) 68; and by J. Daniélou, *Philon d'Alexandrie* (Paris: Arthème Fayard, 1958) 135, 137.

[21] See Wlosok, *Laktanz und die philosophische Gnosis*, 76–107. Wlosok does not distinguish the varius levels of interpretation found in Philo. Nevertheless, these pages are a good description of Philo's allegory of the soul. See also Christiansen, *Die Technik der allegorischen Auslegungswissenschaft bei Philon von Alexandrien*, 134–71.

tion account, only at this level of interpretation does the technical vocabulary of allegory appear. Terms such as ἀλληγορία, ὑπόνοια, σύμβολον are limited to those interpretations which refer to the allegory of the soul.[22] This is true not only of the passages which are interpretations of specific verses from Genesis 1–3; it includes those passages in *De Opificio Mundi* and *Legum Allegoriae* I–III which involve the interpretation of biblical passages other than Genesis 1–3.[23] Philo, in general, uses the technical vocabulary of allegory in his treatises to refer to the internalization of the meaning of the text connected with the allegory of the soul.[24] The same holds true for the *Questions and Answers on Genesis and Exodus.* Those answers characterized as allegorical are almost always part of the allegory of the soul.[25]

[22] ἀλληγορεῖν	*L. A.* 2.5, 10; *L. A.* 3.60
ἀλληγορία	*Op.* 157
ὑπόνοια	*Op.* 157
συμβολικός	*Op.* 154; *L. A.* 1.1, 21, 68, 72; *L. A.* 2.72; *L. A.* 3.159
σύμβολον	*Op.* 157; *L. A.* 1.26, 58, 97; *L. A.* 3.24, 248
τροπικός	*L. A.* 1.45; *L. A.* 2.14
[23] ἀλληγορεῖν	*L. A.* 3.238
ἀλληγορία	*L.A.* 3.236
συμβολικός	*Op.* 164; *L. A.* 2.27; *L. A.* 3.93
σύμβολον	*L. A.* 1.80; *L. A.* 2.89; *L. A.* 3.45, 167, 176, 232

[24] When one examines those passages in Philo which are explicitly identified as allegorical by the use of allegorical terminology (i.e. ἀλλεγορεῖν, ὑπόνοια, συμβολικός, σύμβολον, τροπικός, αἰνίττεσθαι), almost all of these passages have to do with the allegory of the soul. There are a variety of interpretations at this level but the central element of the allegory remains the soul and its fate. The major exception to this is the description of the temple (*Mos.* 2.66–108, 136–40) and the high priest's garments (*Mos.* 2.109–35). In these passages, allegorical terminology (especially σύμβολον) is used to give a cosmic interpretation in which there is little reference to the human soul. These passages, however, must be distinguished from other allegorical interpretations found in Philo. They are examples of a phenomenon common during the Hellenistic and Roman periods in which temples were seen as symbols of the cosmos and vice versa (e.g., Seneca, *Ben.* 7.7.3; Cicero, *Rep.* 3.14; Wis 9:8; 18:24; Josephus, *Ant.* 3.179–87; Heb 8:1–13). It reflects the spiritualization of cult that was taking place during this period (see Festugière, *La Révélation d'Hermès Trismégiste,* 2.234–38). From Josephus (*Ant.* 3.179–87) and Wis 9:8; 18:24, one becomes aware that Philo's interpretation of the temple and the high priest's garments is more of a commonplace, even among Jewish interpreters, than it is an integral part of Philo's own concept of allegory. This development, although not unrelated to other sorts of allegory, is independent of them. The allegorization of the temple and the high priest's garments represents the allegorization of cultic practices. The fact that those cultic buildings and practices are described in a text is irrelevant to the allegory; they could have been allegorized even had there been no text. This is quite different from either Philo's allegory of the soul or from Stoic and Platonic allegories of Homer. These are essentially allegorical interpretations of a text; without the text there would be no allegory.

[25] One of these exceptions is found in *Q. G.* 1.10 in which five explanations of the "tree of life" (Gen 2:9) are given: (1) the earth; (2) the seven circles in the heaven; (3) the sun; (4) the government exercised by the soul; (5) the virtue of piety. Of these five, the first three are not

When Philo claims, then, that an interpretation is allegorical, he usually means something quite specific, that is, the allegory of the soul. The use of allegorical terminology to refer almost exclusively to the allegory of the soul is consistent with what we have seen of previous interpretations. Previous interpreters of the creation account did not use allegorical terminology to describe what they were doing. Although the techniques of allegorical interpretation were used at previous levels of interpretation, the terminology was not. In other words, previous interpreters of the creation account gave no indication that they thought of their interpretations *as* allegorical.[26]

Previous levels of the interpretation of the creation of man drew on the philosophical, especially the Platonic, thought of the period. The same is true for the allegory of the soul, both in terms of content and in terms of pattern.

Philo is working with a tripartite division of the soul in these interpretations: mind (νοῦς), sense perception (αἴσθησις), and the passions (τὰ πάθη). Of the passions, pleasure (ἡδονή) is seen as the starting-point (ἀρχή) and the foundation (θεμέλιος) of the other passions, and so the serpent is seen as a symbol of this particular passion (*L. A.* 3.113). This division of the human soul is not a common Platonic formulation, not even in the *Timaeus*. The division of the soul in the *Timaeus* is not altogether consistent. At times, the division seems to be tripartite: the divine ruling part (θεῖον ἡγεμοῦν) (*Tim.* 41c); the spirited part (θυμός) situated around the heart (*Tim.* 69d–70d); and the appetitive part (τὸ ἐπιθυμητικόν) situated in the belly (*Tim.* 70d–72b). At other times the basic division seems to be bipartite, a division between the immortal part of the soul (the divine ruling part) and the mortal parts of the soul (these would include both the spirited and the appetitive parts).[27] However, in the description of the soul being joined with

directly part of the allegory of the soul. Rather they are much closer to the physical allegory of the Stoics. Interestingly enough, these cosmological allegories are introduced only in conjunction with the allegory of the soul, that is, with interpretations four and five. This same phenomenon occurs in *Som.* 1.133–49, an interpretation of Jacob's ladder (Gen 28:12). In *Som.* 1.133–45 the ladder is interpreted as a figurative (συμβολικῶς) name for air. Again this is quite close to the physical allegory of the Stoics. Yet it is then joined to an allegory of the soul (*Som.* 1.146–49). Jewish interpreters were undoubtedly aware of Stoic allegory and had been so for generations before Philo. But it seems that only with the development of the allegory of the soul were Jewish interpreters willing to accept certain *explicitly* allegorical Stoic interpretations and then only in conjunction with the allegory of the soul. Only in this way can one explain the tremendous emphasis on the allegory of the soul and the occasional use of elements of the physical allegories of the Stoics.

26 Chapter III, 42–44; Chapter IV, 98–99; Chapter V, 130–32.

27 See *Tim.* 41c; 69d. Both of these divisions differ from the division found in the *Republic*. There the division is between the rational part (τὸ λογιστικόν), the spirited part (τὸ θυμοει-

the body, a division is mentioned which is very close to that used by Philo. After the Demiurge has formed human souls (ψυχαί), he shows them the laws of fate (νόμοι εἰμαρμένοι). Among those laws are those concerned with being joined to a body and how the soul should act when united with a body.

> Whenever, therefore, they (the souls) should of necessity have been implanted in bodies, and of their bodies some part should always be coming in and some part passing out, there must needs be innate in them, first, sense perception (αἴσθη-σις), the same for all, arising from violent passions (παθήματα); second, desire (ἔρως) blended with pleasure (ἡδονή) and pain (λύπη), and besides these fear (φόβος) and anger (θυμός) and all that accompany these and all that are of a contrary nature. And if they (the souls) should master these, they would live in righteousness; if they were mastered by them, in unrighteousness. (*Tim.* 42a–b.)[28]

Philo has quite naturally identified the soul from this passage of the *Timaeus* with mind (νοῦς).[29] The other two divisions found in Philo (sense perception and the passions) are the same as those found in this description from the *Timaeus*. In addition, this division, while not common among Middle Platonists either, also appears in Albinus' *Didaskalikos*, a document which has a number of elements in common with the interpretations found in Philo. This section of the *Didaskalikos* is also interpreting *Tim.* 42a–b.

> After he (the Demiurge) had mounted them (the souls), as it were, on a chariot (i.e., an appropriate star), he explained to them, in the manner of a lawgiver, the laws of destiny so that he might not be responsible for the fact that the mortal passions (τὰ πάθη) grow up from the body, first sense perception (αἴσθησις) and then pleasure (ἡδονή) and pain (λύπη) as well as fear (φόβος) and anger (θυμός). (*Didaskalikos* XVI, p. 172, 6–10.)

Although both sense perception and the other four passions are collectively referred to as passions (πάθη), sense perception is distinguished from the other four. Philo's interpretation of man as mind, woman as sense perception, and the serpent as pleasure, then, is the allegorical equivalent of an acceptable, although not common, Middle Platonic interpretation of Plato's *Timaeus*.

Analogies to this pattern of allegorical interpretation are harder to find. The allegories found in Heraclitus, Cornutus, and Pseudo-Plutarch are basi-

δές), and the affective part (τὸ ἐπιθυμητικόν) (*Rep.* 434d–441c). In addition, in the *Republic*, all three parts, and not simply the rational part, are immortal. See A. Graeser, *Probleme der platonischen Seelenteilungslehre* (Zetemata 47; Munich: C. H. Beck, 1969).

[28] Translation from Cornford, 143.

[29] The notion that mind (νοῦς) is the highest part of the soul is already in the *Timaeus* (30b). Various philosophical schools used the term to indicate the highest faculty of man, although each conceived of that faculty differently.

cally Stoic and, more importantly, do not contain interpretations of Homer in which the meaning of the Homeric text becomes an allegory of the soul. In general, these Stoic interpretations are either physical or moral allegories.[30] In physical allegories, the events described are interpreted as the interaction of elements of the physical universe. For example, Apollo shooting his arrows at the Greek ships is intepreted as a plague.[31] In moral allegories, the gods and goddesses represent virtues, but the human figures in the story are not interpreted as aspects of the human soul but rather maintain their own identity. For instance, Athena may be a symbol of wisdom but Achilles does not become a symbol of anger.[32]

Rather, Philo's allegory of the soul is similar to Neoplatonic allegories which cluster around the figure of Odysseus. As Félix Buffière has pointed out, Philo's allegory of the soul "corresponds to the tendency of Neo-platonists who, in their exegesis of Homer, are no longer interested in the physical meaning but find in the adventures of Ulysses the mystical history of the soul on its way to its true homeland."[33] In such interpretations of the *Odyssey*, Odysseus becomes a symbol of the soul imprisoned in the body and his wanderings become symbols for the soul's search to escape from the body and return to its home beyond the material world.[34] As in Philo's allegory of the soul, the Neoplatonic interpreters of the *Odyssey* no longer take the text

---

[30] There is a possible exception, and that is found in Heraclitus, *Quaes. Hom.* 70.1–13. In this section of Heraclitus, the figure of Odysseus comes close to being a symbol for the soul's journey toward virtue. Yet even here, Odysseus is not a symbol of something else. Rather he remains someone who is an ethical ideal; he does not become a symbol for the soul. In *Quaes. Hom.* 70.8, Odysseus' encounter with the dead is described as a descent of prudence (φρόνησις) into the underworld, lest anything remain unexplored. Yet this seems to mean nothing more than that Odysseus, the sage, wanted to know everything, even what was in Hades. See Buffière, *Les mythes d'Homère et la pensée grecque*, 377–86.

[31] *Quaes. Hom.* 6–16.

[32] Ibid., 17–20. Other examples are found in E. Stein, *Die allegorische Exegese des Philo aus Alexandria* (BZAW 51; Giessen: Töpelmann, 1929) 4–6.

[33] Buffière, *Les mythes d'Homère et la pensée grecque*, 39. The role played by Stoic allegory in Philo's allegorical interpretations has been overemphasized by E. Brehier (*Les idées philosophiques et religieuses de Philon d'Alexandrie* [2nd ed.; Paris: Vrin, 1925] 37–39). Brehier (39–43) also points out the similarities of Philo's allegory to that of the *Cebetis Tabula*, a Platonic/Pythagorean work, probably of the first century A.D. The *Cebetis Tabula* is a description and interpretation of a dedicatory plaque placed in a temple. However, the interpretation of the figures on the plaque is in terms of various virtues and vices encountered in one's search for true knowledge. The interpretation of the plaque is not strictly speaking an allegory of the soul since the term "soul" appears nowhere in the document. See R. Joly, *Le Tableau de Cébès* (Coll. Latomus 61; Brussels: Latomus, 1963); and T. Sinko, "De lineamentis platonicis in Cebetis q.v. tabula," *Eos* 45 (1951), 3–31.

[34] Buffière, *Les mythes d'Homère et la pensée grecque*, 413–18.

to refer to events in the external world but concentrate on the internal struggle of every human soul to transcend the material world and the vices connected with it.

While the Neoplatonists developed this type of interpretation of Homer most fully, they were by no means the first to interpret the *Odyssey* in this way. Numenius (fl. A.D. 150) seems to have interpreted the *Odyssey* as an allegory of the soul.[35] However, the most interesting example of this type of allegory for understanding Philo is found in Plutarch's *Questiones Convivales 9*. During a conversation about the relationship of the Muses to the Sirens, Plutarch's teacher M. Annius Ammonius (fl. A.D. 65) talks of the interpretation of the encounter in the *Odyssey* between Odysseus and the Sirens.[36]

> Now Homer's Sirens, it is true, frighten us, inconsistently with the (Platonic) myth; but the poet too conveyed a truth symbolically (αἰνίττεσθαι), namely that the power of their music is not inhuman or destructive; as *souls* (ψυχαί) depart from this world to the next, so it seems, and drift uncertainly after death, it (the power of their music) creates in them a passionate love for the heavenly and divine, and forgetfulness of mortality; it possesses them and enchants them with its spell, so that in joyfulness they follow the Sirens and join them in their circuits. Here on earth a kind of faint echo of that music reaches us, and appealing to our *souls* (ψυχαί) through the medium of words, reminds them of what they experience in an earlier existence. The ears of most souls, however, are plastered over and blocked up, not with wax, but with carnal obstructions and passions (σάρκινα ἐμφράγματα καὶ πάθη). But any soul that through innate gifts is aware of this echo, and remembers that other world, suffers what falls in no way short of the very maddest passions of love, longing and yearning to break the tie with the body but unable to do so. (*Quest. Conv.* 9.14.6)[37]

In this interpretation, the Sirens are the heavenly spheres and their music is the music of the heavenly spheres which either directly attracts the souls upward after their deaths or indirectly reminds them, even while they are in their bodies, of a better mode of existence. Odysseus and his companions are no longer figures of the external world; they have become symbols of souls whose ability to "hear" the harmony of the heavenly spheres is obstructed by being bound to bodies and their passions, symbolized by the wax in their ears. This Homeric allegory is quite similar to the allegory of the soul in Philo.

[35] Numenius, Frg. 33 (des Places).

[36] *Od.* 12.39–54, 153–200.

[37] Translated by F. H. Sandback, *Plutarch's Moralia IX* (LCL) (Cambridge: Harvard University Press, 1961) 279–80 (slightly altered). This comparison with Philo has been emphasized by Boyancé, "Etudes philoniennes," 74–75.

This type of interpretation of the *Odyssey* is quite Platonic in the sense that the patterns of thought used in these interpretations are derived from Plato. Both the harmony of the spheres and the identification of the Sirens with the heavenly spheres and their music are found in Plato.[38] It is not at all accidental, then, that Plutarch places this interpretation on the lips of his teacher, M. Annius Ammonius, a Platonist with whom Plutarch studied in Athens but who was a native of Egypt, probably of Alexandria.[39]

This however is not our only link to Alexandria around the time of Philo. Fragments of basically the same interpretation of the Sirens episode from the *Odyssey* are found in Philo. Philo refers to this interpretation of the *Odyssey* in a discussion of Abraham's sacrifice of a turtle-dove and a dove (Gen 15:9). The two birds are taken as symbols of the harmonious music of the heavenly spheres. He then goes on to mention Homer.

> For it (the music of the heavenly spheres) rouses to madness those who hear it, and produces in the *soul* an indescribable and unrestrained pleasure. It causes them to despise food and drink and to die an untimely death through hunger in their desire for the song. For did not the singing of the Sirens, as Homer says, so violently summon listeners that they forgot their country, their home, their friends and necessary foods? And would not that most perfect and most harmonious and truly heavenly music, when it strikes the organ of hearing, compel them to go mad and to be frenzied? (*Q. G.* 3.3.)

This same Homeric interpretation is alluded to in *Som.* 1.35–36:

> For it is in the heaven and in the mind (νοῦς) that capacity resides to set forth in solemn strains hymns of praise and blessing in honor of the Father who is the author of our being. For man is the recipient of a privilege which gives him distinction beyond other living creatures, that, namely, of worshipping him that is; while the heaven is ever melodious, producing, as the heavenly bodies go through their movements, the full and perfect harmony. If the sound of it ever reached our ears, there would be produced irrepressible yearnings, frantic longings, wild ceaseless passionate desires, compelling to abstain even from necessary food, for no longer should we take in nourishment from meat and drink through the throat after the fashion of mortals, but, as beings awaiting immortality, from inspired strains of perfect melody coming to us through our ears. To such strains it is said that Moses was listening, when, having laid aside his body (ἀσώματος γινόμενος), for forty days and as many nights he touched neither bread nor water at all (Exod 24:18).

---

[38] *Tim.* 35b–36b; *Rep.* X. 617b–d.

[39] Eunapius, *VS* 454. For an analysis of the scant evidence that we have concerning Ammonius, see C. P. Jones, "The Teacher of Plutarch," *Harvard Studies in Classical Philology* 71 (1966) 205–13.

Although fragmentary, the outline of the Homeric interpretation that Philo is aware of is fairly clear and is similar to the one found in Plutarch. The Sirens are the heavenly spheres which draw the soul upward and cause it to forget the sphere of the material. As the comparison with Moses shows (*Som.* 1.36), this harkening to the music of the heavenly spheres is connected with laying aside the body, a conception also found in Plutarch's interpretation.[40] While not identical, the interpretations in Plutarch and in Philo involve the same pattern of interpretation in which the figures in the narrative become symbols for elements of the soul.[41]

This comparison with Plutarch indicates that Philo is aware of Middle Platonic interpretations of the *Odyssey*, interpretations whose patterns are basically the same as those of his own allegory of the soul. These patterns of interpretation of Homer's *Odyssey* may well have served as models for his own allegorical pattern of interpretation, just as earlier Stoic interpretations had served as models for some of his predecessors.[42] These Middle Platonic alllegories may also help us to understand why it is only at the level of Philo's allegory of the soul that we find the technical vocabulary of allegory. In connection with the Platonic interpretations analyzed in Chapters IV and V, I mentioned that one of the reasons that those Platonic interpretations of the creation of man lacked the technical terms of allegory may have been that Alexandria was the center of opposition to Stoic allegory, an opposition that Platonists (following Plato and the New Academy) probably shared.[43] However, the use of the allegorical interpretation of the Sirens episode by both Philo and Plutarch's teacher, Ammonius, indicates that, by the early first century A.D., Alexandrian Middle Platonists had developed a distinct pattern of allegorical interpretation of their own, the allegory of the soul.[44] The

---

[40] Plutarch, *Quaest. Conv.* 9. 14.6.

[41] Buffière (*Les mythes d'Homère et la pensée grecque*, 480) suggests that both Philo and Plutarch may have drawn on the same source for their interpretations, a commentary on Plato's *Phaedrus* (244c). Given the fragmentary character of the interpretations in both Philo and Plutarch, this can remain only a possibility.

[42] Chapter III, 42–44; Chapter IV, 98–99; Chapter V, 130–32.

[43] Pépin, *Mythe et allégorie*, 112–24, 138–43.

[44] Boyancé ("Etudes philoniennes," 73–74) wants to push this pattern of interpretation back to the first half of the first century B.C. He cites a passage from Cicero's *De finibus* (5.48–49) in which Calpurnius Piso, while describing the doctrine of Antiochus, offers the Sirens episode in the Odyssey as an example of the human desire for learning. Boyancé would like to link this passage from Cicero with those from Philo and Plutarch. The interpretation, however, as it is found in Cicero differs in one very crucial respect from both Philo and Plutarch. In Cicero, the interpretation does not involve any allegory of the soul. Rather, the story is about men (*homines*) who were attracted to the rocks by the desire for learning (*discendi cupiditate*), for the Sirens offer knowledge (*scientia*). Cicero, then, does not, by the middle of the

development of this new allegorical pattern also allowed them to make use of allegorical terminology. In the wake of such a development, a Jewish interpreter like Philo could then take up the use of *explicitly* allegorical interpretations, especially since Philo himself was deeply influenced by Alexandrian Middle Platonism. It is important, however, to keep in mind that the extent and the complexity of Philo's allegory of the soul goes well beyond any of the Middle Platonic allegories of the *Odyssey*.[45] While the model for the allegory of the soul was derived from Middle Platonic allegories of the *Odyssey*, its development by Philo and other Jewish allegorical interpreters was quite original and the result of their own reflections on the biblical text.

C. *Levels of Interpretation*

The second significant shift that takes place at this level of interpretation is Philo's attempt to maintain that there are different levels of interpretation, the literal and the allegorical, and that both types of interpretation are, for the most part, valid modes of interpretation. This appears most clearly in the *Questions and Answers on Genesis and Exodus*. In both of these works, literal and allegorical interpretations lie side by side. Philo is obviously more interested in the allegorical interpretations; but, for the most part, the literal interpretations are also considered valid and valuable. The same is true of the interpretations of Genesis 1–3 found in *De Opificio Mundi* and *Legum Allegoriae*. Of the twenty-seven times that allegorical terms appear, only five involve the rejection of a non-allegorical interpretation.[46] The introduction of the allegory of the soul does not lead Philo to reject other sorts of interpretation.

From the way in which allegorical interpretations were used in both patristic and medieval exegesis, Philo's attempt to maintain the overall validity of both allegorical and non-allegorical interpretation seems more obvious to us than it must have seemed to Philo.[47] Allegory, as it was practiced both in the Stoic interpretations of Homer and in the Middle Platonic interpretations of the *Odyssey*, did not include the recognition of different levels of

---

first century B.C., know of an allegorical interpretation of the Sirens episode in the *Odyssey*. Had he known of it, he probably would have made use of it in this passage. The passage in *De finibus* 5.48–49 is about the various parts of the soul (*partes animi*), and so an interpretation of the *Odyssey* which involved an allegory of the *soul* would have been much more appropriate than the interpretation that Cicero did offer.

[45] While the extant Middle Platonic allegories of the Odyssey are fragmentary, this type of allegorization seems to have come into its own only with Numenius in the middle of the second century A.D. See Buffière, *Les mythes d'Homère et la pensée grecque*, 413–18.

[46] *Op.* 154, 157, 164; *L. A.* 3.236, 238.

[47] See H. de Lubac, *Exégèse médiévale* (4 vols.; Paris: Aubier, 1959–64).

interpretation.[48] Rather an allegorical interpretation involved either a rejection of the literal interpretation or at least complete obliviousness to that level. Philo is the earliest example that we have of a writer who tries to maintain the validity of both the allegorical and the non-allegorical levels of interpretation.

Philo's attempt to maintain the validity of both types of interpretation also involved him in controversy. The position which Philo takes in these controversies clarifies his attitude toward previous interpretations of the creation of man and the way in which he made use of them. On the one hand, Philo argues against those who, while interpreting the biblical text allegorically, reject the validity of the literal interpretation. Philo argues this most clearly in *Mig.* 89–93:

> There are some who, regarding laws in their literal sense (ῥητοὶ νόμοι) as symbols (σύμβολα) of matters belonging to the intellect, are overpunctilious about the latter, while treating the former with easy-going neglect. Such men I for my part should blame for handling the matter in too easy and offhand a manner. They ought to have given careful attention to both aims, to a more full and exact investigation of what is not seen and in what is seen to be stewards without reproach.
>
> As it is, as though they were living alone by themselves in a wilderness, or as though they had become disembodied souls, and knew neither city nor village nor household nor any company of human beings at all, overlooking all that the mass of men regard, they explore reality in its naked absoluteness. These men are taught by the sacred word to have thought for good repute, and to let nothing go that is part of the customs fixed by divinely inspired men (θεσπέσιοι) greater than those of our time.
>
> It is quite true that the Seventh Day is meant to teach the power of the unoriginate and the non-action of created beings. But let us not for this reason abrogate the laws laid down for its observance, and light fires or till the ground or carry loads or institute proceedings in court or act as jurors or demand the restoration of deposits or recover loans, or do anything else that we are permitted to do as well on days that are not festival seasons.
>
> It is true also that the keeping of festivals is a symbol of gladness of soul (ψυχικὴ εὐφροσύνη) and of thankfulness to God, but we should not for this reason turn our backs on the general gatherings of the year's seasons.
>
> It is true that receiving circumcision does indeed portray the excision of pleasure (ἡδονή) and all passions (πάθη), and the putting away of impious conceit, under which the mind (ὁ νοῦς) supposed that it was capable of begetting by its own power. But let us not on this account repeal the law laid down for circumcising.

---

[48] J. Tate, "Plato and Allegorical Interpretation," *Classical Quarterly* 23 (1929) 144–45.

Why, we shall be ignoring the sanctity of the Temple and a thousand other things, if we are going to pay heed to nothing except what is shewn us by the inner meaning of things (δι' ὑπονοιῶν). Nay, we should look on all these outward observances as resembling the body, and their inner meanings as resembling the soul. It follows that, exactly as we have to take thought for the body, because it is the abode of the soul, so we must pay heed to the laws in their literal sense (ῥητοὶ νόμοι). If we keep and observe these, we shall gain a clearer conception of those things of which these are the symbols (σύμβολα); and besides that we shall not incur the censure of the many and the charges they are sure to bring against us.

Philo condemns those who want to desert an observance of the Mosaic law based on a literal interpretation. In the three cases which he cites, Philo does not disagree with the allegorical interpretations of the law but rather with the claim that the allegorical interpretation allows one to ignore the literal interpretation of the law. In fact all three interpretations are consistent with Philo's allegory of the soul.[49] Wolfson refers to these interpreters as "extreme allegorists." By that he means that, by their excessive use of philosophic interpretation, they rejected the literal meaning of the law altogether.[50] This characterization is misleading. In the first place, their allegories are no more "extreme" than are those of Philo himself. Secondly, and more importantly, they simply reflect the normal practice of Greek allegory, a practice in which the allegorical interpretation involves at least ignoring the literal meaning of the text and most of the time involves rejecting the literal meaning outright. Put another way, it is not they who have carried a process of interpretation to extremes but Philo who has broken with the normal practice of allegorical interpretation and has maintained the validity and value of the literal interpretation as well.[51]

---

[49] The connection with the allegory of the soul is clearest in the second and third examples, where circumcision is a symbol of the excision of pleasure from the *soul* (cf. *Spec.* 1.8ff.) and the celebration of the festivals is a symbol of the *soul's* rejoicing. In both cases, the Mosaic law is interpreted in terms of what it means for the soul. The parallel with the other two examples indicates that what is allegorical in the first example is not the interpretation of the seventh day of creation as such but the interpretation of the meaning of the fourth commandment, the keeping of the Sabbath. What is allegorical is that the cessation from bodily work is a symbol meant to remind the soul that God alone is truly active. *Post.* 33–39, an interpretation in which Cain's marriage and his begetting of Enoch (Gen 4:17) are symbols of the impious *mind's* belief that it is the originator of its own activities, indicates that this problem was of concern to Philo in his allegory of the soul (cf. *L. A.* 2.31–32, 46–48, 68–69; *L. A.* 3.32–35).

[50] Wolfson, *Philo*, 1.66.

[51] Philo was probably not the only Jewish interpreter to maintain the validity of both levels of interpretation. He does mention other allegorical interpreters without indicating that they rejected the literal level of interpretation (*Post.* 7; *Abr.* 99; *Jos.* 151; *Spec.* 3.178). The way in which he refers to them in *Abr.* 99, *Jos.* 151, and *Spec.* 3.178 suggests that they are his

The reason that Philo wants to maintain the value of both types of interpretation is that without the literal interpretation there would be no way to maintain Judaism as a community. Judaism would be reduced to a series of isolated individuals. The justification that Philo gives for maintaining the validity of the literal interpretations is that they are the work of divinely inspired men (θεσπέσιοι).[52] As is clear from his other uses of this term, Philo includes both literal and allegorical interpreters in the category of θεσπέσιοι.[53] But in *Mig.* 89–93 he is emphasizing the inspired character of the *literal* level of interpretation. Literal interpretations are to be respected because they, like allegorical interpretations, are the work of divinely inspired men.

On the other hand, Philo is forced to argue against those who were unwilling to admit the validity of an allegorical interpretation of the text. For instance, in *Conf.* 190 while admitting the value of the literal interpreta-

---

contemporaries. In all three cases Philo says that he has heard (ἤκουσα) these interpreters himself rather than simply saying that "some have said . . .", which is his usual practice. This too suggests that the use of the alleogry of the soul was a quite recent development. In view of this fact, some of the allegorical interpretations found in Philo may have originated with a group of Jewish interpreters of which Philo was a member rather than with Philo himself. In the case of the allegorical interpretation of the fall, however, Philo gives no indication that this particular interpretation of Genesis 2–3 is derived from some other interpreter. On the contrary, at several points in the *Questions and Answers on Genesis*, he seems to indicate that the interpretation is his own (*Q. G.* 1.8, 13, 31, 41). While Philo probably was not the only one to maintain the validity of both levels of interpretation, he certainly seems to have been the most prominent among them.

[52] Strictly speaking, both the literal and the allegorical interpretations mentioned in *Mig.* 89–93 are concerned with *legal* texts. But there is no reason to think that Philo restricted the use of these principles to legal texts alone. In practice, he certainly applies these same principles to narrative texts, that is, he maintains the validity of both allegorical and literal interpretations of these texts.

[53] *Spec.* 1.8, 314; *Spec.* 3.178; *Virt.* 8. The importance of scriptural interpretation by divinely inspired men for Hellenistic Judaism has been emphasized by D. Georgi (*Die Gegner des Paulus im 2. Korintherbrief* [WMANT 11; Neukirchen: Neukirchener Verlag, 1964] 168–82). The investigation of the relationship of these θεσπέσιοι ἄνδρες to the category of "divine man" (θεῖος ἀνήρ) would go well beyond the bounds of this study. What is important for our purposes is that Philo justifies the validity of multiple interpretations of the biblical text by appealing to the divinely inspired character not only of the text but also of its various interpretations. For a discussion of the wider problem of the "divine man" figure, see, in addition to Georgi, R. Reitzenstein, *Die hellenistischen Mysterienreligionen nach ihren Grundgedanken und Wirkungen* (3rd ed.; Leipzig: Teubner, 1927) 12–19, 37–38; Windisch, *Paulus und Christus*, 90–115; L. Bieler, ΘΕΙΟΣ ΑΝΗΡ (1936; rpt. Darmstadt: Wissenschaftliche Buchgesellschaft, 1967); C. Holladay, *Theios Aner in Hellenistic Judaism, A Critique of the Use of This Category in New Testament Christology* (SBL Dissertation Series 40; Missoula: Scholars, 1977) 103–199; D. Tiede, *The Charismatic Figure as Miracle Worker* (SBL Dissertation Series 1; Missoula: Scholars, 1972).

tion of the story of the Tower of Babel as the origin of the diversity of languages (Gen 11:1–9), he exhorts his fellow interpreters to go beyond the literal to an allegorical level in which the story of the Tower of Babel is seen as God's attempt to break up and then annihilate various vices in the soul.[54] Philo argues against those who maintain that there is only one level of interpretation of a biblical text and that that level is the literal level. While it is impossible to tell precisely who these interpreters were, they could well have been those who could accept the kinds of interpretation that we have analyzed in the previous chapters but who would refuse to accept the allegory of the soul. For them, unlike Philo, there was only one level of interpretation, and that level did not involve the allegory of the soul. Philo had to defend his belief in multiple levels of interpretation not only against those who rejected the literal level but also against those who would accept only the literal level.[55]

This understanding of the process of interpretation is also reflected in Philo's *use* of literal interpretations. At first glance his use of literal interpretations seems ambiguous. Although Philo, for the most part, gives an allegorical interpretation alongside other non-allegorical interpretations, at times he does deny the literal interpretation of a specific text and condemns those who maintain it.[56] His attitude becomes clearer when one remembers what he regards as a literal interpretation. Because allegory basically means the allegory of the soul for Philo, interpretations that are not part of the allegory of the soul are literal interpretations. This can be seen in the *Questions and Answers on Genesis and Exodus.* The basic division in each question is between literal interpretations and allegorical interpretations. With very few exceptions, interpretations which are not part of the allegory of the soul fall within the division of literal interpretations. A "literal" interpretation, then, covers a wide variety of interpretations, from very simple, "literalistic" interpretations to sophisticated interpretations which, however, are still not part of the allegory of the soul. Philo uses the term "literal" (ῥητός) to cover both simplistic interpretations which he rejects and more sophisti-

[54] This same kind of attempt to push interpreters beyond the literal to the allegorical level of interpretation is also found in *Sob.* 33; *Conf.* 190, *Jos.* 125, *Deus* 133, *Abr.* 200–36.

[55] M. J. Schroyer, "Alexandrian Jewish Literalists," *JBL* 55 (1936) 261–84. Schroyer's article is valuable because it deals with a large number of passages where the literal interpretation is either rejected or surpassed. However, Schroyer reduces all literal interpreters to the level of simpletons, narrow conservatives, or vilifiers of the law. This is far too simple and unsympathetic a picture of literal interpreters.

[56] E.g., *Op.* 154; *Som.* 1.92–94; *Det.* 13, 95, 155, 167; *Deus* 133; *Cong.* 44; *Plant.* 32; *Agr.* 131; *L. A.* 3.4.

cated, yet still "literal" interpretations which he finds quite acceptable.[57] For instance, in the interpretation of Gen 2:8, God's planting of the garden in Eden, Philo rejects the literal interpretation as blasphemous because God can have no need of a garden. Rather the verse must be taken figuratively (τροπικῶς) to refer to the planting of virtues in the human soul (*L. A.* 1.43–47). Again, Philo rejects a literal interpretation (τὸ ῥητόν) of Gen 2:21–22 which says that God made Eve from Adam's side. Philo claims that it is ridiculous to think that a woman or any human being was ever created from a man's side (*L. A.* 2.19). Rather the text is talking about the origins of sense perception, symbolized by the woman (*L. A.* 2.24). A literal, or better a literalistic, interpretation is to be rejected when it is either blasphemous or ridiculous. The kind of literal interpretation that is rejected by Philo is the kind of interpretation that was rejected by Jewish interpreters as far back as Aristobulus.[58] Such interpretations would be rejected not only by Philo but also by the sophisticated literal interpreters whose explanations of the creation of man were discussed in the previous chapters. However, a more sophisticated, yet in Philo's mind still literal, interpretation is quite easily accepted and placed beside an allegorical interpretation. For instance, Philo can set a literal interpretation of Abraham's migration as the story of a *wise man's* obedience to God's commands next to an allegorical interpretation of the journey of Abraham as the *virtue loving soul's* search for the true God (*Abr.* 68, 88).

Most of the interpretations of the creation of man which we have analyzed lie outside of the allegory of the soul and so, for Philo, would be literal interpretations. One can see this, for instance, when one compares *Q. G.* 1.6 and *Q. G.* 1.8. In both of these passages, the "symbolic" or allegorical interpretation is that Paradise is a symbol of wisdom. In *Q. G.* 1.6 the "literal" meaning of Paradise is that it is a "dense place full of all kinds of trees." This explicitly literal interpretation of Gen 2:8 is continued in *Q. G.* 1.8a:

> Some, believing Paradise to be a garden, have said that since the molded man is sense-perceptible, he therefore rightly goes to a sense-perceptible place. But the man made in his image, is intelligible and invisible, and is in the class of incorporeal species.

---

[57] For the variety of interpretations to which the term "literal" (ῥητός) is applied, see: *L. A.* 2.14; *Agr.* 157; *Ebr.* 130; *Sob.* 65; *Mig.* 89, 93; *Som.* 1.120; *Abr.* 68, 88, 119, 131, 200, 217, 236; *Jos.* 28, 125; *Spec.* 1.200, 287; *Spec.* 2.29, 147, 257; *Spec.* 3.178; *Praem.* 61, 65; *Cont.* 78 (for a positive use of the term); and *L. A.* 2.19; *Det.* 15, 167; *Agr.* 131; *Plant.* 113, *Fug.* 106; *Som.* 1.101, 102, 164 (for a negative use of the term).

[58] See Chapter III, 50–52.

Even though the interpretation in *Q. G.* 1.8a is not explicitly described as "literal," it is set off against the "symbolic" interpretation of *Q. G.* 1.8b (that is, Paradise as a symbol of wisdom) and continues the literal interpretation of Paradise in *Q. G.* 1.6 as a real garden. The interpretation found in *Q. G.* 1.8a which involves the distinction between the heavenly man created in Gen 1:27 and the earthly man created in Gen 2:7 falls, then, within the area of a literal interpretation.

One must also keep in mind that the allegorical method that Philo used was derived from Greek allegory. That method functioned in such a way that the specific detail in the text that pointed to an allegorical level of interpretation also served to rule out any literal interpretation. Philo is thus using a method of interpretation that works against his own belief in the inspired character of the literal level of interpretation. At times this procedure gives Philo's allegorical interpretations the appearance of rejecting more of the literal interpretation than he actually does.

That fact is perhaps best illustrated by Philo's allegorical interpretation of the serpent as a symbol of pleasure (*Op.* 157–164). In this interpretation, Philo *seems* to be seizing on the absurdity of a talking serpent (*Op.* 156) in order to move to the level of the allegory of the soul in which the serpent is a symbol of pleasure (*Op.* 157). This movement to the allegorical level seems to involve the rejection of the literal interpretation found in *Op.* 156.

> It is said that *in olden times the venomous earthborn crawling thing could send forth a man's voice*, and that one day it approached the wife of the first man and upbraided her for her irresoluteness and excessive scrupulosity in delaying and hesitating to pluck a fruit most beauteous to behold and most luscious to taste, and most useful into the bargain, since by its means she would have power to recognize things good and evil. She, without looking into the suggestion, prompted by a mind devoid of steadfastness and firm foundation, gave her consent and ate of the fruit, and gave some of it to her husband; this instantly brought them out of a state of simplicity and innocence into one of wickedness. Whereat the Father in anger appointed for them the punishments that were fitting. For their conduct well merited wrath, inasmuch as they had passed by the tree of life immortal, the consummation of virtue, from which they could have gathered an existence long and happy. Yet they chose that fleeting and mortal existence which is not an existence but a period of time full of misery. (*Op.* 156.)

This passage is part of a literal interpretation of the fall in which the man, the woman and the serpent maintain their identities as figures in the external world. It is of a piece with the literal interpretations of the fall found in *Op.* 151–152 and 167–170a. In addition, this literal interpretation is by no means a simple-minded literalistic one. It presents a rather sophisticated analysis of the motivation behind the fall. However, Philo does not reject this literal interpretation of the fall when it appears in *Op.* 151–152 and 167–170a; he *seems* to reject only the notion of the talking serpent mentioned in *Op.* 156. A further complication is that in *Q. G.* 1.32, Philo accepts the same explanation that in days of old serpents could talk, an explanation which he seems to reject in *Op.* 157.

When one looks again at *Op.* 157 with these problems in mind, one notices that Philo mentions nothing specifically as being a "mythical fiction" (μύθου πλάσμα), not even the notion of a talking serpent. In the hands of any Greek allegorist, the notion of a talking serpent would have been precisely the detail that he would have seized on to reject the literal meaning of the text and move to an allegorical interpretation. Philo, however, does not really want to reject the literal interpretation of the fall found in *Op.* 151–152, 156, 167–170a and *Q. G.* 1.32. At the same time, he needs some reason, some "opportunity" (ἀφορμή) offered by the text, which would enable him to move to the allegorical level.[59] So, instead of seizing on the notion of the talking serpent, he simply rejects in very general terms any literal interpretation of Gen 3:1 which would involve a "mythical fiction." This general rejection serves as his "opportunity" to move to the allegorical level. In this way he can hold on to the literal interpretation of the fall of which *Op.* 156 is a part and yet still offer an allegorical interpretation (*Op.* 157). The whole process, however, illustrates the problem that Philo faced in trying to maintain the validity of the literal level of interpretation while making use of an allegorical method that had developed by rejecting that same literal level.

Philo's understanding of the process of interpretation is thus an inclusive one in which several interpretations of the same text are to be considered valid and valuable. In practice, this also extends to different interpretations, *all* of which are at the literal level. For instance, in the *Questions and Answers on Genesis* which deal with Genesis 1–3, Philo not uncommonly mentions *several* valid literal interpretations, with or without an allegorical interpretation.[60] In other words, *several* literal interpretations, in addition to the allegorical interpretation, fall within Philo's notion of inspired interpretations. The biblical text, then, looks rather different to Philo than it did to his predecessors whose work was analyzed in the preceding chapters. The biblical text has a density and depth to it which allows it to be interpreted at several different levels, all of which are valid. This sense of depth and density also allows Philo to bring to bear on a biblical text a number of different interpretations which are of different origins.

---

[59] *Plant.* 36; *Conf.* 191. See Pépin, "Remarques sur la théorie de l'exégèse allegorique chez Philon," 161–62.

[60] *Q.G.* 1.3, 5, 7, 18, 21, 32, 52.

D. *Philo's Use of Previous Interpretations*

Philo's belief in the inspired character of literal interpretations of the biblical text influences the way in which he makes use of previous interpretations of the creation of man. The sense of the biblical text's density allows Philo to treat the literal interpretations of the creation of man differently than his predecessors did. Previous interpreters were aware of working within a tradition and felt a responsibility toward it. Because of this, previous interpretations of the account of the creation of man were preserved intact. In addition, each successive interpretation preserved basically the same Middle Platonic thought structure. Yet each successive interpretation also contained an implicit critique of the previous interpretation. For instance, the interpretation of Gen 1:27 and Gen 2:7 as a description of the creation of two different men involves an implicit critique of the previous interpretation in which these two verses were taken as complementary descriptions of a single act of creation. Both *Op.* 134–135 and *L. A.* 31–32 argue that Gen 1:27 and Gen 2:7 do *not* refer to the creation of the same man but to the creation of two different men, one heavenly and the other earthly.[61] One interpretation seems to have superseded the previous interpretation. There is no indication that these interpreters had a sense that *all* of these interpretations were valid. But the situation changes with Philo. Because Philo thought that all of these interpretations were inspired, all of them could be accepted as valid interpretations. Philo does find some interpretations more congenial than others. These interpretations are basically the Platonic interpretations of the creation of man and especially the allegory of the soul. Yet his own allegory of the soul, for instance, is not a critique of previous interpretations. It is rather an additional interpretation that can be set side by side with other interpretations. Because of this he can make use of other interpretations without revising them to fit in with his own interests or preferences.

Philo's use of previous interpretations becomes clearer when one looks at the way in which he arranged the various interpretations of Gen 1:26–27 and Gen 2:7 in *De Opificio Mundi* and *Legum Allegoriae* 1. The following outline will illustrate his arrangement of previous interpretations.

I. *De Opificio Mundi:*
   A. Gen 1:26–27; *Op.* 69–88

---

[61] One should keep in mind that both Stoic and Middle Platonic allegories of Homer involved a critique of non-allegorical interpretations. Philo is different because he is willing to allow that several different interpretations of the same biblical passage are *all* valid.

1. *Op.* 69–71: Man's mind is made as an image of God; as God is to the universe, man's mind is to his body. (III.A)[62]
2. *Op.* 72–75: What is the meaning of "Let *us* make man"? God's helpers make the lower parts of man so that God is not responsible for the evil man does. (III.A)
   Op. 76: "Generic" man versus "specific" man. (V.B)
3. *Op.* 77–88: Why does God create man last in the order of creation?
   a. *Op.* 77–78: So that all might be prepared for man.
   b. *Op.* 79–81: Had man stayed rational, all would have stayed prepared for him; instead he gave in to pleasure and so now must work.
   c. *Op.* 82: God wanted to unite the beginning of creation (the heaven) and the end of creation (man as a miniature heaven).
   d. *Op.* 83–86: That all animals might be amazed and do him homage.
   e. *Op.* 87–88: Man is not inferior because he was created last. Drivers and pilots are not inferior because they come "after" what they control.
B. Gen 2:7; *Op.* 134–147
   1. *Op.* 134–135: Creation of the earthly man as distinct from the heavenly man of Gen 1:27. (V.B)
   2. *Op.* 136–137: The first earthly man was beautiful in *body*. Three proofs for this:
      a. In the beginning the material was pure and easy to work with.
      b. God chose to use the best clay.
      c. God excelled in skill.
   3. *Op.* 138–139: The first earthly man was beautiful in *soul* because it was a likeness (ἀπεικόνισμα) of the *Logos* and divine spirit was breathed into its face. (IV.C)
   4. *Op.* 140–141: The devolution of man
   5. *Op.* 142–144: Man as a citizen of the world (κοσμοπολίτης).
   6. *Op.* 145–146: Men of later generations have a kinship with their first father because their minds are allied to the *Logos* and are copies (ἐκμαγεῖα) and fragments (ἀποσπάσματα) of the blessed nature and their bodies are allied to the earth. (IV.C)
   7. *Op.* 147: Man is at home among all of the elements.
II. *Legum Allegoriae* 1:
   A. Gen 1:26–27; Missing.[63]
   B. Gen 2:7; *L. A.* 1.31–42
      1. *L. A.* 1.31–32: Creation of the earthly man as distinct from the heavenly man of Gen 1:27 (V.B)

---

[62] The numbers in parentheses refer to the chapters and sections in this study where these passages are analyzed in detail.

[63] See footnote 12.

2. *L. A.* 1:33–42: Four questions about the interpretation of Gen 2:7
   a. *L. A.* 1.34–35: Why was the earthly mind given the divine spirit and
      not the mind made after God's image (Gen 1:27)? He leaves no soul
      barren of virtue and only one into whom real life has been breathed
      can experience virtue. (IV.C)
   b. *L. A.* 1.36–38: What is the meaning of "breathed in"? He breathes
      in "spirit." (III.A)
   c. *L. A.* 1.39–41: What is the meaning of "into the face"? "Physically"
      it refers to the senses; "ethically" it refers to the human mind, which
      is (1) God to the rest of the human being (Exod 7:1); and (2) is,
      unlike the rest of man, created both by (ὑπό) and through (διά) God
      (Gen 2:8). (IV.B)
   d. *L. A.* 1.42: Why is "breath" (πνοή) and not "spirit" (πνεῦμα) used in
      Gen 2:7, especially because Moses knows of the "spirit" borne over
      the waters (Gen 1:2)? "Spirit" belongs to the heavenly mind
      (Gen 1:27) while only "breath" belongs to the earthly mind (Gen
      2:7). (VI.A)

The principle of organization of these interpretations of the creation of
man is that of a series of discrete interpretations grouped around the appropriate biblical verse. This principle of arrangement is most obvious in
Op. 77–78 which contains five different answers to the question of why man
was created last; in *L. A.* 1.33–42 which consists of answers to four different
questions about the interpretation of Gen 2:7; and in *Op.* 136–139 which
consists of proofs for the beauty of the body and soul of the first
earthly man.

However, in each of the three sets of interpretations, there is one main
interpretation, which is then followed by questions about particular aspects
of any given verse. In *Op.* 69–88 the main interpretation of Gen 1:27 is that
man's mind is an image of God. This is then followed by attempts to answer
specific questions, one about the meaning of "Let *us* make man" (*Op.* 72–75)
and the other about the reason why man was created last (*Op.* 77–88). In
Op. 134–147, the main interpretation involves the distinction between the
heavenly man and the earthly man (*Op.* 134–135). It is then followed by a
series of proofs of the beauty of man's body and soul (*Op.* 136–139) and by
interpretations of man's devolution and place in the world (*Op.* 140–147).
Finally, in *L. A.* 1.31–42 the main interpretation again involves the distinction between the heavenly man and the earthly man (*L. A.* 1.31–32) and is
followed by a series of questions and answers about particular aspects of the
interpretation of Gen 2:7 and its relationship to Gen 1:27.

The main interpretation in each of these three cases is Platonic. Stoic
interpretations, on the other hand, such as *L. A.* 1.36–38, 39–41, and
Op. 147, and even partially Stoic interpretations such as *Op.* 138–139 and

Op. 145–146 are in subordinate positions. Even by his arrangement of the various interpretations Philo shows himself part of a Platonizing tradition of interpretation. He also shows his uneasiness about the Stoic interpretations of the creation of man by placing them in subordinate positions. This uneasiness is consistent with the kinds of adjustments that he makes in Stoic interpretations of the creation of man found elsewhere in his works.[64]

Philo also shows his hand by introducing into these interpretations of the creation of man a passage which serves to prepare the reader for the allegory of the soul, which really begins only with the interpretation of Gen 2:8 (*L. A.* 1.43). In *L. A.* 1.42 Philo explains that "spirit" (πνεῦμα) is given only to the "*mind* made according to the image and the idea" (ὁ κατὰ τὴν εἰκόνα γεγονὼς καὶ τὴν ἰδέαν νοῦς) (Gen 1:27) while only "breath" (πνοή) is given to the "*mind* made from matter" (ὁ ἐκ τῆς ὕλης νοῦς) (Gen 2:7).[65] This procedure is also consistent with Philo's technique of introducing into the interpretation of Gen 2:8, 15, 16–17 the distinction between a heavenly mind and an earthly mind rather than a distinction between a heavenly man and an earthly man.[66] In this way, Philo also shows his own particular preference for the allegory of the soul.

Although Philo does show his own preferences for the Platonic model of creation and for the allegory of the soul, nevertheless, the various interpretations of the creation of man are not revised so that they are consistent with Philo's own preferences. As one looks over the arrangements of the interpretations of Gen 1:27 and 2:7, one sees immediately that all of the levels of interpretation that have been analyzed in this study are represented.

1. Anti-anthropomorphic interpretations (Chapter III):
   Op. 69–71; 72–75; *L. A.* 1.36–38
2. Single creation of man (Chapter IV): *Op.* 138–139; 145–146;
   L. A. 1.34–35.
3. Double creation (Chapter V):
   a. of man: *Op.* 76, 134–135; *L. A.* 1.31–32.
   b. of mind: *L. A.* 1.42.

[64] *Mut.* 223; *Plant.* 18–20; *Her.* 283; *Det.* 83.

[65] He (Moses) uses the word "breath" not "spirit", implying a difference between them; for "spirit" is conceived of as connoting strength and vigour and power, while a "breath" is like an air or a peaceful and gentle vapour. The *mind* that was made after the image and original might be said to partake of spirit, for its reasoning faculty possesses robustness; but the *mind* that was made out of matter must be said to partake of the light and less substantial air, as of some exhalation, such as those that rise from spices, for if they are kept and not burned for incense there is still a sweet perfume from them. (*L. A.* 1.42.)

[66] *L. A.* 1.53–55, 88–89, 90–96; *Plant.* 44–46.

At the same time, the conflicts among them remain. For instance, *Op.* 138–139 and 145–146, in their present context are interpretations of the earthly man created in Gen 2:7. Yet the interpretations themselves make use of language appropriate only to the *heavenly* man created in Gen 1:27, that is, language of likeness to the *Logos.* Again, *L. A.* 1.42 which claims that only the heavenly mind created in Gen 1:27 was given the "spirit" is clearly at odds with *L. A.* 1.36–38 where the central point of the interpretation is that man's mind is inbreathed with "divine spirit." Finally, all of the interpretations in *Op.* 69–88 are about the creation of man prior to any distinction between a heavenly man and an earthly man. Yet in their present context they should be interpretations that apply only to the creation of the heavenly man in Gen 1:27. There can be no doubt that Philo was aware that these various interpretations were not of a piece. Yet his belief in the inspired character of all of these interpretations led him to place them side by side without any real revision. Philo then, unlike his predecessors, thought that there were multiple, valid interpretations of the text, and this enabled him to see the biblical text as a multifaceted reality which yielded a number of inspired interpretations.

One must also be aware, however, that the way in which Philo uses the various literal interpretations of the creation of man differs from the way in which he makes use of allegorical interpretations. The contrast of style illustrates Philo's own preference for the allegorical method of interpretation. In the literal interpretations of the creation of man which were given above, the compositional technique was to bring together various literal interpretations of a given biblical verse. In addition, the literal interpretations were given in a very descriptive style. They were not at all homiletic in style. There was nothing in them of diatribe or parenesis, no attempt to draw moral consequences from the interpretations. In contrast, allegorical interpretations tend to involve a single interpretation of a biblical verse followed by similar interpretations of other biblical verses. The homiletical character of these interpretations is also prominent.[67]

This contrast of style is illustrated when one compares the literal interpretations of Gen 2:7 found in *L. A.* 1.31–42 with the allegorical interpretation of Gen 2:8 found in *L. A.* 1.43–52. As I indicated above, the literal interpretations of Gen 2:7 form a series of discrete interpretations of the creation of man grouped around the appropriate biblical verse. The allegorical interpretation of Gen 2:8 found in *L. A.* 1.43–52, however, is composed

---

[67] For a detailed study of the use of diatribe and parenesis in Hellenistic Jewish homilies, see H. Thyen, *Der Stil der jüdisch-hellenistischen Homilie* (Göttingen: Vandenhoeck & Ruprecht, 1955) 40–63, 85–116.

quite differently. In *L. A.* 1.43–47, the trees of the garden of paradise are interpreted figuratively (τροπικῶς) as virtues planted in the soul. In *L. A.* 1.48–52 Philo goes on to interpret three other biblical verses (Deut 16:21; Exod 20:23; Lev 19:23) in a way that develops the thought found in the allegorical interpretation of Gen 2:8. All three of these interpretations develop in a homiletic fashion the proper attitude that one should have toward God in one's practice of virtue. Instead of a series of discrete interpretations of one biblical verse, one has interpretations of several biblical verses, all of which are part of the allegory of the soul and all of which develop points that are considered important in one's moral or spiritual development.[68] While Philo collects and organizes various literal interpretations of the creation of man, it is the allegory of the soul that brings out his concern with both the integration of the interpretation of disparate texts and the ethical and religious consequences to be drawn from those interpretations.

The acceptance of multiple interpretations also appears in Philo's interpretations of the creation of the world. It would be impossible to go through all of those interpretations in this study. Yet the point can be illustrated by showing how several recent attempts to make Philo's interpretation of the creation of the world read consistently have failed. As in his understanding of the creation of man, so too in his understanding of the creation of the world, there are multiple, inspired, and valid interpretations.

The first of these attempts was by H. A. Wolfson. He suggested that Philo's interpretation of the creation of the world and of man be read in the following way.

> Philo's interpretation of the story of the six days of creation is thus as follows. On the first day, God created the intelligible world of ideas, of which Scripture mentions specifically seven ideas, namely, the idea of what Plato calls the "receptacle," the ideas of the four elements, the idea of the celestial bodies, and the idea of mind and soul. Then he created a copy of the idea of the "receptacle" and, within it, copies of the ideal four elements, both of which together constituted what is known as formless matter, out of which he created the four elements. Out of the element of fire He then created, on the second day, the corporeal heaven; on the third day, land and sea and trees and plants; on the fourth day, the sun and moon and stars; and on the fifth day, aquatic animals and birds of the air. Finally, on the sixth day, He created land animals, the mind of man or the ideal man, which is referred to in the first account of the creation of man, and the corporeal or individual man, which is referred to in the second

---

[68] Other examples of this homiletically colored allegory of the soul are found in *L. A.* 1.80–84; *L. A.* 2.27–29, 46–48, 51–52, 54–63, 77–106; *L. A.* 3.12–27, 32–43, 69–74, 77–96, 119–37; 140–59, 162–81, 191–99, 225–33, 236–45.

account of the creation of man. This interpretation in his *De Opificio Mundi* differs only in slight details from that in his other works.[69]

However, there are two details of more than slight importance that render this harmonization impossible. In the first place, the creation of the "corporeal or individual man" (Gen 2:7/ *Op.* 134–135) is mentioned only *after* a description and interpretation of the seventh day (Gen 2:1–3/ *Op.* 89–128) and so the creation of the earthly man could have taken place only on the seventh day (*Q. G.* 2.56). Secondly, Wolfson overlooked *Op.* 129–130 in which Gen 2:4–5 is taken to mean that everything created in Gen 1:1–31 was part of the world of "incorporeal and intelligible ideas" (*Op.* 129). This interpretation is in agreement with that found in *L. A.* 2.12–13 and *Q. G.* 1.2, 19 in which Gen 1:1–31 refers to the creation of the intelligible world and Gen 2:6–25 refers to the creation of the sensible world. These three interpretations (*Op.* 129–130; *L. A.* 1.12–13; *Q. G.* 1.2, 19) quite clearly clash with *Op.* 13–35 in which only what is created on "day one" is part of the intelligible world. Wolfson's interpretation is unable to reconcile those differences.

An alternative suggestion has been proposed by R. Arnaldez in his edition of *De Opificio Mundi.*[70] In it he tries to overcome the difficulties presented by *Op.* 129–130, *L. A.* 2.12–13, and *Q. G.* 1.2, 19. He claims that there were really three steps in the creation of the world: (1) on "day one" the *Logos* and the world of ideas were created; (2) on the second through the sixth days the *types* or *forms* of sensible objects (including man) were created; and (3) on the seventh day, the actual sensible realities (including man) were created.[71] The second step is what distinguishes Arnaldez's attempt at interpretation from that of Wolfson. It is specifically devised to integrate *Op.* 129–130, *L. A.* 2.12–13, and *Q. G.* 1.2, 19 into the scheme of creation. Arnaldez's interpretation rests on an interpretation of a specific phrase in *Op.* 130:

> We must suppose that in the case of all other objects also, on which the senses pronounce judgment, the elder *forms* (τὰ πρεσβύτερα εἴδη) and measures (μέτρα), in keeping with which all things that come into being have shape and size, subsisted before them (προϋπῆρχε).

The crucial term is "forms" (εἴδη). Appealing to Albinus and Atticus, Arnaldez claims that the "forms" do not refer to the Platonic "ideas" but to

---

[69] Wolfson, *Philo*, 1.310.

[70] R. Arnaldez, "Introduction generale," in Vol. 1 of *Les Oeuvres de Philon d'Alexandrie* (Paris: Cerf, 1961).

[71] Ibid., 136–37.

those ideas as they are attached to matter.[72] They are the specifications of the ideas with a view to their being attached to sensible objects.[73] They are halfway between the intelligible ideas and sensible objects. According to Arnaldez, these "forms," intermediate between the ideas and sensible objects, were created on days two through six, while the ideas were created on "day one," and the sensible objects were created on the seventh day.[74] In this way, Arnaldez hoped to solve the problem created by such passages as *Op.* 129–130, *L. A.* 1.12–13, and *Q. G.* 1.2, 19.

As I pointed out in Chapter V, the use of the term "form" (εἶδος) in the sense suggested by Arnaldez was quite acceptable by the late first century B.C. in Middle Platonic circles.[75] This term also appears with the same meaning in interpretations of the creation of man found in Philo.[76] However, from *Op.* 129 it is clear that the phrase "the *elder* forms and measures" is equivalent in meaning to the phrase "incorporeal and intelligible ideas." The adjective "elder" (πρεσβύτερα) is being used precisely to distinguish these forms from those which are attached to sensible objects. Since *Op.* 129-130 does refer to the creation of the intelligible world and so is still in conflict with *Op.* 13-35, Arnaldez's attempt at harmonization is no more successful than was Wolfson's.[77]

The third and most recent attempt to offer a consistent interpretation of *De Opificio Mundi* has been made by V. Nikiprowetzky in his article, "Problèmes du 'Récit de la Création' chez Philon d'Alexandrie."[78] Of the three, Nikiprowetzky's attempt to offer a consistent reading of Philo's interpretation of the creation of the world comes closest to being convincing. According to Nikiprowetzky, Philo divides the account of creation into two parts. The first part involves days one through six. Day one is the creation of the *intelligible* model of the world; the second day is the creation of the *sensible* heaven; the third day of the sensible earth and the *generic* (κατὰ γένος) plants; the fourth day of the *sensible* heavenly bodies and time; the fifth day of the *generic* (κατὰ γένος) fish and birds; and the sixth day of the *generic* (κατὰ γένος) land animals and "the man made according to the image." The

---

[72] Ibid., 137.

[73] Ibid., 136.

[74] Ibid., 136–37.

[75] See Chapter V, 114–19.

[76] *Op.* 76; *Her.* 163–64.

[77] The interpretation of *Op.* 129-30 was analyzed more fully in Chapter V, 123–25. The discussion of *Op.* 129–30 in this chapter depends on that analysis.

[78] Nikiprowetzky, "Problem du 'Récit de la Création' chez Philon d'Alexandrie," 271–306.

second part includes God's rest on the seventh day and the production of the *sensible* living creature (plants, birds, etc.) and the *sensible* earthly man.[79]

In contrast to Arnaldez's interpretation, Nikiprowetzky's arrangement has the merit of seeing that the term "genus" (γένος) used in *Op.* 76, 134, and *L. A.* 2.12–13, to describe the plants, fish, birds, animals, and the man created in Gen 1:27 means "ideal" or "intelligible."[80] In his interpretation most of the intelligible world is created on "day one." On days two through six the sensible world is created, with the exception of the plants, fish, birds, animals, and man. For these, only their paradigms or *genera* (κατὰ γένος in Gen 1:11, 12, 21, 24, 25) are created on days three through six. The man created in Gen 1:27 is one of those paradigms. Only on the seventh day are the sensible copies of those paradigms created (i.e., the sensible man at Gen 2:7 and the sensible living creatures at Gen 2:19.)[81]

There are, however, serious problems even with Nikiprowetzky's interpretation. In the first place, *Op.* 36 states quite clearly that the incorporeal world (ἀσώματος κόσμος) was completed on "day one" and that the sensible world was begun on the second day. *Op.* 36 leaves no room for the creation of those further paradigms, either of living creatures or of man, which Nikiprowetzky claims were created on days three through six. In addition *Op.* 36–38 clearly describes only the creation of the sensible world; no paradigms are even hinted at. In other words, *Op.* 36–88 is simply irreconcilable with the interpretations found in *Op.* 76, 134–135, *L. A.* 1.12–13, and *Q. G.* 1.2, 19.

Secondly, he misinterprets *L. A.* 1.1, 19–27 by failing to see that these two passages still refer to creation in the intelligible world alone.[82] These two passages take Gen 2:1, 4–5 as a summary of Gen 1:1–31 which refers to the creation of the idea of mind, the idea of sense perception, and the *ideas* of things intelligible and things sensible. In *L. A.* 1.1, 19–27 all of Genesis 1 is taken to refer to the creation of the ideal or intelligible world. This outlook is also irreconcilable with *Op.* 15–88.

Finally, Nikiprowetzky misinterprets *Op.* 129–130, also an interpretation of Gen 2:4–5:

> In his concluding summary of the story of creation he says: "This is the book of the genesis of heaven and earth, when they came into being, in the day in which (ἢ ἡμέρᾳ) God made the heaven and the earth, and every herb of the field before it appeared upon the earth, and all grass of the field before it sprang up"

[79] Ibid., 292–93.
[80] Ibid., 283–89.
[81] Ibid., 292–93.
[82] Ibid., 291–92.

(Gen 2:4–5). Is he not manifestly describing the incorporeal ideas present only to the mind (τὰς ἀσωμάτους καὶ νοητὰς ἰδέας), by which as by seals, the finished objects that meet our senses were molded? For before the earth put forth its young green shoots, young verdure was present, he tells us, in the nature of things without material shape, and before grass sprang up in the field, there was in existence an invisible grass.

We must suppose that in the case of all other objects also, on which the senses pronounce judgment, the elder forms and measures (πρεσβύτερα εἴδη καὶ μέ-τρα), in keeping with which all things that come into being have shape and size, subsisted before them; for even if he has not dealt with everything together according to genus (κατὰ γένος), aiming as he does at brevity in a high degree, nevertheless what he does say gives us a few indications of universal Nature, which brings forth no finished product in the world of sense without using an incorporeal pattern.

Nikiprowetzky wants to take the phrase "on the day when" to refer to "day one" of creation (Gen 1:1–5). In this way, the *idea* of green herbs and the *idea* of the grass of the field were created on "day one" while their sensible counterparts were created later, on the third day (Gen 1:12). In this way the distinction between "day one" and the other six days is preserved.[83] However, as I indicated in chapter V, *Op.* 129–130 places the line of demarcation between the creation of the intelligible world and the creation of the sensible world not at Gen 1:5 but at Gen 2:5, that is, between the sixth day and the seventh day.[84] The phrase "on the day when" does not enter into the interpretation of Gen 2:4–5 in *Op.* 129–130; it is taken to mean nothing more than "at the time when . . ." The green herbs and the grass of the field are simply examples used to indicate that everything created in Gen 1:1–31 was part of the intelligible world. Not everything is mentioned because Moses aims at "brevity in a high degree" (*Op.* 130). The basic conflicts, then, between the various levels of interpretation remain and Nikiprowetzky's attempt is no more successful than the other two.

All of this indicates that Philo has treated previous interpretations of the creation of the world in the same way that he treated previous interpretations of the creation of man. Since all of the interpretations were inspired, all of them found a place in his description of the creation of the world. While Philo's inclusive notion of the types of valid interpretations may seem strange to us, it does represent a consistent vision of the biblical text. This vision allows him to develop consistently the allegory of the soul without

[83] Ibid., 288–89.

[84] Part of the problem with Nikiprowetzky's interpretation is that he does not deal with the textual problem found in *Op.* 130 (κατὰ γένος rather than κατὰ μέρος). See Chapter V, footnote 61.

rejecting previous types of interpretation. The tradition of interpretation can develop in significantly new ways (e.g., the allegory of the soul) and at the same time maintain continuity with its past.

E. *Transmission and Institution*

Both the analysis of the exegetical traditions discussed in the previous three chapters and that of Philo's use and reinterpretation of those traditions discussed in this chapter point to a well developed framework for the transmission and development of such traditions. With the exception of the early Stoic interpretations of Gen 2:7, all of the interpretations reflect the Middle Platonism of the latter half of the first century B.C. and the early part of the first century A.D. From these analyses two questions arise about the overall development of the interpretations of the creation of man: (1) Were these interpretations passed on orally or were they passed on in written form; and (2) what was the institutional framework within which these interpretations developed?

Evidence suggests that we are dealing primarily with the history and development of written interpretations. In general, the extent and complexity of Philo's treatises and his *Questions and Answers on Genesis and Exodus* point to a well developed tradition of written interpretations. The *Questions and Answers on Genesis and Exodus* represent a massive collection of interpretations from various sources, and the various Philonic treatises represent complex, well developed styles of interpretation. It is unlikely that such a highly developed *corpus* of interpretations emerged in written form only with Philo. The written character of these interpretations should not surprise us since we know that interpretations of biblical texts were written down by Alexandrian Jews at least as early as the middle of the second century B.C., that is, at the time of Aristobulus.

More specifically, the interpretations of the creation of man are not simply a collection of unconnected interpretations. Rather, in Philo they represent *levels* of interpretations. The analysis of Philo's interpretations of the creation of man reveals more than simply the level of interpretation immediately prior to Philo's own allegory of the soul. It reveals interpretations, the earliest of which probably go back several generations before Philo. In addition, one does not have to sort through layers of revision in order to get at these earlier levels of interpretations. These interpretations show up in Philo's treatises, and especially in the *Questions and Answers on Genesis and Exodus*, in an unrevised form. For instance, one does not have to sort through layers of revision in order to get at the earliest, antianthropomorphic interpretations of Gen 1:27 and Gen 2:7 found in *Op.* 69–71 and *L. A.* 1.36–38.[85] This does not mean that Philo is quoting these

---

[85] See Chapter III, section A.

interpretations *verbatim*. But he does preserve the original structure, content, and key vocabulary of each of these interpretations to such an extent that these interpretations must have been available to him in their original form. The presence of such interpretations points to a written form of transmission in which these various interpretations could be transmitted in the stable form in which one finds them in Philo.[86]

The answer to the first question has consequences for how one answers the second question about the institutional framework within which these interpretations developed. The written preservation of levels of interpretation which extended over several generations and which are in continuity with one another suggests that we are dealing with a "school" tradition of some sort. In the early part of this century Wilhelm Bousset suggested that behind the writings of Philo lay the work of an "exegetical school" which, by Philo's time, had already existed for a generation or two.[87] Just as there was a Christian catechetical school in Alexandria at the time of Clement, so too there probably was an exegetical school in Alexandria at the time of Philo.[88] The problem with Bousset's position is that, while we do have evidence for a Christian catechetical school in Alexandria at the time of Clement, the evidence for a Jewish exegetical school at the time of Philo is more ambiguous.

Yet both Philo and the traditions that he used do point to some kind of institutional framework of transmission and development. As Dieter Georgi has shown, Philo himself indicates that such an institutional framework was provided by the synagogue.[89] In a passage from *De Vita Mosis*, Philo describes Moses' regulations for the observance of the Sabbath. While the regulations are ostensibly about the observance of the Sabbath at the time of Moses, they clearly reflect, if in a somewhat idealized form, the synagogue service as Philo understood it (*Mos.* 2.216).

> Moses, great in everything, determined that all whose names were written on his holy burgess-roll and who followed the laws of nature should hold high festival through hours of cheerful gaity, abstaining from work and profit-making crafts and professions and business pursued to get a livelihood, and enjoy a respite from labour released from weary and painful care. But this leisure should be occupied, not as by some in bursts of laughter or sports or shows of mimes and dancers on which stage-struck fools waste away their strength almost to the point of death, and through the dominant senses of sight and hearing reduce to

---

[86] This is not to deny the oral character of the interpretation and instruction that took place. It simply means that, in addition, the interpretations were stabilized and passed on in written form.

[87] Bousset, *Jüdisch-christlicher Schulbetrieb in Alexandria und Rom*, 2.

[88] Ibid., 2.

[89] Georgi, *Die Gegner des Paulus im 2. Korintherbrief*, 87–100.

slavery their natural queen, the soul, but by the pursuit of wisdom only (μόνῳ τῷ φιλοσοφεῖν).

For it was customary on every day when opportunity offered, and pre-eminently on the seventh day, as I have explained above, to pursue the study of wisdom (φιλοσοφεῖν) with the ruler expounding and instructing the people what they should say and do, while they received edification and betterment in moral principle and conduct.

Even now this practice is retained, and the Jews every seventh day occupy themselves with the philosophy of their fathers (πάτριος φιλοσοφία), dedicating that time to the acquiring of knowledge and the study of truths of nature. For what are our places of prayer throughout the cities but schools of prudence and courage and temperance and justice and piety, holiness and every virtue by which duties to God and men are discerned and rightly performed? (*Mos.* 2.211, 215–216.)

From *Hypothetica* 7.13, it is clear that what is meant by the exposition of the philosophy of the fathers is the interpretation of scripture.[90] What is of interest to us is that Philo casts the interpretation of scripture that takes place in the synagogue in the image of the kind of instruction that takes place in a philosophical school. The ideology of the synagogue service is that of the pursuit of wisdom (τὸ φιλοσοφεῖν) that takes place in a school setting (διδασκαλεῖον).

This fits in well with what little we know of the philosophical schools of the period. Philosophical speculation and philosophical instruction, at least in the first century B.C., seem to have taken place by means of commenting on and interpreting a text. For instance, one of the speakers in Cicero's *De Oratore* (I. 47) remembers how he "read" Plato's *Gorgias* with Charmadas, meaning that he listened to Charmadas' comments on the *Gorgias*.[91] As Pierre Boyancé has pointed out, "the habitual manner of teaching a doctrine such as that of Plato must have been, well before Neoplatonism, the commentary."[92] The same is true of philosophical speculation in its written form; it took the form of an interpretation of a Platonic text. Eudorus (*fl.* 30 B.C.) and Thrasyllus (d. A.D. 36), both philosophers connected with Alexandria,

---

[90] And indeed they (Jews) do always assemble and sit together, most of them in silence except when it is the practice to add something to signify approval of what is read. But some priest who is present or one of the elders reads the holy laws to them and expounds them point by point (καθ᾽ ἕκαστον ἐξηγεῖται) till about the late afternoon, when they depart having gained both expert knowledge of the holy laws and considerable advance in piety. (*Hyp.* 7.13.)

[91] Boyancé, "Etudes philoniennes," 80.

[92] Ibid., 81.

wrote commentaries of some sort on the texts of Plato.[93] In addition, works such as the *Timaeus Locrus* and Arius Didymus' *On the Doctrines of Plato* were manuals which may well have been based on commentaries on Plato. We do not know what these interpretations of the text of Plato looked like, that is, whether they were line-by-line commentaries or broader interpretations of the Platonic texts. However, what is important for a comparison with Philo and the tradition to which he belonged is that the developments in Middle Platonism during this period were rooted in the interpretation of the texts of Plato. Because both the philosophical speculation and the philosophical instruction of the period were carried on by means of written and oral interpretations of texts, the comparison of the synagogue with a philosophical school is not at all artificial.

The comparison, however, should not be confined to the synagogue service itself but should also include the synagogue as an institution. By that I simply mean that the comparison must take in more than the synagogue service itself, that one must also look to other activities connected with the synagogue.[94] Philo himself hints at this in *Mos.* 2.215 when he claims that, while the interpretation of the biblical text takes place pre-eminently on the Sabbath, it also takes place whenever the opportunity presents itself. The various levels of interpretation of the creation of man that we have analyzed point in the same direction. These interpretations represent the sustained attempt of Jewish interpreters to appropriate the philosophical developments of the period, an attempt that lasted over several generations. In addition, the texts that we have studied indicate a very close reading of the biblical text as well as a great deal of concern for the preservation of the exegetical traditions of previous generations. It is difficult to imagine that all of this was the result of the interpretations of Scripture that took place in the synagogue service itself. Rather, the synagogue as a larger, complex institution must have served as a place where Jewish exegetes, who were deeply influenced by the philosophical developments of the period, could have developed their interpretations of Scripture and where exegetical traditions

---

[93] Plutarch, *De Anima Proc. in Tim.* 1013B, 1019E, 1020C; Porphyry, *Plot.* 20; D.L. 3.56–57.

[94] See S. Safrai, "The Synagogue," *The Jewish People in the First Century* (ed. S. Safrai and M. Stern; Philadelphia: Fortress, 1976) 2.942–43. Almost all of what we know of the synagogues in Alexandria (and that is not much) comes from Philo. There is a highly legendary description of what may be a synagogue in *t. Sukk.* 4.6 (Zuck. 198) (variant versions in *y. Sukk.* 5.31a–b and *b. Sukk.* 51b). For the evaluation of the evidence, see E. R. Goodenough, *Jewish Symbols in the Greco-Roman Period* (New York: Pantheon, 1953) 2.85–86; and S. Krauss, *Synagogale Altertümer* (Berlin: Benjamin Harz, 1922) 261–63.

could have been preserved and transmitted. The strong, well developed sense of tradition, of "school," points to exegetical activity that goes well beyond the bounds of interpretations given in a synagogue homily.[95] The form of Philo's treatises also points in this direction. Even if one grants that some of the treatises reflect the interpretations given at the Sabbath synagogue service, they were certainly revised and recast in order to be put into "publishable" form.[96] The interpretation of Scripture at the synagogue service was of a piece then with the activities of the synagogue as a broad, diversified institution.

It is impossible to say how widespread this conception of the synagogue was. But one can say, at least, that it represented the conception of the synagogue to which Philo and his fellow allegorical interpreters were attached.[97] Nor can one say with much precision for how long this conception of the synagogue had been in existence. One can say, however, that it must have been in existence for at least a generation before Philo, since the Platonic interpretations of the creation of man and of the world of the generation prior to Philo call for the same kind of developed synagogue structure which Philo himself points to. Bousset, then, was correct in maintaining that the interpretations found in Philo assumed a developed institutional structure, but he was wrong only in looking to a separate "school" for this rather than in looking to the institution of the synagogue itself for such a structure.

---

[95] The relationship of the treatises of Philo to the synagogue homily is disputed. Georgi thinks that the relationship was rather close (*Die Gegner*, 94–96). For an opposing view, see Nikiprowetzky, *Le commentaire sur l'écriture*, 174–77.

[96] Georgi emphasizes the importance of the synagogue service itself (*Die Gegner*, 87–100). That is probably correct since, as he shows, the interpretation of Scripture was a highly religious act. My point is a complementary one. The institutional framework necessary to support such a well developed process had to go well beyond the service itself. This necessity seems to me to be the value of Bousset's suggestion about a "school" tradition. The highly developed nature of these interpretations, the amount of erudition contained in them, and their accurate transmission point to an institutional framework considerably wider than that of the synagogue service itself. In that sense Thyen's attempt (*Der Stil der jüdisch-hellenistischen Homilie*, 8–9, 79–81) to choose one (the synagogue homily) rather than the other (the school lecture) seems to me to be artificial.

[97] Philo indicates that there were a number of synagogues in Alexandria (*Leg.* 132; *Flacc.* 47), but there is no way to tell how many other synagogues saw themselves as Philo and his fellow interpreters saw their synagogue(s). Given Philo's prominent place in the Jewish community in Alexandria, there probably was some influence on the self-understanding of other synagogues, but there is no way to gauge the extent of that influence.

CONCLUSIONS AND LIMITATIONS

Since the eighteenth century poets have tended to think of the accomplishments of their predecessors as a burden from which they had to escape. They felt that they had to find a voice of their own.[1] The same is true of many modern writers. Whether in terms of thought or in terms of technique, modern authors try to set themselves apart from their predecessors, to emphasize their uniqueness. But the Jewish interpreters whose work we have analyzed in this study saw things quite differently. For them previous interpretations were something to which they felt a responsibility, something which therefore could not be easily or openly rejected. Their patterns of thought were rooted, as were those of their non-Jewish contemporaries, in an ideology of continuity.[2] Yet they were not content simply to repeat the interpretations of their predecessors. Rather they developed interpretations of their own, interpretations that went beyond or subtly changed the work of those who went before them. This tension between continuity and change has left its mark on the work of Philo and has enabled us to recognize not only Philo's interpretation of the creation of man but also those of his predecessors whose work he incorporated into his own. In addition, because he incorporated the work of his predecessors basically intact, we have been able to sort out *levels* of interpretation.

The interpretation of the creation of man developed in two major phases. The first of these major phases involved the development of a consistent, Platonically oriented interpretation of the creation of man, an interpretation that was coordinated with an equally Platonically oriented interpretation of the creation of the world. Within this phase one finds both the interpretation of Gen 1:27 and Gen 2:7 as the creation of a *single* man and later the interpretation of Gen 1:27 and Gen 2:7 as the creation of *two* men, one heavenly and the other earthly. Both of these developments represent

[1] Cf. W. J. Bate, *The Burden of the Past and the English Poet* (Cambridge: Harvard University Press, 1970) and H. Bloom, *The Anxiety of Influence: A Theory of Poetry* (New York: Oxford University Press, 1973).

[2] This outlook is true of the ancient world in general.

177

attempts to interpret the account of the creation of man in a way that is consistent with analogous developments within the Middle Platonism of the latter half of the first century B.C. in Alexandria. The second major phase, the level of Philo himself, involves the introduction of the allegory of the soul. In this type of interpretation, the text of Genesis is taken to refer not to events of the external world but to conflicting elements within the individual human being, especially to the soul. The man becomes a symbol of mind, the woman of sense perception, and the serpent of pleasure. This type of interpretation is similar to the Middle Platonic interpretations of the *Odyssey* which seemed to have made their appearance toward the end of the first century B.C. But unlike the allegorical interpretations of Homer, Philo's use of the allegory of the soul did not involve the rejection of the literal level of interpretation. Both levels were to be maintained since both levels of interpretation were divinely inspired.

As has been obvious throughout this study, these developments in the interpretation of the creation of man were not isolated, inner-Jewish developments. Rather they represent a conscious attempt to appropriate analogous philosophical developments that were taking place in Alexandria during the latter half of the first century B.C. and the early part of the first century A.D.[3] Yet these Jewish interpretations of the creation of man are not simply imitations of Middle Platonic models, whether interpretations of Plato's *Timaeus* or of Homer's *Odyssey*. For instance, the intermediate *Logos* figure is similar to but never identical with intermediate figures in Middle Platonism. More strikingly, the allegory of the soul, while similar to the allegorical interpretations of Homer's *Odyssey*, goes well beyond them, both in scope and complexity. These Jewish interpreters of Genesis appropriated the patterns of thought of their milieu but turned them to their own purposes. This is also seen in the care with which they read the text of Genesis. Their methods of interpretation, although quite different from our own, are nevertheless rooted in observations on critical details in the biblical text. Each interpretation is argued on the basis of the text and not simply imposed on the text without a reason being given. Given their presuppositions, these interpretations represent both a sophisticated understanding of the biblical text and a critical appropriation of the patterns of thought available to them.

The results, then, of this study are based both on an analysis of the relationship of the various interpretations of the creation of man among themselves and on an analysis of the relationship of these interpretations to

---

[3] These interpretations, however, were an inner-Jewish development in the sense that, while Jewish interpreters were affected by the philosophical milieu of Alexandria, there is no evidence that they in turn significantly influenced the philosophical milieu.

CONCLUSIONS AND LIMITATIONS

the philosophical milieu of Alexandria during that period. These two types of analysis have been complementary. Through an analysis of the relationship of these various levels of interpretation to contemporary philosophical developments we have been able to explain *why* the interpretations of the account of the creation of man developed in the way that they did. One can discover not simply the *fact* that there were levels of interpretation but also *why* the interpreters moved from one level of interpretation to the next. The results of one type of analysis have confirmed the results of the other.

There are, of course, limitations to a study of this sort, and those limitations ought to be kept in mind. The most obvious limitation appeared in Chapter VI. The allegorical method of interpretation was discussed primarily in so far as it helped us to understand either the allegorical interpretation of the creation of man or the way in which Philo was able to accept multiple levels of interpretation of the texts of Genesis about the creation of man. Yet the allegorical method of interpretation, since it is a type of interpretation that runs through most of Philo's treatises and involves both narrative and legal texts, is a far more complex type of interpretation than could be dealt with in a study of this sort. The history of the introduction and use of allegory in Alexandrian Judaism would undoubtedly be clarified by a careful study of its uses in Philo's other treatises.[4] Nevertheless, an understanding of how the allegory of the soul was introduced and used in the interpretation of the creation of man contributes, in however limited a fashion, to an overall conception of allegorical interpretation as it was used in Alexandrian Judaism.

The same holds true for the various types of non-allegorical interpretations that are found in Philo's treatises. Figures such as Abraham and Moses are interpreted not only as elements in the allegory of the soul but also as real historical figures who serve as exemplars of various private and public virtues. In addition, legal texts in treatises such as *De Decalogo* and *De Specialibus Legibus 1–4* are more often than not interpreted literally rather than allegorically. Finally, the Jewish wisdom tradition played a far more important role in the interpretations of these narratives and legal texts than it did in the interpretation of the creation of man.[5] Since many of these interpretations are pre-Philonic, any attempt to understand the overall history of Hellenistic Jewish exegesis would have to do justice to these types of interpretation and to the role played by the Jewish wisdom tradition. The

---

[4] See Mack, "Weisheit und Allegorie," for an analysis of *De Congressu Quaerendae Eruditionis Gratia.*

[5] See Mack, *Logos und Sophia*; and Georgi, *Die Gegner des Paulus im 2. Korintherbrief,* 138–87.

goal of this particular study of the interpretations of the creation of man has, for good reason, been far more limited. But precisely because of that, one must not take the part for the whole and must realize that this study is a contribution to the interpretation of a larger and more complex whole, the history of Hellenistic Jewish exegesis.

A third and final limitation is that the interpretations which we have analyzed are of the *creation* account. Philo saw this account as distinct both from the historical and from the legislative sections of the Pentateuch.[6] His predecessors probably maintained much the same distinction. In addition, the interpretations of neither the historical nor the legal sections of the Pentateuch were as closely related to the interpretation of a Greek philosophical text (Plato's *Timaeus*) as were the interpretations of both the creation of the world and of man. For these two reasons, the history of the interpretation either of the creation of man or of the creation of the world cannot be used as *the* paradigm for the history of the interpretation of either the historical or the legal sections of the Pentateuch. The history of the interpretation of these sections must be approached by the exploration of genres and models appropriate to them. However, once this is granted, the history of the interpretation of the creation of man can, no doubt, be helpful in the reconstruction of the history of the interpretation of other parts of the Pentateuch. This is especially so because the interpretation of the creation account, as an interpretation of the basic structure of reality, is obviously going to influence the interpretation of both the historical and the legal parts of the Pentateuch.

There is then much more to be done if one is to understand the history of Hellenistic Jewish exegesis in all of its complexity. One can only hope that an analysis of the various interpretations of the creation of man found in Philo is a worthwhile contribution to that effort. The effort is also worthwhile since an analyisis of this process of interpretation can contribute to a better understanding of Early Christianity, a religious tradition whose development was rooted in the interpretation of biblical texts and whose interpretations of those texts were influenced by the work of Philo and other Jewish interpreters.

---

[6] *Op.* 1–3; *Praem.* 1–3.

BIBLIOGRAPHY

Primary Sources

Albinus. *Eisagoge and Didaskalikos. Platonis dialogi secundum Thrasylli tetralogias dispositi.* Ed. C. F. Hermann. Leipzig: Teubner, 1902. Vol. 6, 147–89.

Apocalypsis Henochi Graece. Ed. M. Black. *Fragmenta pseudepigraphorum quae supersunt Graeca.* Ed. A. M. Denis. PVTG 3; Leiden: Brill, 1970.

Apocryphon Johannis, the Coptic Text of the Apocryphon Johannis in the Nag Hammadi Codex II. Ed. S. Giversen. Copenhagen: Munksgaard, 1963.

Apuleius. *Opuscules philosophiques et fragments.* Ed. J. Beaujeu. Paris: Société d'édition "Les Belles Lettres," 1973.

Aristeas to Philocrates (Letter of Aristeas). Ed. M. Hadas. New York: Harper and Row, 1951.

Aristotle. *Du ciel.* Ed. P. Moraux. Paris: Société d'édition "Les Belles Lettres," 1965.

Augustine. *De civitate dei libri XXII.* 2 vols. Ed. B. Dombart and A. Kalb. Leipzig: Teubner, 1928–29.

Cebetis Tabula. Ed. C. Praechter. Leipzig: Teubner, 1893.

Cicero. *Scripta quae manserunt omnia.* 48 fasc. Ed. F. Marx et. al. Leipzig: Teubner, 1911–69.

————. *De natura deorum and Academica.* LCL. Trans. H. Rackham. London: Heinemann, 1933.

————. *Brutus.* LCL. Trans. G. H. Hendrickson. Cambridge: Harvard University Press, 1939.

————. *De finibus bonorum et malorum.* LCL. Trans. H. Rackham. London: Heinemann, 1914.

————. *Orator.* LCL. Trans. H. M. Hubbell. Cambridge: Harvard University Press, 1939.

————. *De oratore.* LCL. 2 vols. Trans. H. Rackham. Cambridge: Harvard University Press, 1942.

————. *Tusculan Disputations.* LCL. Trans. J. E. King. Cambridge: Harvard University Press, 1945.

Cornutus. *Theologiae Graecae compendium.* Ed. Carl Lang. Leipzig: Teubner, 1881.

Corpus Papyrorum Judaicarum. 3 vols. Ed. V. A. Tcherikover and A. Fuks. Cambridge: Harvard University Press, 1957–64.

Diogenes Laertius. *Vitae philosophorum.* 2 vols. Ed. H. S. Long. Oxford: Clarendon Press, 1964.

_____ . *Lives of Eminent Philosophers.* LCL. 2 vols. Trans. R. D. Hicks. Cambridge: Harvard University Press, 1959.

Doxographi Graeci. Ed. H. Diels. 1879; rpt. Berlin: de Gruyter, 1929.

Heraclitus. *Allegories d'Homère.* Ed. F. Buffière. Paris: Société d'édition "Les Belles Lettres," 1962.

Hermès Trismégiste. 4 vols. Ed. A. D. Nock and A. J. Festugière. Paris: Société d'édition "Les Belles Lettres," 1946-54.

Horace. *Opera.* Ed. E. C. Wickham and H. W. Garrod. Oxford: Clarendon Press, 1901.

The Nag Hammadi Library. Ed. J. M. Robinson. New York: Harper and Row, 1977.

Numenius. *Fragments.* Ed. E. des Places. Paris: Société d'édition "Les Belles Lettres," 1973.

Philo Alexandrinus, *Opera quae supersunt.* 7 vols. Ed. L. Cohn and P. Wendland. Berlin: de Gruyter, 1896-1930.

_____ . LCL. 12 vols. Trans. F. H. Colson, G. H. Whitaker, and R. Marcus. Cambridge: Harvard University Press, 1929-62.

_____ . *Les oeuvres de Philon d'Alexandrie.* 35 vols. to date. Ed. R. Arnaldez, J. Pouilloux, and C. Mondésert. Paris: Cerf, 1961-.

Plato. *Opera.* 6 vols. Ed. J. Burnet. Oxford: Clarendon Press, 1900-13.

_____ . *The Collected Dialogues Including the Letters.* Bollingen Series 71. Ed. E. Hamilton and H. Cairns. Princeton: University Press, 1961.

Plutarch. *Moralia.* 7 vols. Ed. W. R. Paton et al. Leipzig: Teubner, 1925-1960.

_____ . *Moralia.* LCL. 16 vols. Trans. F. C. Babbitt et al. Cambridge: Harvard University Press, 1927-1976.

Plutarch's De Iside et Osiride. Ed. and trans. J. G. Griffiths. Cardiff: University of Wales Press, 1970.

Pseudo-Plutarch. *De vita et poesi Homeri.* In *Plutarchi Chaeronensis Moralia.* Ed. G. N. Bernardakis. Leipzig: Teubner, 1896. Vol. 7, 329-462.

Posidonius. Vol. I: The Fragments. Ed. L. Edelstein and I. G. Kidd. Cambridge: University Press, 1972.

The Pythagorean Texts of the Hellenistic Period. Acta Academiae Aboensis, Humaniora 30/1. Ed. H. Thesleff. Abo: Abo Akademi, 1965.

Quellen zur Geschichte der christlichen Gnosis. Ed. W. Völker. Tübingen: J. C. B. Mohr, 1932.

Seneca. *Ad Lucilium epistulae morales.* 2 vols. Ed. L. D. Reynolds. Oxford: Clarendon Press, 1965.

_____ . *Ad Lucilium epistulae morales.* LCL. 3 vols. Trans. R. M. Gummere. London: Heinemann, 1917-25.

Stobaeus, Ioannes. *Anthologii libri duo priores.* 2 vols. Ed. K. Wachsmuth. Berlin: Weidmann, 1884.

Stoicorum Veterum Fragmenta. 4 vols. Ed. H. von Arnim. Leipzig: Teubner, 1905-24.

Timaeus Locrus. *De natura mundi et animae.* Philosophia Antiqua 24. Ed. W. Marg. Leiden: Brill, 1972.

Veröffentlichungen aus der Heidelberger Papyrussammlung. Vol. I: Septuaginta-Papyri und andere altchristliche Texte. Ed. A. Deissmann. Heidelberg, 1905.

Walter, N. "Fragmente jüdisch-hellenistischer Exegeten: Aristobulos, Demetrios, Aristeas." JSHRZ 3/2. Gütersloh: Gerd Mohn, 1975.

Zosimus of Panopolis. *On the Letter Omega.* Texts and Translations 14. Ed. and trans. H. M. Jackson. Missoula: Scholars, 1978.

Secondary Sources

Aall, A. *Geschichte der Logos Idee in der griechischen Philosophie.* Leipzig: Reisland, 1896.

Babut, D. *Plutarque et le Stoïcisme.* Paris: Presses Universitaires de France, 1969.

Baer, R. A. *Philo's Use of the Categories Male and Female.* ALGHJ 3. Leiden: Brill, 1970.

Baltes, M. *Timaios Lokros: Über die Natur des Kosmos und der Seele.* Philosophia Antiqua 21. Leiden: Brill, 1972.

————. *Die Weltentstehung des platonischen Timaios nach den antiken Interpreten.* Philosophia Antiqua 30/1. Leiden: Brill, 1976.

Bieler, L. ΘΕΙΟΣ ANHP. *Das Bild des "Göttlichen Menschen" in Spätantike und Frühchristentum.* 2 vols. 1935–36; rpt. Darmstadt: Wissenschaftliche Buchgesellschaft, 1967.

Bousset, W. *Hauptprobleme der Gnosis.* Göttingen: Vandenhoeck & Ruprecht, 1907.

————. *Jüdisch-christlicher Schulbetrieb in Alexandria und Rom. Literarische Untersuchungen zu Philo und Clemens von Alexandria, Justin und Irenäus.* Göttingen: Vandenhoeck & Ruprecht, 1915.

Boyancé, P. "Echo des exégèses de la mythologie grecque chez Philon." *Philon d'Alexandrie.* Colloques nationaux du Centre National de la Recherche Scientifique, Lyon, 11–15 Sept. 1966. Lyon, 1967, 169–88.

————. "Etudes philoniennes." *REG* 76 (1963) 64–110.

————. "Philon d'Alexandrie." *REG* 72 (1959) 377–84.

————. "La Religion astrale de Platon à Ciceron." *REG* 65 (1952) 312–50.

Brandenburger, E. *Adam und Christus. Exegetisch-religionsgeschichtliche Untersuchung zu Röm. 5, 12–21 (1, Kor. 15).* Neukirchen: Neukirchener Verlag, 1962.

Bréhier, E. *Les idées philosophiques et religieuses de Philon d'Alexandrie.* 2nd ed. Paris: J. Vrin, 1925.

Bruns, J. E. "Philo Christianus: the Debris of a Legend." *HTR* 66 (1973) 141–45.

Büchsel, F. "ἀλληγορέω." *TDNT* 1 (1964) 260–63.

Buffière, F. *Les mythes d'Homère et la pensée grecque.* Paris: Société d'édition "Les Belles Lettres," 1956.

Bultmann, R. *The Gospel of John. A Commentary.* Philadelphia: Westminster, 1971.

Burkert, W. *Lore and Science in Ancient Pythagoreanism.* Cambridge: Harvard University Press, 1972.

Cazeaux, J. "Aspects de l'exégèse philonienne." *RSR* 47 (1973) 262–69.

Chadwick, H. "Philo." *The Cambridge History of Later Greek and Early Medieval Philosophy.* Ed. A. H. Armstrong. Cambridge: University Press, 1967, 137–57.

Charlesworth, J. H. *The Pseudepigrapha and Modern Study.* Missoula: Scholars, 1976.

Cherniss, H. *The Riddle of the Early Academy.* Berkeley: University of California Press, 1945.

Christiansen, I. *Die Technik der allegorischen Auslegungswissenschaft bei Philon von Alexandrien.* Beiträge zur Geschichte der biblischen Hermeneutik 7. Tübingen: J. C. B. Mohr, 1969.

Colpe. C. *Die religionsgeschichtliche Schule. Darstellung und Kritik ihres Bildes vom gnostischen Erlösermythus.* Göttingen: Vandenhoeck & Ruprecht, 1961.

Dalbert, P. *Die Theologie der hellenistisch-jüdischen Missionsliteratur unter Ausschluss von Philo und Josephus.* Hamburg: Herbert Reich, 1954.

Daniélou, J. *Philon d'Alexandrie.* Paris: Arthème Fayard, 1958.

Daube, D. "Rabbinic Methods of Interpretation and Hellenistic Rhetoric." *HUCA* 22 (1949) 239–64.

Delling, G. *Bibliographie zur jüdisch-hellenistischen und intertestamentarischen Literatur 1900–1970.* TU 106/2. Berlin: Akademie Verlag, 1975.

———. "Wunder-Allegorie-Mythus bei Philon von Alexandreia." *Gottes ist der Orient.* Berlin: Evangelische Verlag, 1959, 42–68.

Dillon, J. *The Middle Platonists.* Ithaca: Cornell University Press, 1977.

Dodd, C. H. *The Bible and the Greeks.* London: Hodder and Stoughton, 1934.

Dodds, E. R. "The *Parmenides* of Plato and the Origin of the Neoplatonic 'One,'" *Classical Quarterly* 22 (1928) 129–42.

Dölger, F. J. *Sphragis: Eine altchristliche Taufbezeichnung in ihren Beziehungen zur profanen und religiösen Kultur des Altertums.* Studien zur Geschichte und Kultur des Altertums 5/3.4. Paderborn: Schöningh, 1911.

Dörrie, H. "Albinos." *PW.*Sup 12 (1971) 14–22.

———. *Platonica Minora.* Munich: Wilhelm Fink, 1976.

———. "Zur Methodik antiker Exegese." *ZNW* 65 (1974) 121–38.

Edelstein, L. "The Philosophical System of Posidonius." *American Journal of Philology* 57 (1936) 286–325.

Elbogen, I. *Der jüdische Gottesdienst in seiner geschichtlichen Entwicklung.* 2nd ed. Frankfurt: J. Kauffmann, 1924.

Eltester, F. W. *Eikon im Neuen Testament.* Berlin: Töpelmann, 1958.

Farandos, G. D. *Kosmos und Logos nach Philon von Alexandria.* Amsterdam: Rodopi, 1976.

Festugière, A. J. *La Révélation d'Hermès Trismégiste.* 4 vols. Paris: Gabalda, 1944–54.

Fraser, P. M. *Ptolemaic Alexandria.* 3 vols. Oxford: Clarendon Press, 1972.

Freudenthal, J. *Der Platoniker Albinus und der falsche Alkinoos.* Hellenistische Studien 3. Berlin: Calvary, 1879.

Friedländer, M. *Geschichte der jüdischen Apologetik als Vorgeschichte des Christentums. Eine historisch-kritische Darstellung der Propaganda und Apologie im Alten Testament und in der hellenistischen Diaspora.* 1903; rpt. Amsterdam: Philo Press, 1973.

————. *Der vorchristliche jüdische Gnosticismus.* Göttingen: Vandenhoeck & Ruprecht, 1898.

Früchtel, U. *Die kosmologischen Vorstellungen bei Philo von Alexandrien. Ein Beitrag zur Geschichte der Genesisexegese.* ALGHJ 2. Leiden: Brill, 1968.

Georgi. D. *Die Gegner des Paulus im 2. Korintherbrief. Studien zur religiösen Propaganda in der Spätantike.* WMANT 11. Neukirchen: Neukirchener Verlag, 1964.

Giblet, J. "L'homme image de Dieu dans les commentaires littéraires de Philon d'Alexandrie." *Studia Hellenistica* 5. Louvain: Bibliotheca Universitatis Lovanii, 1948, 93–118.

Goodenough. E. R. *By Light Light. The Mystic Gospel of Hellenistic Judaism.* New Haven: Yale University Press, 1935.

————. *Introduction to Philo Judaeus.* New Haven: Yale University Press, 1940.

————. *Jewish Symbols in the Greco-Roman Period.* 12 vols. New York: Pantheon, 1953–65.

————. *The Politics of Philo Judaeus.* New Haven: Yale University Press, 1938.

Graeser, A. *Probleme der platonischen Seelenteilungslehre. Überlegungen zur Frage der Kontinuität im Denken Platons.* Zetemata 47. Munich: C. H. Beck, 1969.

Gronau, K. *Poseidonios und die jüdisch-christliche Genesisexegese.* Berlin: Teubner, 1914.

Gross, J. *Philons von Alexandreia Anschauungen über die Natur des Menschen.* Tübingen: Tübinger Chronik, 1930.

Hamerton-Kelly, R. G. "Sources and Traditions in Philo Judaeus: Prolegomena to an Analysis of His Writings." *SP* 1 (1972) 3–16.

Hani, J. *La religion égyptienne dans la pensée de Plutarque.* Paris: Société d'édition "Les Belles Lettres," 1976.

Hanson, A. "Philo's Etymologies." *JTS* 18 (1967) 128–39.

Hanson, R. P. C. *Allegory and Event. A Study of the Sources and Significance of Origen's Interpretation of Scripture.* Richmond: John Knox Press, 1959.

Harder, R. "Timaios 4." *PW* 6A (1937) 1203–1226.

Hegermann, H. *Die Vorstellung vom Schöpfungsmittler im hellenistischen Judentum und Urchristentum.* TU 62. Berlin: Akademie Verlag, 1961.

Heinemann, I. *Altjüdische Allegoristik.* Breslau: Marcus, 1936.

————. *Philons griechische und jüdische Bildung. Kulturvergleichende Untersuchungen zu Philons Darstellung der jüdischen Gesetze.* Breslau: Marcus, 1932.

Hengel, M. *Judaism and Hellenism. Studies in their Encounter in Palestine during the Early Hellenistic Period.* 2 vols. Philadelphia: Fortress, 1974.

Holladay. C. *Theios Aner in Hellenistic Judaism. A Critique of the Use of This Category in New Testament Christology.* SBLDS 40. Missoula: Scholars, 1977.

Horovitz, J. *Untersuchungen über Philons und Platons Lehre von der Weltschöpfung.* Marburg: N. G. Elwert, 1900.

Hruby, K. *Die Synagogue: Geschichtliche Entwicklung einer Institution.* Zurich: Theologischer Verlag, 1971.

Jaeger, W. *Nemesios von Emesa. Quellenforschungen zum Neuplatonismus und seinen Anfängen bei Poseidonios.* Berlin: Weidmann, 1914.

Jervell, J. *Imago Dei. Gen. 1.26f im Spätjudentum, in der Gnosis und in den paulinischen Briefen.* Göttingen: Vandenhoeck & Ruprecht, 1960.

The Jewish People in the First Century. Historical Geography, Political History, Social, Cultural and Religious Life and Institutions. Compendia Rerum Iudaicarum ad Novum Testamentum. Vols. 1–2. Ed. S. Safrai, *et al.* Philadelphia: Fortress, 1974–76.

Joly, R. *Le Tableau de Cebes.* Coll. Latomus 61. Brussels: Latomus, 1963.

Jonas, H. *Gnosis und spätantiker Geist.* 2 vols. Göttingen: Vandenhoeck & Ruprecht, 1934–64.

————. *The Gnostic Religion.* Boston: Beacon Press, 1963.

Jones, C. P. "The Teacher of Plutarch." *Harvard Studies in Classical Philology* 71 (1966) 205–13.

Jones, R. M. *The Platonism of Plutarch.* Menasha, Wisconsin: George Banta Publishing Company, 1916.

————. "Posidonius and the Flight of the Mind through the Universe." *Classical Philology* 21 (1926) 97–113.

Katz, P. *Philo's Bible. The Aberrant Text of Bible Quotations in Some Philonic Writings and Its Place in the Textual History of the Greek Bible.* Cambridge: University Press, 1950.

Kelber, W. *Die Logoslehre von Heraklit bis Origenes.* Stuttgart: Urachhaus, 1976.

Klein, F. N. *Die Lichtterminologie bei Philon von Alexandrien und in den hermetischen Schriften.* Leiden: Brill, 1962.

Kraeling, C. H. *Anthropos and the Son of Man.* Columbia University Oriental Series 25. New York: Columbia University Press, 1927.

Krämer, H. J. *Platonismus und hellenistische Philosophie.* Berlin: de Gruyter, 1971.

————. *Der Ursprung der Geistmetaphysik. Untersuchungen zur Geschichte des Platonismus zwischen Platon und Plotin.* Amsterdam: P. Schippers, 1964.

Krauss, S. *Synagogale Altertümer.* Berlin: Benjamin Harz, 1922.

Laffranque. M. *Poseidonios d'Apamée.* Paris: Presses Universitaires de France, 1964.

Leisegang, H. "Der Gottmensch als Archetypus." *Eranos Jahrbuch 18* (1950) 9–45.

Lesky, A. *A History of Greek Literature.* New York: Crowell, 1966.

Long, A. A. *Hellenistic Philosophy. Stoics, Epicureans, Sceptics.* London: Duckworth, 1974.

Lubac, H. de. *Exégèse médiévale.* 4 vols. Paris: Aubier, 1959–64.

Luck. G. *Der Akademiker Antiochos.* Noctes Romanae 7. Bern: Paul Haupt, 1953.

McCasland, S. V. "The 'Image of God' According to Paul." *JBL* 69 (1950) 85–100.

Mack. B. L. "Exegetical Traditions in Alexandrian Judaism: A Program for the Analysis of the Philonic Corpus." *SP* 3 (1974–75) 71–112.

————. *Logos und Sophia. Untersuchungen zur Weisheitstheologie im hellenistischen Judentum.* Göttingen: Vandenhoeck & Ruprecht, 1973.

————. "Weisheit und Allegorie bei Philo von Alexandrien." *SP* 5 (1979) 57–105.

Merki. H. ΟΜΟΙΩΣΙΣ ΘΕΩ, *von der platonischen Angleichung an Gott zur Gottähnlichkeit bei Gregor von Nyssa.* Fribourg: Paulusverlag, 1952.

Moraux, P. "Quinta Essentia." *PW* 24 (1963) 1171–1263.

Nikiprowetzky, V. *Le commentaire de l'écriture chez Philon d'Alexandrie. Son caractère et sa portée. Observations philologiques.* ALGHJ 11. Leiden: Brill, 1977.

_____ . Problèmes du 'Recit de la Creation' chez Philon d'Alexandrie." *REJ* 124 (1965) 271–306.

_____ . "La spiritualization des sacrifices et le culte sacrificiel au temple de Jérusalem chez Philon d'Alexandrie." *Semitica* 17 (1967) 97–116.

Nilsson, M. *Geschichte der griechischen Religion* Vol. 2. 3rd ed. Munich: C. H. Beck, 1974.

Nock, A. D. *Essays on Religion and the Ancient World.* 2 vols. Ed. Z. Stewart. Cambridge: Harvard University Press, 1972.

Olerud, A. *L'idée de macrocosmos et de microcosmos dans le Timée de Platon.* Uppsala: Almqvist & Wiksells, 1951.

Otte, K. *Das Sprachverständnis bei Philo von Alexandrien. Sprache als Mittel der Hermeneutik.* Tübingen: J. C. B. Mohr, 1968.

Pépin, J. *Mythe et allégorie. Les origines grecques et les contestations judéochrétiennes.* Paris: Aubier, 1958.

_____ . "Remarques sur la théorie de l'exégèse allégorique chez Philon." *Philon d'Alexandrie.* Colloques nationaux du Centre National de la Recherche Scientifique, Lyon, 11–15 Sept. 1966. Lyon, 1967, 138–168.

Quispel, G. "Der gnostische Anthropos und die jüdische Tradition." *Eranos Jahrbuch* 22 (1953) 195–234.

Reinhardt, K. *Kosmos und Sympathie. Neue Untersuchungen über Poseidonios.* Munich: C. H. Beck, 1926.

_____ . *Poseidonius.* Munich: C. H. Beck, 1921.

_____ . "Poseidonios." PW 22 (1953) 558–826.

Reitzenstein, R. *Die hellenistischen Mysterienreligionen nach ihren Grundgedanken und Wirkungen.* 3rd ed. Leipzig: Teubner, 1927.

_____ . *Das iranische Erlösungsmysterium.* Bonn: Marcus & Weber, 1921.

_____ . *Das mandäische Buch des Herrn der Grosse und die Evangelienüberlieferung.* SHAW 12. Heidelberg, 1919.

_____ . *Poimandres. Studien zur griechisch-ägyptischen und frühchristlichen Literatur.* Leipzig: Teubner, 1904.

_____ and H. H. Schaeder. *Studien zum antiken Synkretismus aus Iran und Griechenland.* Leipzig: Teubner, 1926.

Robin, L. *La théorie platonicienne des idées et des nombres d'après Aristote.* Paris: Alçan, 1908.

Rokeah, D. "A New Onomasticon Fragment from Oxyrhynchus and Philo's Etymologies." *JTS* 19 (1968) 70–82.

Rudolph, K. *Die Gnosis: Wesen und Geschichte einer spätantiken Religion.* Göttingen: Vandenhoeck & Ruprecht, 1977.

Russell, D. A. *Plutarch.* London: Duckworth, 1973.

Sandmel, S. "Philo's Knowledge of Hebrew." *SP* 5 (1978) 107–12.

Schenke, H.-M. *Der Gott "Mensch" in der Gnosis. Ein religionsgeschichtlicher Beitrag zur Diskussion über die paulinische Anschauung von der Kirche als Leib Christi.* Göttingen: Vandenhoeck & Ruprecht, 1962.

Schmidt, H. *Die Anthropologie Philons von Alexandria.* Würzburg: Triltsch, 1933.

Schmitt, A. "Interpretation der Genesis aus hellenistischen Geist." *ZAW* 86 (1974) 137–63.

Schroyer, M. J. "Alexandrian Jewish Literalists." *JBL* 55 (1936) 261–84.

Schürer, E. *The History of the Jewish People in the Age of Jesus Christ (175 B.C. -A.D. 135).* 2 vols. Revised and edited by G. Vermes and F. Millar. Edinburgh: T. & T. Clark, 1973–79.

Scroggs, R. *The Last Adam. A Study in Pauline Anthropology.* Philadelphia: Fortress, 1966.

Siegfried, C. *Philo von Alexandria als Ausleger des Alten Testaments an sich selbst und nach seinem geschichtlichen Einfluss betrachtet.* Jena: Hermann Dufft, 1875.

Sinko, T. "De lineamentis platonicis in Cebetis q.v. tabula." *Eos* 45 (1951) 3–31.

Staehle, K. *Die Zahlenmystik bei Philon von Alexandria.* Berlin: Teubner, 1931.

Stein, E. *Die allegorische Exegese des Philo aus Alexandria.* BZAW 51. Giessen: Töpelmann, 1929.

————. *Philo und der Midrasch.* Giessen: Töpelmann, 1931.

Sukenik, E. L. *Ancient Synagogues in Palestine and Greece.* London: British Academy, 1934.

Tate, J. "The Beginnings of Greek Allegory." *Classical Review* 41 (1927) 214–15.

————. "On the History of Allegorism." *Classical Quarterly* 28 (1934) 105–14.

————. "Plato and Allegorical Interpretation." *Classical Quarterly* 23 (1929) 142–54.

Taylor, A. E. *A Commentary on Plato's Timaeus.* Oxford: Clarendon Press, 1928.

Tcherikover, V. *Hellenistic Civilization and the Jews.* New York: Atheneum, 1959.

————. "Jewish Apologetic Literature Reconsidered." *Eos* 48/3 (1956) 169–193.

Theiler, W. *Forschungen zum Neoplatonismus.* Berlin: de Gruyter, 1966.

————. "Philo von Alexandreia und der Beginn des kaiserzeitlichen Platonismus." *Untersuchungen zur antiken Literatur.* Berlin: de Gruyter, 1970, 484–501.

————. *Die Vorbereitung des Neuplatonismus.* Berlin: Weidmann, 1930.

Thesleff, H. *An Introduction to the Pythagorean Writings of the Hellenistic Period.* Acta Academiae Aboensis, Humaniora 24/3. Abo: Abo Akademi, 1961.

Thompson, C. *Stoic Allegory of Homer. A Critical Analysis of Heraclitus' Homeric Allegories.* Diss. Yale University, 1973.

Thyen, H. *Der Stil der jüdisch-hellenistischen Homilie.* Göttingen: Vandenhoeck & Ruprecht, 1955.

Tiede, D. L. *The Charismatic Figure as Miracle Worker.* SBLDS 1. Missoula: Scholars, 1972.

Völker, W. *Fortschritt und Vollendung bei Philo von Alexandrien. Eine Studie zur Geschichte der Frömmigkeit.* TU 49/1. Leipzig: J. C. Hinrich, 1938.

Wallis, R. T. *Neoplatonism.* London: Duckworth, 1972.

Walter, N. *Der Thoraausleger Aristobulos. Untersuchungen zu seinen Fragmenten und zu pseudepigraphischen Resten der jüdisch-hellenistischen Literatur.* TU 86. Berlin: Akademie Verlag, 1964.

————. "Zu Pseudo-Eupolemus." *Klio* 43/45 (1965) 282–90.

Weiss, H.-F. *Untersuchungen zur Kosmologie des hellenistischen und palästinischen Judentums.* TU 97. Berlin: Akademie Verlag, 1966.

Widengren. G. *The Gnostic Attitude.* Santa Barbara, 1973.

Willms, H. EIKΩN. *Eine begriffsgeschichtliche Untersuchung zum Platonismus. I. Teil: Philon von Alexandreia.* Münster: Aschendorff, 1935.

Wilson, R. McL. "The Early History of the Exegesis of Gen 1:26." *Studia Patristica I.* Ed. K. Aland and F. L. Cross. Berlin: Akademie Verlag, 1957, 420–437.

Windisch, H. *Paulus und Christus. Ein biblischreligionsgeschichtlicher Vergleich.* UNT 24. Leipzig: J. C. Hinrich, 1934.

Winston, D. *The Wisdom of Solomon. A New Translation with Introduction and Commentary.* AB 43. Garden City: Doubleday, 1979.

Witt, R. E. *Albinus and the History of Middle Platonism.* Cambridge: University Press, 1937.

Wlosok, A. *Laktanz und die philosophische Gnosis. Untersuchungen zu Geschichte und Terminologie der gnostischen Erlösungsvorstellung.* Heidelberg: Carl Winter, 1960.

Wolfson, H. A. *Philo. Foundations of Religious Philosophy in Judaism, Christianity and Islam.* 2 vols. Cambridge: Harvard University Press, 1947.

INDEX OF PASSAGES FROM PHILO

190

INDEX OF ANCIENT AUTHORS OTHER THAN PHILO

INDEX OF MODERN AUTHORS

198

Thyen, H., 166, 176
Tiede, D., 157
Walter, N., 10, 11, 50, 54
Weiss, H. F., 63
Wendland, P., 63
Widengren, G., 105
Willms, H., 64, 65

Wilson, R. McL., 7, 106
Windisch, H., 157
Winston, D., 86
Witt, R. E., 65
Wlosok, A., 11, 74, 75, 141, 146
Wolfson, H. A., 1, 3, 6, 57, 64, 168